DECISION MAKING AND JUVENILE JUSTICE

DECISION MAKING AND JUVENILE JUSTICE

AN ANALYSIS OF BIAS IN CASE PROCESSING

PAUL E. TRACY

PRAEGER

Westport, Connecticut
London

Library of Congress Cataloging-in-Publication Data

Tracy, Paul E.
Decision making and juvenile justice : an analysis of bias in case processing / Paul E. Tracy.
p. cm.
Includes bibliographical references and index.
ISBN 0–275–97651–3 (alk. paper)
1. Juvenile justice, Administration of—Decision making. 2. Discrimination in juvenile justice administration. I. Title.
HV9069.T78 2002
364.36'068'4'4'—dc21 2001055150

British Library Cataloguing in Publication Data is available.

Library of Congress Catalog Card Number: 2001055150
ISBN: 0–275–97651–3

First published in 2002

Praeger Publishers, 88 Post Road West, Westport, CT 06881
An imprint of Greenwood Publishing Group, Inc.
www.praeger.com

Printed in the United States of America

The paper used in this book complies with the Permanent Paper Standard issued by the National Information Standards Organization (Z39.48–1984).

10 9 8 7 6 5 4 3 2 1

Contents

Illustrations

FIGURES

TABLES

Acknowledgments

I gratefully acknowledge the assistance of many people without whom this research would not have been possible. I am grateful to several groups and individuals who facilitated and assisted in the conduct of the research. Special thanks are owed to the Honorable Karen Green, Judge 282nd Criminal District Court of Dallas County, and former Director of the Criminal Justice Division of the Governor's Office. Judge Green and her staff, Nancy Hugon, Glenn Brooks, Jim Kester, Melissa Foley, and Ed Santiago provided invaluable support in facilitating the successful completion of such an ambitious study. Thanks are also offered to the staff of the Texas Juvenile Probation Commission, the Texas Youth Commission, the Texas Criminal Justice Policy Council, and the District and County Attorneys' Association. They greatly assisted in the planning and logistics for the survey of juvenile justice practitioners. I also greatly appreciate the time and courtesy of the judges, prosecutors, defense attorneys, probation department staff, and law enforcement officers who participated in the survey. The survey process was not always unobtrusive, and yet, they willingly gave their time, usually when it was least convenient during their busy professional lives.

This study required the assistance of juvenile justice officials in the three counties where intensive case-level data collection occurred. It would be appropriate to thank these persons by name and location, but the promise of keeping the county identities confidential precludes such personalized acknowledgments. I trust that these juvenile justice officials know just how much I appreciate their help and guidance.

Special recognition is due to the staff at the Public Policy Research Institute at Texas A&M University. This project could not have been possible without the tireless efforts of Dr. J. Randy Booher, Dr. Radmila Prislin, Dr. Rickie Fletcher, Jeffrey A. Jordan, Lisa Halperin, Mark Bell, and Carla Glover who assisted at various stages of the research. Dr. Ben Crouch and Guy Whitten were invaluable in resolving many substantive questions and methodological issues. Greg Muller, Elaine Jude Leyda, Linda A. Baez, and Ross Blakely helped prepare the original report and provided editorial assistance. Last, Dr. Ramdas Menon, the Principal Investigator on the project, deserves special mention for his high level of dedication and collegiality throughout the project. This research would have been neither conceived nor successfully accomplished were it not for his unparalleled skills and professionalism.

Special gratitude is also owed to Judge Harold C. Gaither Jr. of the 304th Juvenile District Court of Dallas County. Throughout our work on the Governor's Juvenile Justice Task Force, and in numerous conversations over the years, Judge Gaither has offered valuable insights into the dynamics of juvenile court administration, and more importantly, the extent to which recognition of the due process rights of juveniles and adherence to statutory provisions in the law are the proper basis on which juvenile case processing decisions should be rendered.

1

Introduction

The overrepresentation of minorities in the criminal and juvenile justice systems is an issue that arises again and again in the popular media and the scholarly literature (albeit, more so in the media). The explanation usually proffered for the racial and ethnic disparities in criminal justice data is that the agents of the criminal justice system are biased and discriminate against racial and ethnic minorities. It is argued, quite simply, that minorities are targeted for arrest, prosecution, conviction, and subsequent imprisonment merely because they are persons of color. The issue has recently been addressed by R. Clegg in a thought-provoking article (*Legal Times,* 17 July 2000). Clegg notes that:

> No one disagrees that a disproportionate number of African Americans are arrested, tried, and convicted of crimes. But, there are two ways to explain this fact. It might be argued that it results entirely from discrimination in the criminal justice system: that whites are just as likely to commit crimes, but that police, prosecutors, and juries are all looking the other way. Or it may be claimed that there is no discrimination in the system and that the disparity results entirely from more lawbreaking among blacks.

Of course, the situation is not this simple. To be sure, the issue of race/ethnicity and possible systemic biases in the criminal justice decision-making process is very important and the dynamics are certainly complex. Unfortunately, prior research has generally not addressed this issue in a sufficiently rigorous fashion, and consequently, a highly inconsistent and inconclusive body of results has accumulated. This work will attempt to show that previous research concerning the overrepresentation of minorities in the justice system is beset with serious methodological and statistical analysis problems. It is the central thesis of this work that the available research is largely inconclusive, and despite the absence of a coherent body of results, the federal agency responsible for monitoring disproportionate minority confinement has exaggerated, if not mischaracterized, the issue of racial bias in the juvenile justice system.

The perspective maintained in this work is in agreement with Clegg when he observed that prior studies are uniformly unpersuasive in both their findings of pervasive bias and their proposed solutions (*Legal Times,* 17 July 2000). Yet, despite the failure of prior research to uncover widespread and systematic differential handling of minority youth, a few authors as well as the Office of Juvenile Justice and Delinquency Prevention (OJJDP), a federal agency in the Department of Justice authorized to deal with juvenile justice issues, have essentially indicated to the contrary—that juvenile justice systems across the country are racist and engage in discriminatory practices. That is, despite the fact that scientifically rigorous evidence is lacking, OJJDP, and a group of researchers, often supported by OJJDP funding, have argued that minority youngsters (simply because of their race or ethnicity), as compared to white youth, are more likely to be (1) arrested; (2) detained in secure lock-up facilities prior to their juvenile court trials; (3) adjudicated (conviction terminology in juvenile courts); and (4) sentenced to secure punishment facilities. The important point here is that these discriminatory practices have been portrayed by OJJDP as frequent, pervasive, and systematic despite the fact that the majority of research does not substantiate such claims. Yet, these portrayals continue to be made and the states are federally mandated to prove that they are neither racist nor biased in their juvenile justice policies and practices.

In particular, this research attempts to address the question of racial disparity in the juvenile justice system. The allegations of racial bias are lodged more frequently against the juvenile justice system than against the adult component of the system, and when such allegations are indeed lodged, they are often levied with the authority of federal law. The specific focus of this study is the investigation of disproportionate minority confinement (DMC) in the Texas juvenile justice system. The disproportionate minority confinement issue has also been referred to by other phrases such as "disproportionate minority representation" or "minority overrepresentation." Investigations of the extent to which minorities are disproportionately represented in the juvenile justice system, given their underlying percentage distribution in the at-risk youth population, is certainly a legitimate and important area of scholarly inquiry in criminology. The essence of the issue is whether members of certain race or ethnic youth groups are more likely to be kept in secure detention at the preadjudication stage and/or given a final disposition of incarceration in a secure facility at the adjudication stage. In many ways, the disproportionate minority confinement issue is reminiscent of the debate which began in the 1960s concerning the "dark figure of crime" and the effort to discover the "real" relationship surrounding race and involvement in delinquency and crime (Hindelang, 1978; Tracy, 1978, 1987; Elliott and Ageton, 1980). That is, researchers became concerned that official delinquency statistics overrepresented the involvement of minority youth in crime, and proposed instead the development of self-reported delinquency studies to produce "unbiased" estimates of delinquency which would be free from system decisions which produced race effects that were not genuine.

However, unlike the evolution of self-reported delinquency studies, the disproportionate minority confinement issue, and objective scholarly inquiry into its extent and possible causes, has been rendered more complicated than should be the case by the highly politicized, and often ideological, manner by which the issue has arisen and has been studied. That is, most criminological research is usually conducted by independent scholars based in academia or research organizations. The research is usually guided by one or more theories or conceptualizations of the phenomenon with subsequent tests of attendant hypotheses. In this pursuit, the researcher attempts to be scientific and objective, and has only the cannons of science as operative constraints. Unfortunately, the issue of disproportionate minority confinement in the juvenile justice system has not been allowed to proceed in the usual scientific mode—that is, unfettered by government intrusion. The research surrounding minority overrepresentation has been severely affected by federal mandates, and regrettably, greatly influenced by the attendant socio-political interests (and even lobbying) which often accompanies such mandates. In effect, unlike the vast majority of criminological research, not only has the federal government been highly active in raising and publicizing the issue of disproportionate minority confinement, but federal authorities have secured legislative mandates that require states wishing to participate in certain formula funding programs to study and assess disproportionate minority confinement as part of the qualification process. Further, federal mandates have even prescribed the manner in which the problem should be identified, assessed, and subsequent interventions initiated.

It will be argued here that these federal mandates and constraints are manifestly political rather than scientific, border on the ideological rather than the substantive, and have thereby tainted the usual process of objective scientific inquiry. Owing to government intrusion into the research process, the quality of research undertaken concerning the topic of disproportionate minority confinement has been diminished. Most important, although the available research has yielded findings which are inconclusive, and does not provide strong evidence of systematic racism or discrimination, numerous government publications as well as some researchers sponsored by federal funding portray the results to the contrary. This only serves to further complicate, confound, and politicize the issue. Ultimately, it will be argued that this pursuit necessarily deflects attention, and most importantly funding, away from the most important policy issues: (1) the investigation of why minority youth disproportionately commit more frequent and more severe crimes in the first place; and (2) research-based development of effective prevention programs to remedy the disproportionate criminality.

ORIGIN OF DISPROPORTIONATE MINORITY CONFINEMENT: FEDERAL MANDATES

The federal mandates surrounding disproportionate minority confinement arise as a function of the fact that the federal government, through specific subdivisions of the United States Department of Justice, makes funds available to the states for both criminal justice and juvenile justice initiatives and programs. The federal agency which has jurisdiction over and provides formula funding to the states with respect to juvenile delinquency, juvenile justice, and related issues is the Office of Juvenile Justice and Delinquency Prevention (OJJDP). The enabling legislation under which OJJDP functions is the Juvenile Justice and Delinquency Prevention Act of 1974 (the Act), as amended.

OJJDP has mandated various requirements that the states must follow in order to receive federal funds available under the Act. One of these requirements concerns the issue of disproportionate minority representation in the juvenile justice system. The operative factors concerning the issue of minority overrepresentation in the juvenile justice system may be found in Title II, Section 223 (a) (23), of the Juvenile Justice and Delinquency Prevention Act of 1974, as amended, 1988. This section of the Act provides that states should address efforts to reduce the proportion of juveniles detained or confined in secure detention facilities, secure correctional facilities, jails, and lockups who are members of minority groups, if such proportion exceeds the proportion that such groups represent in the general population.

In order that states would approach the determination of minority overrepresentation in a focused, comprehensive and systematic manner, OJJDP published in the *Federal Register*, August 8, 1989, a set of rules or requirements for implementing Title II, Section 223 (a) (23). The OJJDP guidelines call for a two-stage process which states must follow. First, states must provide documentation in their program plans indicating whether minority juveniles are disproportionately detained or confined in secure detention or correctional facilities, jails, or lockups, in relation to their proportion of the at-risk youth population. Second, if documentation on the specific issues listed previously is unavailable, or alternatively, if it is available and demonstrates that minorities are disproportionately detained or confined in relation to their proportion in the at-risk youth population, states must provide a strategy for addressing the disproportionate representation of minority juveniles in the juvenile justice system.

OJJDP subsequently decided that the original guidelines were insufficient and promulgated another set of regulations. OJJDP published a revised set of rules and guidelines for implementing Title II, Section 223 (a) (23) of the Act in the *Federal Register,* May 31, 1995 (see also, Devine, Coolbaugh, and Jenkins, 1998; Hsia and Hamparian, 1998). The essential differences between the original set of rules and the revised rules are as follows:

1. states must demonstrate specific efforts to reduce the proportion of juveniles detained or confined in secure facilities who are members of minority groups if such proportion exceeds the proportion such groups represent in the general population;
2. states must provide quantifiable documentation in the determination of minority detention and/or confinement overrepresentation;
3. where quantifiable documentation does not exist, the State must provide a time-limited plan of action, not to exceed six months, for developing and implementing a system for the ongoing collection, analysis, and dissemination of information regarding minorities;
4. states must provide a completed assessment of disproportionate minority confinement including the identification and explanation of differences in:
   a. arrest, diversion, and adjudication rates;
   b. court dispositions other than incarceration;
   c. the rates and periods of prehearing detention in and dispositional commitments to secure facilities; and
   d. transfers to adult court.
5. when disproportionate minority confinement is found, the State must provide a time-limited plan of action for reducing disproportionate confinement including:
   a. diversion;
   b. prevention;
   c. reintegration;
   d. policies and procedures; and
   e. staffing and training.

In essence, the OJJDP guidelines assume that the mere presence of disproportionate minority confinement is prima facie evidence that such overrepresentation is *illegitimate,* and is therefore discriminatory, and further, represents evidence of biased decision making, and the states are required to address the problem. Alternatively, of course, is the equally valid proposition that disproportionate minority confinement in the juvenile justice system, including rates of disproportionate detention prior to adjudication and post-adjudication confinement, may be quite legitimate and legally quite explainable and justified. There are two alternative scenarios available. On one hand, there is a "differential selection" thesis which suggests that minority youth are arrested, detained, adjudicated, and incarcerated *regardless* of the nature, extent, and quality of their current delinquent acts together with the frequency and severity of their prior criminal history. Alternatively there is also a "differential involvement" thesis which argues that minority youth are differentially handled by the system owing to a variety of factors such as a more serious current offense (e.g., a delinquent offense involving personal violence or drug violations, violations which the system may be targeting), a longer delinquency career, a more extensive prior record, accelerating recidivism, or even a history of previous lenient dispositions which have failed to curb the offender's recidivism. All of these factors would be legally probative in making a determination of how to handle the offender for his/her current offense. Thus, unlike the differential selection thesis which posits racial bias or the stereotyping of minorities as more dangerous and deserving of harsh treatment per se, the differential involvement approach posits legitimate and legally permissible factors which result in the handling of certain cases more harshly than others.

It is interesting that OJJDP has essentially adopted the differential selection thesis, despite the absence of overwhelming evidence to support its validity. How did such a particular view on the disproportionate minority confinement issue become part of a federal legislative mandate? Two notable commentators, Feyerherm (1995) and Howell (1997) on the history of OJJDP, and especially the various mandates surrounding the Juvenile Justice and Delinquency Prevention Act, have demonstrated that the origins of the disproportionate minority confinement issue can be traced to specific developments in the late 1980s. Feyerherm (1995) has pointed out that the first reference to the DMC issue in legislative annals was the testimony of Ira Schwartz in 1986 before the United States House of Representatives, Subcommittee on Human Resources. Feyerherm notes that Schwartz informed Congress that:

> Minority youth now comprise more than half of all the juveniles incarcerated in public detention and correctional facilities in the United States and that despite widely held perceptions to the contrary, there is recent research showing that minority youth do not account for a substantially disproportionate amount of serious crime. However, minority youth stand a much greater chance of being arrested than white youth, and once arrested, appear to be at great risk of being charged with more serious offenses than whites who are involved in comparable levels of delinquency. (Schwartz, 1986: 5, as cited in Feyerherm, 1995: 7–8)

At about the same time, Schwartz, Fishman, Hatfield, Krisberg, and Eisikovits (1987) appear to have dismissed the role of delinquency history as a relevant explanatory factor in disproportionate minority confinement by suggesting that:

This situation deserves the attention of juvenile justice researchers; many questions about law enforcement and detention practices are raised by the possibility that minority over-representation in detention centers does not seem to be a function of greater minority involvement in serious juvenile crime. (1987: 233)

Feyerherm (1995) and Howell (1997), former director of the National Institute of Juvenile Justice and Delinquency Prevention and Deputy Director of OJJDP, are in agreement that another crucial development concerning the origins of the disproportionate minority confinement mandates was the lobbying efforts of the National Coalition of State Juvenile Justice Advisory Groups (now called The Coalition for Juvenile Justice). Feyerherm (1995: 9) has indicated that the Coalition began raising the problem of disproportionate minority confinement in two annual reports (1987, 1989) to Congress, and as a featured topic during its 1988 annual meeting. Howell has shown that the Coalition informed Congress in the 1989 annual report that 55% of incarcerated youth were minorities and the percentage had been increasing since 1979 (1997: 37). Howell has even suggested that one of the Coalition's most important accomplishments was convincing Congress to amend the JJDP Act by adding the disproportionate minority confinement mandate (1997: 37).

It is clear that the disproportionate minority confinement issue did not arise from a body of accumulating research literature indicating that, while minorities were not responsible for a greater share of crime, they nonetheless were being processed differently by agents of the criminal and juvenile justice systems. Instead, the disproportionate minority confinement initiative results from the lobbying of a few persons and organizations who maintained that differential involvement does not explain the differential handling of minorities. I am not suggesting that the differential handling of any identifiable group of young persons such that they are disproportionately confined is not a significant problem. Rather, my concern is that the reasons why such persons are differentially available for subsequent differential handling must be investigated properly or else the field runs the risk of misdiagnosing the problem, and consequently, any proposed remedies may be ineffective.

EXTENT OF DISPROPORTIONATE MINORITY CONFINEMENT: THE FEDERAL VIEW

The Office of Juvenile Justice and Delinquency Prevention can exert strong influence over the states by its ability to withhold, if not just delay, a state's formula funding if the disproportionate minority confinement issue is not investigated and documented in accord with OJJDP guidelines, and then subsequently resolved to OJJDP's satisfaction. Even though a particular state's disproportionate minority confinement data may be entirely legitimate and explainable, the state must develop plans for reducing disproportionate minority confinement or else sacrifice its formula funds. In addition to the legal mandates and the threat of frozen formula funds, the Office of Juvenile Justice and Delinquency Prevention promulgates reports and bulletins which provide a distorted picture of disproportionate minority confinement nationally. These reports serve to reinforce the notion that minorities are experiencing differential and selective processing for their delinquent behavior. The message which is conveyed, whether actually intended or not, is that a more harsh or more severe or more selective treatment represents racial bias on the part of the various agents of the juvenile justice system across the country. By so doing, OJJDP perpetuates a climate which makes it difficult and burdensome for a state to defend itself and demonstrate that the disproportionate minority confinement statistics result from valid and appropriate decision making on the basis of real and legally permissible differences in offending behavior. When such decision making is based on legally relevant factors, then the handling of the case does not represent discriminatory handling of minority youth.

There are numerous examples of questionable OJJDP reporting concerning the existence and extent of disproportionate minority confinement. There is a widely distributed bulletin series, *Minorities in the Juvenile Justice System* (e.g., Bilchik, 1999). In the latest such report, Shay Bilchik (the former OJJDP administrator) draws upon a national study of descriptive data concerning juvenile offenders, victims, and juvenile justice system parameters that was conducted on behalf of OJJDP (*Violence and Victims,* Snyder and Sickmund, 1999). Bilchik notes that:

> The most recent statistics available reveal significant racial and ethnic *disparity* in the confinement of juvenile offenders. In 1997, minorities made up about one-third of the juvenile population nationwide but accounted for nearly two-thirds of the detained and committed population in secure facilities. For black juveniles, the disparities were most evident. While black juveniles ages 10 to 17 made up about 15% of the juvenile population, they accounted for 26% of the juveniles arrested and 45% of delinquency cases involving detention. About one-third of adjudicated cases involved black youth, yet 40% of juveniles in secure residential placements were black. *These are numbers that cannot be ignored.* (1999: 1, emphasis added)

These numbers should not be ignored and Bilchik (drawing upon Snyder and Sickmund, 1999: 192) should be credited for distinguishing among overrepresentation, disparity, and discrimination, as he appropriately notes that these terms have different meanings, and that overrepresentation is not necessarily the result of discrimination (1999: 2). Yet, the bulletin, like the national report, is filled with descriptive data, persuasively formatted and highlighted, which nonetheless seems to convey the message that discrimination may be a significant causal factor. That is, the report details the disparities which exist, especially for black youth, at all stages of the juvenile justice system. Of course, reaching the conclusion that minority youth are treated differently just because they are African American or Hispanic requires statistically rigorous analyses of the data—not just descriptive tables and charts. Bilchik (1999) and Snyder and Sickmund (1999) do admit that detailed causal analysis is necessary to resolve whether minority disparity in juvenile justice has its origins in discrimination as opposed to behavioral and legal factors. However, Bilchik (1999: 3) and Snyder and Sickmund (1999: 193) suggest that, "on a national level, such detailed analysis is not possible with the data that are available." If the OJJDP bulletins stopped here and clearly conveyed the inability of available data to permit any causal conclusions, then concerns about sending the wrong message would be unnecessary. However, my objection is that, although the requisite data are supposedly not available on a national level, Bilchik (1999) and Snyder and Sickmund (1999) still make inferences which are not supported by either the OJJDP data that are used in the report, or by citations to recently published literature that reflects the required rigorous analyses. For example, Bilchik (1999: 3) and Snyder and Sickmund (1999: 193) readily admit that research findings on disproportionate minority confinement are not consistent, but still offer the conclusive observation that data available for most jurisdictions across the country indicate that minorities are overrepresented in the juvenile justice system, especially in secure facilities. It is one thing to point out overrepresentation when the data support such a claim, but it is an entirely different matter when, despite failing to present the necessary data or providing citations or references to published studies which would substantiate their claims, these authors still declare that:

> Some research also suggests that differences in the offending rates of white and minority youth cannot explain the minority overrepresentation in arrest, conviction, and incarceration counts. (Bilchik, 1999: 3; Snyder and Sickmund, 1999: 193)

Further, after referring to a literature review previously conducted for OJJDP (Pope and Feyerherm, 1990a, 1990b, 1992, 1993) that is now nine years old, the authors indicate, again with no apparent citations, that:

> Since that research, a rather large body of research has accumulated across numerous geographic regions that reinforces these earlier findings. Thus, existing research suggests that race/ethnicity does make a difference in juvenile justice decisions in some jurisdictions at least some of the time. (Bilchik, 1999: 3; Snyder and Sickmund, 1999: 193)

A few key references to this accumulating literature would be necessary to support the opinions being offered, especially since the literature has been typified as a rather "large body of research." Yet, no such citations are provided.

The making of unsupported claims of what the extant research literature suggests concerning disproportionate minority confinement is a frequent problem in OJJDP reports. Such claims are unacceptable in such a high profile government report. Similarly, offering an excuse that the right kind of data or proper analyses are not available to determine the "real" situation surrounding disproportionate minority confinement is problematic and unacceptable especially when the reports speculate about the topic anyway. The fundamental question arises then, why base such an important national level report on only aggregate level, descriptive data? Why not utilize a detailed analysis of high quality, individual-level case data that are available for a particular jurisdiction so that a proper test of causal factors could be done? If such data, or such a detailed causal study do not exist, then OJJDP could devote some of its considerable resources to funding such a study through the usual Request For Proposals (RFP) process. As it turns out, however, such detailed studies did exist (e.g., the present research) and OJJDP was aware of the final report of this study as it had been submitted to OJJDP for approval in order to bring Texas into compliance with the disproportionate minority confinement mandates reviewed previously.

One has to wonder why OJJDP is reluctant to publicize studies which provide alternative findings about the differential selection versus differential involvement of minorities and crime, and similarly, why OJJDP seems to ignore the contrary evidence and continues to maintain the position that, "questions regarding the causes of the observed disparity and overrepresentation remain unanswered" (Bilchik 1999: 3; Snyder and Sickmund, 1999: 193). It is especially surprising that Snyder would adopt this particular stance concerning the possible causes of overrepresentation, because he has properly noted elsewhere that some causes lie in the differential criminal records of minority and white youth when he suggested that:

> Nonwhites were more likely to be detained than whites. Detention occurred in 29% of nonwhite delinquency cases, compared to 23% of white delinquency cases. A part of this differential handling can be attributed to the findings that *nonwhite youth were more likely to have prior court referrals and were more likely to be referred to court for more serious offenses.* (Snyder, 1990: 2–3, emphasis added)

In addition to the national report series, OJJDP maintains another widely distributed series called *Fact Sheets*. The fact sheets contain descriptive data concerning a wide array of juvenile justice issues. One of these fact sheets, *Residential Placement of Adjudicated Youth, 1987–1996* (MacKenzie, 1999), reports a few descriptive data across three time periods. Despite the absence of any rigorous statistical tests that would be crucially necessary to support the observations offered, the report nevertheless suggests the following:

> While these data cannot control for the severity of the offense or the court histories of the youth, the disproportionate representation of minorities in out-of-home placement is a national concern. Suggestions of court bias in assessing the home conditions of minority youth and the lack of available community resources to provide needed supports have been raised as possible factors contributing to disparities in placement practices. (1999: 2)

It is problematic that the report makes reference to "suggestions" of court bias, but no citations to these sources are included in the report. How is one supposed to gauge the validity of these suggestions of court bias when no information is provided? It should dismay anyone concerned about fair, objective, and scientifically responsible reporting of federally sponsored research, especially through a federally disseminated and endorsed publication, that none of MacKenzie's observations are supported by any evidence (either direct, or even inferential). Unfortunately, there seems to be a tendency in these publications to include a caveat indicating that certain observations and conclusions are not warranted given the nature and quality of the data available, but the publication nonetheless proceeds to offer definitive observations as if the data limitations just raised were not relevant. Again, it is simply unacceptable for government-sponsored research and attendant publications to speculate about such important and highly controversial topics as "court bias" in the processing of juveniles in the absence of necessary data and appropriately rigorous analyses of these data. It is problematic to suggest that something as important as "court bias" exists and yet fail to provide methodologically and statistically sound evidence in support of such a thesis.

MINORITIES AND CRIME

Differential Involvement

The disproportionate minority confinement issue and the comparative validity of the "differential involvement" versus "differential selection" theses within the juvenile justice system cannot be properly examined within a vacuum, but rather, must be viewed within the historical context of the extant criminological literature. This is especially the case for the research that was readily available at the time the disproportionate minority confinement mandates first arose and Congress was lobbied to enact the legislation. In this light, it is more than arguable whether the observations of Schwartz and his colleagues about the relative criminality of minority youth as opposed to white youth, and in particular, the comparability of levels of offending were valid portrayals of the state of the knowledge at the time. There was available, prior to, and about the same time as Schwartz's congressional testimony, substantial evidence which disputes the conclusions

Schwartz offered to the Congress. This evidence was available with respect to the following: (1) racial overrepresentation in arrest and prison data (see, for example Blumstein, 1982); (2) studies of official delinquency (see, for example Wolfgang et al., 1972; Hindelang, 1978; Hamparian et al., 1978, 1985; Shannon, 1980; and particularly, Tracy et al., 1985); and (3) even self-report studies of delinquency (see, for example Tracy, 1978; Hindelang et al., 1979, 1981; and Elliott and Ageton, 1980). In fact, my research (Tracy et al., 1985) with the 1958 Philadelphia birth cohort was funded by OJJDP and the findings were well publicized by OJJDP prior to the Schwartz testimony. One might legitimately expect that experts would have been well aware of such high profile studies when composing their congressional testimony so as to render it as up-to-date as possible.

It is disconcerting, therefore, that expert testimony given to Congress seems to be based on such a selective awareness of what was called "recent" evidence when Congress was lobbied to authorize the Office of Juvenile Justice and Delinquency Prevention to adopt the presumptive disproportionate minority confinement mandates. Moreover, there appears to be a substantial and ill-advised reluctance among criminologists to confront the full range of available information concerning the race and crime issue. Sampson and Wilson, in commenting on the available data pertaining to race and violent crime, have recently suggested the following:

> Despite these facts, the discussion of race and crime is mired in an unproductive mix of controversy and silence. At the same time that articles on age and gender abound, criminologists are loath to speak openly on race and crime for fear of being misunderstood or labeled racist. (2000: 126)

They have also argued, quite convincingly, that:

> Still others engage in subterfuge, denying race-related differentials in violence and focusing instead on police bias and the alleged invalidity of official crime statistics—this in spite of evidence not only from death records but also from survey reports showing that blacks are disproportionately victimized by, and involved in, criminal violence. . . . [C]riminologists have, with few exceptions, abdicated serious scholarly debate on race and crime. (2000: 126–127)

I agree completely with this view and would also suggest that, in an effort to subscribe to the dictates of political correctness, criminologists have avoided confronting the overwhelming evidence surrounding race and differential involvement in crime, particularly violent crimes against the person, drug-related offenses, weapons offenses, and other serious crimes that come to the attention of the police most often, thus necessitating an official police response. Researchers have focused instead on alleged system biases and racial discrimination in the processing of offenders like those that are hypothesized in the disproportionate minority confinement initiative of OJJDP. Unfortunately, the consequence of avoiding the readily available research evidence, and subscribing instead to a politically correct agenda, is the diversion of scholarly attention (particularly funded research) away from the crucial questions surrounding race, ethnicity, and crime and the pursuit of highly peripheral issues that bring us further and further away from the "right stuff." There is sufficient evidence available over the past 30 years, and even longer (see, LaFree, 1995), that there is a significant association between race and criminality. The following represent the conclusions reached by a few of the researchers who felt compelled to stimulate the research community to confront the issue of race and crime as part of a comprehensive agenda that acknowledges the reality of the race and crime connection rather than the myth of a racist system. In their classic work on the subculture of violence, Wolfgang and Ferracuti noted over 30 years ago that:

> Statistics on homicide and other assaultive crimes in the Unites States consistently show that Negroes have rates between four and ten times higher than whites. Aside from a critique of official arrest statistics that raises serious questions about the rate of Negro crime, there is no real evidence to deny the greater involvement that Negroes have in assaultive crimes. (1969: 264)

Similarly, in a volume specifically focused on explicating the race and crime relationship, Wolfgang and Cohen have shown that:

> With monotonous regularity in methodologically well designed studies of delinquency, from Shaw and McKay in Chicago to Lander in Baltimore, and in many less capably performed analyses, the disparity between white and Negro rates of juvenile violence has been duly spread before scholars and citizens. It should be kept in mind, however, that none of these figures demonstrates that Negroes as a race are more prone to crime. They do demonstrate that the average black citizen is more likely than the average white citizen to be exposed to a plethora of conditions that result in his being arrested, convicted and imprisoned. Most of these conditions are inherent in the social structure and are not subject to control by an individual. (1970: 34)

The Rand Corporation conducted a comprehensive research study for the National Institute of Corrections. The report, in an effort to confront the issue of race and criminality at the outset, indicated in the introductory section the following:

> [B]lacks make up only 12 percent of the U.S. population, but 48 percent of the prison population. This seemingly outrageous disparity has prompted allegations that the police overarrest minorities, prosecutors pursue their cases more vigorously, judges sentence them more severely, and corrections officials make sure they stay

incarcerated longer than whites. However, it is difficult to believe that discrimination in the United States is so vast as to produce such a disparity. (Petersilia, 1983: 1)

In a similar vein, a noted criminologist has concluded that, "The main reason that black incarceration rates are substantially higher than those for whites is that black crime rates for imprisonable crimes are substantially higher than those for whites" (Tonry, 1995: 79).

Twenty years after Wolfgang and Ferracuti first developed their thesis on a subculture of violence, a subculture which they believed may disproportionately recruit or affect members of minority populations, Curtis (1989) argued for the development of a more informed social policy concerning violence, especially concerning the poverty, unemployment, and other social ills suffered by the underclass in America. Curtis observed that:

Violent crime is too complex for any brief statement to be entirely accurate in explaining disproportionate minority involvement in violent and related crimes. But no explanation since the Violence and Kerner Commissions better explains the available statistics on levels of violence, trends in violence, the role of relative economic deprivation, and the independent determinant of race. (1989: 141)

A similar concern about race and violence was raised by Prothrow-Stith (1991) within the context of public health issues surrounding homicide in the African-American community. Prothrow-Stith, then the Assistant Dean at Harvard University's School of Public Health, noted that:

Black men are far more likely than whites to be the victims and the perpetrators of violent acts. This racial correlation is not new. Since 1929, when the FBI began keeping racially segregated homicide statistics, black males have run a 6 to 12 times greater risk of dying the victim of homicide. While blacks are approximately 12 percent of the population, they generally comprise half of all those arrested for murder and nonnegligent homicide and half of the homicide victims. (1991: 65)

The evidence for the differential involvement thesis is effectively summarized in the writing of another noted African-American scholar, Randall Kennedy, a law professor at Harvard Law School. In a treatise that provides a comprehensive analysis of the relationships among race, crime, and the law, Kennedy offers the following observations. Kennedy notes a problematic tendency for scholars to engage in denial owing to a need to rebut the race crime connection. He writes:

This explains why some observers, even in the face of overwhelming evidence, deny claims that blacks commit a disproportionate percentage of street crime. Some deniers maintain that the apparent disproportionate prevalence of black street criminals is an illusion created by the news and popular entertainment media. Others maintain that an exaggerated image of the black man as criminal stems from a racially discriminatory criminal justice system apparatus that systematically disadvantages black men by watching them more closely than whites, by arresting them more frequently under circumstances in which whites are not arrested, and by treating them more harshly than similarly situated whites. (Kennedy, 1997: 22)

Kennedy's response to these denials and explanations is to offer the following rendition of what the real evidence suggests:

That relative to their percentage of the population, blacks commit more street crime than do whites is a fact not a figment of a Negrophobe's imagination. Although blacks constitute only around 12 percent of the national population, in 1992, 44.8 percent of all persons arrested for crimes were black. Blacks made up 55.1 percent of those arrested for homicide, 42.8 percent of those arrested for rape, and 60.9 percent of those arrested for robbery. Even after one makes a reasonable discount to offset some degree of racial discrimination in law enforcement, a strikingly large disproportionality remains. (Kennedy, 1997: 23)

Differential Selection

It was noted earlier that criminology, beginning in the 1960s, became concerned that official delinquency data may distort the actual criminality of minorities. The proponents of the self-report method have argued that official crime and delinquency data reflect class and associated race biases on the part of the official agents of control, rather than a measurable and valid difference in the actual behavior of persons of minorities or lower social strata. The self-report approach is an attempt by criminologists to use alternative data sources that would possibly produce "unbiased" estimates of delinquency which would be free from system decisions and bias that were responsible for race and ethnicity effects that were not genuine. For some criminologists, self-reported delinquency data are not just an alternative measure of delinquent behavior but are really preferred measures that tap somewhat different domains of delinquency and crime. The direct consequence of this has been the development of two distinct research camps—one using official archival data and the other employing the self-report method.

It is clear that official crime data are not perfect. According to Hawkins, Laub, Lauritsen, and Cothern (2000), system effects, which can bias estimates of racial differences, can arise for a number of reasons. First, official crime data pertain only to offenses and offenders that come to the attention of the police. Second, different race and ethnic groups may vary in their inclination to report crimes to the authorities. Third, crimes committed by certain ethnic groups may be more likely to result in an arrest (Hawkins, Laub, Lauritsen, and Cothern, 2000: 1). Last, they note that "police themselves may be biased in their arrest policies and may handle offenders differently (e.g., arresting rather than warning) depending on the offender's racial or ethnic background" (Hawkins, Laub, Lauritsen, and Cothern, 2000: 1; see also Hagan and Peterson, 1995; Mann, 1993). Yet, the problem with the differential selection thesis is that the potential for showing a lack of congruence between the official and self-reported estimates of delinquency is more apparent than real. That is, there are few self-report studies that have produced reliable and valid evidence that official data are as biased as the critics would suggest. Until recently, it was clear that the domains were different. Self-reports tended to address more trivial and less serious offensive behaviors, while official data usually reflected more serious criminal activity. The findings which emerged from the use of these two kinds of data were usually quite different. Research drawn from official offense data generally indicated that males, nonwhites, and persons of lower social class were more likely to be offenders with records of less serious offenses, while on the other hand, self-report research did not find sex, race, and social class differences of great magnitude, thus leading to the conclusion that official data must be in error.

Over time, however, research has tended to show that with more sophisticated self-report inventories and survey administration procedures, and with more representative samples, the results of self-report research are much more congruent with those of official data studies. For example, Elliott and Ageton (1980) have reported from the National Youth Survey that self-report and official correlates of and conclusions about delinquent behavior are quite similar. Similar findings have also been reported by Farrington (1973) and Hindelang, Hirschi, and Weiss (1979). In addition, my research with the 1945 Philadelphia birth cohort employed a self-report inventory which permitted direct comparisons between official and unofficial measures, and my findings support many of those reported by Elliott and Ageton. Essentially, my research found that the socio-demographic groups with high arrest rates were also likely to self-report the highest frequencies and severity of hidden offenses (Tracy, 1987). Similarly, recent results from three longitudinal studies being conducted in Rochester, Denver, and Pittsburgh on behalf of the causes and correlates program of OJJDP, would seem to confirm the validity of official crime research (Kelley, Huizinga, Thornberry, and Loeber, 1997). That is, the researchers constructed a measure of self-reported serious violence that incorporated aggravated assault, robbery, rape, and gang fights and the questions were asked at each interview session and examined differences in serious violence prevalence rates across ethnic groups. The results indicated that a greater proportion of minorities were involved in self-reported violence. With the single exception of 18-year-olds in Rochester, the violence prevalence rates were higher among minority groups than among Caucasians at each age and site and the differences were often substantial (Kelley, Huizinga, Thornberry, and Loeber, 1997: 5).

Alternatively, an often cited study in support of a discrepancy between official and unofficial data is Elliott's (1994) more recent analyses of the

National Youth Survey. Elliott has noted that at the peak age of offending (i.e., age 17), 36% of black males and 25% of white males reported that they had committed one or more serious violent offenses (1994: 5). The supposedly significant point about this finding is that it is represents a smaller differential than is usually found in studies that employ official delinquency records thus leading to a question about the validity of the official data. Further, Elliott also found that nearly twice as many blacks as whites continued violent offending into early adulthood, and that the male race differential up to age 30 is close to that observed in official data (1994: 7–8). Thus, Elliott's results are more useful to explain the white versus minority differentials for adult crime than for the juvenile venue of such activity.

The promise of self-report research is yet to be achieved and some of the reasons are clear. First, although the self-report technique is generally believed to provide more complete data on an offender's delinquency career owing to the absence of the possible selection effects present in official data, it is clear that retrospective self-reports from respondents are affected by other effects such as recall errors and the general inability for respondents to provide a precise sequencing of the illegal acts reported, especially when the subject reports many offenses per year per offense type. This raises the issue of the validity of self-reports, especially across race groups (see Hindelang, Hirschi, and Weis, 1979; 1981). Second, the usually small sample sizes and the absence of sufficient numbers of high-rate offenders preclude the generalization of results to offender groups that represent the most meaningful study subjects for research on juvenile and criminal careers (Cernkovich, Giordano, and Pugh, 1985).

At this point it is difficult to conclude that self-report and official measures are or are not congruent, particularly in terms of the correlates of delinquency, because of the lack of concurrent official and self-report data (on sufficient sample sizes) in prior research. It is obvious that this knowledge gap strongly suggests the use of multiple measures of illegal behavior. The use of such data allows a cross-validation check of official delinquency measures and provides for the analysis of a host of research issues that would not be possible with only one kind of offense data. Yet, at this point in time, it must be concluded, as has a recent assessment of the literature by Hawkins, Laub, and Lauritsen (1998), that the predominant involvement of African Americans in delinquency and crime cuts across the major sources of data on crime and offenders: (1) official crime data; (2) self-report studies; and (3) victimization surveys (see also Hawkins, Laub, Lauritsen, and Cothern, 2000).

The findings in some prior research with respect to officially recorded delinquency are especially pronounced. For example, I have reported evidence from the analysis of delinquency careers in the 1958 birth cohort study in Philadelphia, that nonwhite males in the cohort compared to white males (1) were twice as likely to be recorded as delinquent; and (2) had offense rates that were 2.6 times higher for overall offenses, 3.7 times higher for UCR index offenses, and 8.3 times higher for UCR violent crimes (Tracy, 1990). These findings come from a delinquency career analysis using longitudinal data on an entire birth cohort in a particular city and do not suffer from the generalizability problems of cross-sectional research which uses small samples. Consequently, my colleagues and I were able to study the racial and social class parameters of delinquency careers themselves (Tracy, Wolfgang, and Figlio, 1990) and the transition of delinquents to adult criminality (Tracy and Kempf-Leonard, 1996).

Perhaps at this point in time, criminologists will muster the fortitude to confront the results surrounding race and involvement in serious crime, however unpleasant this task may be, and whatever misguided criticisms may be levied against this effort. Clearly, a competent research agenda must be developed to investigate the causes and correlates of the race effects that have so often been found, rather than continue to focus on collateral issues, or else criminologists risk succumbing to the denial syndrome raised earlier by Kennedy (1997).

PRESENT RESEARCH

The previous sections establish the federally promulgated climate surrounding disproportionate minority confinement in the juvenile justice system. Essentially this climate is one in which differential processing data (especially statistics concerning confinement) for minority as opposed to white youth are immediately suspect. The present study was one component of a comprehensive, multi-year effort by the Criminal Justice Division of the state of Texas to fulfill its statutory mandates under the JJDP Act to investigate the processing of juvenile delinquency cases through the various agencies of the juvenile justice system and to analyze the various decision points at which juvenile justice officials determine whether and how juveniles should be handled. The ultimate goals of the research were to utilize this statewide study as a basis to measure disproportionate minority confinement, analyze its correlates, and help the state develop appropriate program initiatives as needed. Thus, this research project was conducted to meet the requirements of the federal mandates, rules and guidelines, detailed in this chapter concerning disproportionate minority confinement (Public Policy Research Institute, 1997).

The volume is organized as follows. Chapter 2 provides a review of prior research and the limitations surrounding prior investigations of disproportionate minority processing in the juvenile justice system. Chapter 3 discusses the methods that were used to select the counties for analysis and the measurement of the independent and dependent variables used in the analyses. Chapter 4 provides the results concerning the identification of minority overrepresentation in Texas using aggregate data, as opposed to case-level data. Chapters 5, 6, and 7 provide a case-level assessment of whether minority overrepresentation can be explained through legally permissible factors such as current offense and prior delinquency history, including severity of prior acts and the frequency with which prior acts were committed. Chapter 8 introduces the second phase of the research—a statewide survey of juvenile justice practitioners in Texas—and presents the results of the statewide survey of practitioners. Last, Chapter 9 provides a summary and the implications of the study.

2

Prior Research

Contrary to numerous characterizations in the literature, and especially in government-sponsored publications that are widely disseminated, the most striking aspect of the research concerning minorities and the juvenile justice system is not that it has provided substantial evidence of significant differentials by race or ethnicity in the handling of cases by juvenile court systems, but rather, that it is inconclusive and provides consensus on one issue, and one issue only. The sole aspect of the problem upon which prior research is in general agreement concerns the finding that the proportion of minorities processed through the various decision stages exceeds the proportion that minority youth represent in the at-risk youth population. Simply, prior research indicates minorities are overrepresented in cases handled by juvenile justice agencies. Unfortunately, the disproportionate minority processing research is inconclusive in all other respects. Prior research has provided neither methodologically nor statistically adequate documentation of the extent of the racial/ethnic differentials. More important, prior research has not brought forth a sufficiently competent body of research data concerning the causes of the disparity in processing.

There are crucial questions which remain unanswered. Are minorities overrepresented in juvenile justice statistics because they commit a disproportionate share of juvenile delinquency? Alternatively, are minorities overrepresented in juvenile justice data because the juvenile justice system exposes minority youth to differential handling which selects them for processing, in the first place, and continues to expose them to harsher treatment at successive processing stages, because and simply because, they are members of racial or ethnic minorities? Some research suggests that race/ethnicity is a significant factor in how dispositions are handled within the juvenile justice system, while other research examining the influence of race/ethnicity on dispositions has shown little or no race/ethnicity effect on case processing. Although often characterized to the contrary, the most significant aspects of the minority overrepresentation issue remain unresolved.

The inconclusiveness of prior research is often hidden, or even masked, owing to the fact that, despite serious deficiencies surrounding the methodological and statistical rigor of both the prior studies themselves and the widely cited assessment of the research literature, the research has been repeatedly characterized as if it has conclusively demonstrated that minority youth do indeed receive differential handling by juvenile justice authorities. Such characterizations have spawned, and continue to perpetuate, an image that the juvenile justice system is beset with racism and discrimination. Problematically, once such allegations become prevalent, it becomes exceedingly difficult to disprove them. Indeed, juvenile justice officials are placed in the unwarranted position of having to prove a negative—that is, that they are not guilty of racist and discriminatory practices, rather than the so-called experts having to prove that the allegation is indeed valid. Given the power of the OJJDP mandates reviewed in the previous chapter, the states are thus forced to defend themselves against a modern day "witch-hunt."

A highly referenced assessment (Pope and Feyerherm, 1990a, 1990b, 1992, 1993) of the minority processing research has played both a passive and an active role in the perpetuation of a distorted, or at least only a partial, image of the findings from the research on minorities and juvenile justice. Thus, this review must necessarily devote more than the usual critical scrutiny to the Pope and Feyerherm work than might usually be accorded to a single piece of prior research in a volume such as this. Thus, the Pope and Feyerherm study is highlighted because it is singularly important and because it is frequently cited as providing strong evidence that minorities are treated differently (i.e., more harshly). The study is almost always cited in OJJDP publications concerning disproportionate minority confinement, and the citations are usually employed to bolster an argument that there is substantial and widespread evidence of significant minority differentials in the system. A few examples of how OJJDP rely on the Pope and Feyerherm research will suffice to demonstrate this mischaracterization.

In a widely publicized and extensively distributed OJJDP report concerning *Juvenile Offenders and Victims* (and its companion piece, *Minorities in the Juvenile Justice System,* by Bilchik, 1999), Snyder and Sickmund (1999) offer the following:

> Further, there is *substantial* evidence that minority youth are often treated differently from majority youth within the juvenile justice system. In a review by Pope

and Feyerherm of existing literature, approximately two-thirds of the studies examined showed that racial and/or ethnic status did influence decision-making within the juvenile justice system. (1999: 193, emphasis added)

Snyder and Sickmund also portray the Pope and Feyerherm study as having established evidence of regional correlates of the differential handling. They note that:

Pope and Feyerherm found that research reveals *substantial variation* across rural, suburban, and urban areas. . . . For example, cases in urban jurisdictions are more likely to receive severe outcomes at various stages of processing than are cases in nonurban areas. Because minority populations are concentrated in urban areas, this effect may work to the disadvantage of minority youth and result in greater overrepresentation. (1999: 193, emphasis added)

Similarly, in another of OJJDP's Disproportionate Minority Confinement bulletins, Devine, Coolbaugh, and Jenkins (1998) use only one research citation (to Pope and Feyerherm, 1990a, 1990b, 1993) to provide support for the following appraisal:

A growing body of literature has focused on the problem of selection bias in juvenile justice systems. Much of this literature suggests that processing decisions in many State and local juvenile justice systems are not racially or culturally neutral. Minority juveniles are more likely than other juveniles to become involved in the system. The overrepresentation is apparent at various decision points in the juvenile justice system (arrest, detention, prosecution, and so forth) and may intensify as juveniles continue through the system. (1998: 2)

It will be demonstrated that the Pope and Feyerherm study does not provide sufficiently definitive findings that would permit claims as grandiose and as definitive as the selections previously offered by Snyder and Sickmund, Bilchik, and Devine, Coolbaugh, and Jenkins. Moreover, not only has the research community been guilty of exaggerating and embellishing the findings, but more importantly, Pope and Feyerherm themselves have offered changing characterizations of their results. For example, Pope and Feyerherm (1990a) have indicated that, "roughly one-third of the studies reviewed found no evidence of discrimination." On the contrary, the Pope and Feyerherm "Research Literature Matrix" (see 1990b, 1992) actually indicates that 19 research articles, or 41.3% of the literature studied, found no evidence of differential handling. Forty-one percent is a far cry from the one-third figure offered by the authors. In addition, there were a number of studies which could provide only "mixed" results for the race/ethnicity-based handling hypothesis. That is, nine studies found evidence of differential handling at a particular decision stage but not at others, while 18 studies found overall race/ethnicity effects. Thus, the majority of the research reviewed, 28 separate studies (or 60.8% of all studies examined), either provide no support or only partial support for the race/ethnicity hypothesis. Thus, the reality of prior research is in sharp contrast from the conclusion offered by Pope and Feyerherm that, "there is substantial support for the statement that there are race effects in operation within the juvenile justice system" (1990a: 325). In fact, one might even suggest that the Pope and Feyerherm study provides substantial evidence that race or ethnicity-based decision making was a significant overall problem in only a minority (39.2%) of the jurisdictions studied.

Another disturbing situation surrounding the portrayal of the Pope and Feyerherm research concerns the fact that the findings seem to change over time, or perhaps in emphasis, depending upon the context in which they are offered. That is, Pope and Feyerherm made a special point of mentioning in their final report that, "studies that found evidence of selection bias are generally no less sophisticated in methodology than those that found no such evidence" (1993: 2; see also 1992: 39). Yet, just a few years later, one of the authors indicated that, "In the more sophisticated and methodologically sound studies, we found the following set of possible explanations for overrepresentation" (Feyerherm, 1995: 11). Apparently, the "no less sophisticated" have now become "more sophisticated and methodologically sound." Clearly, the Pope and Feyerherm assessment of the literature requires close scrutiny so that what it does and does not definitively establish will be fully explicated and observers can judge for themselves the extent to which broad generalizations of system bias are warranted.

POPE AND FEYERHERM ASSESSMENT OF THE LITERATURE

Pope and Feyerherm have framed the necessity of their assessment of the juvenile literature as follows:

> It is critically important to examine this body of literature so that strengths and weaknesses can be determined and gaps in our knowledge base be identified. Although racial effects on the adult criminal justice system have undergone thorough review, no one has yet applied rigorous methodology to inquiring just what effect minority status has on juvenile justice. (1993: 1)

Unfortunately, Pope and Feyerherm's fifteen-month study conducted for OJJDP does not deliver the rigorous methodology in assessing the literature concerning minorities and juvenile justice that was promised. The study did, however, have the potential to provide a meaningful analysis and assessment of the research literature, but this potential is unfulfilled. The researchers first identified 250 potentially relevant articles dealing with minority processing. Articles were eliminated if they did not focus on minority status or if specific juvenile justice decision points were not included.

This resulted in a pool of 46 articles which became the basis of the assessment. The researchers coded the following important aspects of the studies under review: (1) sample size; (2) sampling method; (3) method of data collection; (4) type of statistical analysis; (5) measurement of independent and dependent variables; (6) definitions of minority status; and (7) specific processing stage (arrest, detention, informal/formal adjudication, and sentencing). The coded data were transferred to an SPSS file for analysis. Despite what appears to be a comprehensive content analysis of the research literature, including the coding of crucial design and statistical analysis features of the studies, the Pope and Feyerherm study is basically descriptive, is practically devoid of analysis (at least it reports no analytical results), and thus, provides little more than a cataloguing of prior research. The specific deficiencies of the study are as follows.

First, Pope and Feyerherm, in order to guard against the problem of "selection bias" themselves, should have provided a more detailed discussion of the exclusion process by which the original pool of 250 studies was reduced to the sub-sample of 46. In the absence of such information, it is not possible to determine exactly how or why any given study was excluded. Thus, a listing of the entire set of 250 articles along with the reason for its inclusion/exclusion would facilitate an independent assessment of the appropriateness of their decision that a particular study should be included or excluded. After all, 204 studies were excluded from the analysis. What effect did this exclusion have on the results?

Second, despite the coding of highly useful and analytically valuable information about the studies, there is no assessment of the connection between such information about the study and the results that were and were not obtained. Given the availability of such data on all the studies, Pope and Feyerherm should have utilized such classificatory information to analyze the studies so as to demonstrate that particular findings, whether they supported or did not support the differential handling of the juveniles, were or were not correlated with certain design or analysis features. The following represent but a few of the particulars which should have been assessed by Pope and Feyerherm in order that they be in a position to deliver the rigorous methodology they promised.

Research Setting

The research setting of the studies should have been investigated extensively. Research studies were conducted in various jurisdictions: small and large, rural/urban, and northern, southern, midwestern, and eastern jurisdictions. Were any of these location types correlated with the findings? Surely, these locations represent a sufficient cross-section of jurisdictions providing for a non-negligible likelihood of various Issues which would vary considerably across these types of locations. Issues, such as the extant crime rate, extent of juvenile crime problem, relative concentration of minorities, workloads in the juvenile court, and so on, are all-important aspects of the location, and thereby the study itself, which may have been related to findings of differential handling. Yet, Pope and Feyerherm did not assess these characteristics.

Sample Selection

The type of sampling designs should have been analyzed. Was the sample statewide or from a particular jurisdiction? Was this jurisdiction chosen randomly? Was the sample of cases drawn from the front end of system processing like intake, or was it drawn from a later stage, like cases eligible for adjudication, and data on earlier decision points were collected retrospectively? It is clear that the extent to which cases are drawn earlier rather than later may be related to the capability of the research to document differential handling. As cases are drawn later and later, the cases become more and more homogenous and the variance surrounding the independent variables becomes concomitantly reduced, thereby attenuating the predictive power of the measures (simply, predictor variables with small variance have little predictive efficiency). Further, were findings of racism and discrimination more likely in smaller samples or larger samples, samples from one county versus statewide? In the absence of any analysis of sampling designs or sample characteristics, it cannot be determined with any degree of confidence whether particular findings might be merely an artifact of particular research designs or sampling methods rather than genuine findings of discrimination.

Measurement of Variables

It is crucial to investigate and analyze the manner in which the studies measured the variables of interest and the extent to which such measurement issues might be related to differential handling. Studies which used binary measures for the decisions at various processing stages are able to use (and should have utilized) particular statistical analysis techniques as compared to other studies which scaled the dependent variables as ordinal measures (and could not and should not have analyzed the data with certain techniques). Further, a highly significant aspect of the studies concerns the manner in which prior record, prior offense severity, and current offense severity were measured. Were quantitative scales used for assessing severity? Or, was offense seriousness measured by an offense category hierarchy like felony versus misdemeanor? The extent to which these measurement issues were associated with the results should have been assessed. In the absence of such analyses, it is difficult to assess the relative quality of the measurement models, or the extent to which variation in such measurement quality may have influenced the finding of racism or discrimination against minority youth. Again, it is not possible to resolve whether differential handling was real or merely an artifact of the research process.

Mode of Statistical Analysis

A crucial aspect of the studies being assessed concerns the rigor, power, and appropriateness of the statistical analyses that were performed. It would be essential to go well beyond the characterization of sophisticated/unsophisticated used by Pope and Feyerherm. Instead, they should have assessed whether analyses were bivariate versus multivariate and the correlation of such techniques to the findings. Then further, Pope and Feyerherm should have scrutinized the multivariate techniques indicating whether (1) the analyses were appropriate (ordinary least squares regression, for example, is inappropriate with a binary dependent variable); and (2) certain statistical tests were more likely to find differential handling or not compared to other techniques, which albeit multivariate, are less powerful. Thus, statistical analysis techniques could be sophisticated in Pope and Feyerherm's terminology, and yet, be inappropriate for the type of data that were being analyzed.

Those examples represent only a small sample of the necessary analyses and assessment issues that should have been conducted in evaluating the juvenile processing literature. Further, these analyses could have quite easily been accomplished as follows. The assessment could have coded each article as a dummy variable indicating whether the article reported finding discrimination or not (0 = "did not find"; 1 = "found" differential handling). One would then have regressed, using a logit model, the various article characteristics on the binary dependent variable, which would have produced a set of coefficients (and accompanying standard errors and t-scores) telling us which design features were significantly associated with the binary dependent variable concerning discrimination. Similarly, the dependent variable could also have been coded as a tri-level measure (1 = "did not find"; 2 = "found mixed"; and 3 = "found overall" evidence of discrimination) and the data then analyzed using an "ordered probit model," a discriminant function analysis, or a cluster-type routine so that predictive or discriminating characteristics could be identified.

The Pope and Feyerherm assessment conducted none of these analyses and did not appear to have utilized the characteristics of the studies in any rigorous fashion to assess the quality of the underlying research. It seems questionable, therefore, for anyone to claim as has been reported previously, that the Pope and Feyerherm results provide *substantial evidence* of differential handling of minority youth, or that the study has shown that *cases in urban jurisdictions are more likely to receive severe outcomes at various stages of processing than are cases in non-urban areas.* There is no statistically meaningful way in which such characterizations can be validly gleaned from the Pope and Feyerherm study.

While Pope and Feyerherm are quite right that "It is critically important to examine this body of literature so that strengths and weaknesses can be determined and gaps in our knowledge base be identified," their study does not identify the strengths, weaknesses, or knowledge gaps in the minority overrepresentation research.

Other Assessments

The Pope and Feyerherm (1990a, 1990b) assessment of the literature on minority processing in the juvenile justice system has been augmented by other OJJDP commissioned reviews. Feyerherm (1993) has completed a review of efforts by the states to comply with OJJDP Disproportionate Minority Confinement mandates. This review was augmented by a similar assessment by Community Research Associates, Inc. (Hamparian and Leiber, 1997). Neither of these reviews provides a substantive or methodological assessment of the research being conducted by the states to document their efforts to comply with the OJJDP mandates. The reviews are nothing more than descriptions of state plans and the compilation of aggregate measures of minority overrepresentation. Unfortunately, therefore, OJJDP has sacrificed two more valuable opportunities to commission rigorous assessments of the nature and extent of differential minority handling in the juvenile justice system across the country and has provided instead sheer descriptive presentations.

PRIOR RESEARCH

Despite many federal government publications which strongly suggest a very different view of the literature, the minority processing research is inconclusive and has established no consistent body of findings. While some research suggests that race/ethnicity is a significant factor in how dispositions are administered (see, e.g., Bishop and Frazier, 1988a, 1996; Bortner, Sunderland, and Winn, 1985; Fagan, Slaughter, and Hartstone, 1987; Feyerherm, 1981; Johnson and Secret, 1992), other research examining the influence of race/ethnicity on dispositions has shown little or no race/ethnicity effect (Bailey and Peterson, 1981; Bortner and Reed, 1985; Cohen and Kluegel, 1978, 1979; Horwitz and Wasserman, 1980; Kowalski and Rickicki, 1982).

There are, however, a few commonalities which have emerged concerning possible explanations for the inconclusiveness of previous research efforts (Feyerherm, 1995; Kempf, Decker, and Bing, 1990; Bridges, Conley, Beretta, and Engen, 1993; Kempf-Leonard, Pope, and Feyerherm, 1995). One reason suggested for the variability of the findings is that many of the early studies of disproportionality focused on only one specific stage of the juvenile justice decision-making process. Restricting the scope to include only one decision point limits the capacity to detect differential treatment at different stages of the system (Pope, 1984; Pope and Feyerherm, 1990a, 1990b; Kempf-Leonard and Sontheimer, 1995). Few of the early studies have examined the treatment of youth at multiple process points. Recent research has attempted to overcome this major deficiency and has focused on four general decision points within the juvenile justice system where racial bias may occur: (1) police/referral decision; (2) detention at intake; (3) prosecutor's decision; and (4) court dispositions. In the present study, focus is on the decision areas subsequent to arrest. In order to shed light on police arrest decisions as an underpinning for the data on juvenile justice processing, the present study analyzed aggregate data by race/ethnicity and gender to determine trends in arrests and referrals for juvenile justice processing statewide, and in the three counties under investigation (see Chapter 4).

A brief discussion of the trends in the literature examining race/ethnicity and discrimination at three crucial decision points follows: (1) detention at intake; (2) prosecutor's decision; and (3) court dispositions. The literature includes published studies and unpublished reports (usually conducted by individual states as part of the compliance process for OJJDP minority overrepresentation mandates).

Detention at Intake

At the detention stage of juvenile justice processing, cases are typically reviewed by an intake officer, who decides whether to detain or release the juvenile. Youth who are released are often placed in the custody of their parents or other responsible adult(s). Some youth are detained temporarily, pending transfers to other agencies or jurisdictions; others are detained in secure facilities for days and possibly weeks. In Texas, as in other states, a juvenile may be held in detention (incarceration) after intake for up to two working days before being brought before a judge or referee. While in such short-term detention, a juvenile is brought before a judge or referee, who determines if continued detention is warranted, or if the juvenile will be placed in (protective) custody or released (often to parents), pending adjudication and disposition of the case.

The decision to detain has significant implications for subsequent stages of the decision-making process (Bridges et al., 1993). Consequently, it is one of the most important junctures in the process. Youth who are detained are more likely than youth who are not detained to have their cases forwarded for prosecution. A number of studies have found that a juvenile's race/ethnicity is a significant predictor of the decision to detain. Although many of these studies are unpublished reports of research conducted for state juvenile justice commissions, some are nonetheless rigorous assessments.

For example, Kempf et al. (1990) studied youth processed in the juvenile justice system in Missouri. They used a sophisticated stratified sampling design and covered both urban and rural court jurisdictions. They found that African Americans in rural areas were significantly less likely than whites to be detained, while in urban courts, white youth were significantly less likely than African-American youth to be detained. However, Kempf et al. found that a juvenile's prior referrals and the presence of legal counsel were the strongest predictors of detention, followed by the absence of parents in court, felony referrals, violence, race/ethnicity, status offenses, and non-police referrals. In addition to race, Kempf et al. determined that juvenile girls were less likely to be detained. However, other studies have shown that females do not receive more lenient treatment (Johnson and Secret, 1992; Leiber, 1992). Kempf (1992; see also Kempf-Leonard and Sontheimer, 1995) conducted a similar study in Pennsylvania. A stratified sample of 1,797 cases was drawn from urban, suburban, and rural courts. The results showed that, given similar other factors, detention was more common for Latino and African-American youth.

Leiber (1992) conducted a comprehensive assessment of minority overrepresentation in three Iowa counties. In County A Leiber found that race was not predictive of detention status. Instead, significant effects were obtained for prior contacts, currently under court authority for a previous offense, charges for multiple offenses, and severity of offense. In County B, in addition to the offense conduct type measures, Native American youth were more likely to be detained than white juveniles. In County C, blacks were more likely (marginally significant, $p < .10$) to be detained.

In their study of juvenile justice processing in Washington State, which included 1,777 juvenile justice cases, Bridges et al. (1993) reported that older non-Anglo youth were more likely than Anglo youth to be detained, even when researchers controlled for a number of differences between cases and personal characteristics of the youth. This study also suggested that youth with irregular school attendance and from single-parent households were significantly more likely to be detained than youth with good attendance and from two-parent households. To the extent that minorities are more likely than Anglos to come from single-parent families and are more likely to have irregular school attendance, they are at greater risk than Anglos for being detained for committing similar offenses.

In addition to race/ethnicity, family structure has been shown to have an effect on a juvenile's processing outcomes. Researchers suggest that youth from female-headed households, particularly minority households, may receive more intrusive treatment and sanctions, due to a perceived lack of adequate parental supervision (Pope and Feyerherm, 1992). Black and Smith's (1981) research suggests that a juvenile's living arrangements (not living with natural parents) and prior record were the two most important variables in the decision to detain a juvenile.

A juvenile's criminal history can (and legally should be allowed to) influence the manner in which subsequent offenses are handled. A number of studies provide evidence that findings of racial discrimination at various processing stages have been confounded by the effects of a juvenile's previous detention (Bishop and Frazier, 1988a; Johnson and Secret, 1992; Kempf et al., 1990; Lockhart, Kurtz, Stutphen, and Gauger, 1991; Leiber, 1992). This research suggests that, as youth with multiple prior offenses typically receive harsher treatment than first-time offenders, studies of racial disparity must take into account the number and severity of past offense for each juvenile record examined. Bortner and Reed (1985) found that the two strongest predictors of the assignment of youth to detention at intake were the number of prior referrals that a juvenile had accumulated and his/her access to legal counsel. Youth with prior referrals were more likely to be detained for the current offense than were youth without prior referrals. Other research confirms the importance of prior referrals and the presence of counsel in the decision to detain (Frazier and Bishop, 1995).

Bishop and Frazier (1988b) examined the disposition of 161,369 juvenile justice cases in Florida between 1985 and 1987 and found that race/ethnicity was predictive of being held in secure detention, even after researchers controlled for prior record, offense severity, and other important background variables. The typical non-Anglo juvenile in this study had a 16% probability of being placed in detention, compared to a 12% probability for Anglo youth. Like other researchers, they also found that the presence of a prior record was one of the leading predictors of detention.

Other researchers, however, have found little evidence that race/ethnicity affects how youth are assigned to detention. Using case records from Alabama (Jefferson County), McCarthy (1985) found that a juvenile's prior offenses and the severity of the current offense explained detention status, whereas race/ethnicity was not a significant predictor. McCarthy and Smith (1986) have also conducted a very sophisticated path analysis of juvenile justice decision making, including detention and disposition. Unfortunately, the authors used "days of detention" rather than detention status, and an ordinal "disposition scale" rather than discrete dispositions. The results which do indicate some race differentials are not comparable to other studies and the design suffers from "omitted variable bias" as severity of prior offenses was not included in the analysis.

Prosecutor's Decision

Further penetration in the juvenile justice system is achieved when petitions are filed by the prosecuting attorney. The decision to file petitions with the juvenile court for adjudication of youth is generally made by the prosecuting attorney. The most consistent finding at this decision point is that, regardless of their race/ethnicity, youth who are detained prior to adjudication are much more likely to be subsequently charged with offenses and confront court hearings than youth who are not detained (Bridges et al., 1993; Kempf, 1992).

However, prior research has not documented a consistent association between race/ethnicity and the decision to file court petitions. Kempf et al. (1990) did not find a relationship between race and the petition decision in Missouri. Yet, Kempf (1992) found that, in both urban and rural juvenile justice jurisdictions, petitions were filed more often for African-American youth than for Anglo youth. In addition, youth from single-parent households or youth with alcohol abuse problems were more likely to have petitions filed against them. Bridges et al. (1993) examined factors associated with court referrals of felonies and violent offenses and found that non-Anglo youth were more likely than their Anglo peers to be charged with an offense, even when controls for case-specific differences were taken into account. However, other findings in this same study suggested that, in some instances, non-Anglo youth were less likely to have petitions filed against them. Non-Anglo youth, especially Hispanics with prior records of being diverted (away from prosecution) were more likely than Anglo youth to be diverted for subsequent offenses. The petition stage results are clouded even further by the Leiber (1992) study which found that in County A there was no race effect, while in County B minority youth were significantly less likely to be petitioned to court compared to whites.

Bishop and Frazier's (1996) examination of juvenile cases in Florida indicates that, like the decision to detain, prosecutorial decision making is significantly influenced by the seriousness of the offense and by prior records for a given juvenile case, yet it is only slightly influenced by race/ethnicity. They report that in relation to its impact on detention status, "The impact of race is very modest: the typical white youth has a 32% chance of being referred to court, compared to a 34% chance for the typical nonwhite youth" (p. 404). They also indicate that both gender and age influence the probability of court referrals.

Disposition

A review of the literature suggests, but not very conclusively, that the dispositions of juvenile court hearings disfavor minority youth and that sentences resulting in confinement are disproportionately higher for minority youth than for Anglo youth. Researchers have found that, when compared with Anglo youth, African-American youth are more likely to have their cases adjudicated (Huizinga and Elliot, 1987; Fagan et al., 1987) and are less likely to have their cases dismissed (Kempf et al., 1990). Among a sample of juvenile cases examined by Fagan et al. (1987), African Americans were less likely than Anglos to have their cases dismissed, except in more serious offenses. Kempf et al. (1990) suggest that the differential treatment of youth might be explained by the type of counsel they have access to, and that "there is evidence that black youths who commit serious offenses are more likely to admit their guilt, while their white counterparts may plead to lesser charges with a private attorney" (1990: 17).

Race/ethnicity has been found to be a predictor of dispositions, even with controls for relevant legal criteria such as prior record, severity of the offense, and the type and level of injury or damage (Bishop and Frazier, 1988a, 1988b, 1996; Bortner, Sunderland, and Winn, 1985; Fagan et al., 1987). Bridges et al. (1993) found that race/ethnicity was directly related to confinement sentences, a pattern that persisted even after adjustments were made in the seriousness of offenses, prior record, juvenile's age, and other legally relevant characteristics.

Other research concerning the likelihood of an adjudication or a disposition which imposes confinement has not found consistent racial differentials. Kempf et al. (1990) did not find significant race effects in Missouri for either dispositions or sentences. Similarly, in Kempf's (1992; Kempf-Leonard and Sontheimer, 1995) research in the Pennsylvania study, race was not only unrelated to adjudication and sentencing, but African-American youth were significantly less likely than whites to receive unfavorable court adjudications. The absence of race effects at adjudication and sentencing has also been reported by Leiber (1992).

As in the analysis of other stages of juvenile justice processing, higher rates of detention among minority youth increase the likelihood of their being sentenced to confinement following adjudication. Bridges, Conley, Engen, and Price-Spratlen (1995) found that minority youth in their sample were, on average, prosecuted at substantially higher rates than Anglos. They attributed this finding to the significantly increased likelihood of prosecution for minority youth with prior records of juvenile court referral, and for youth detained prior to adjudication. As minority youth are much more likely than their Anglo counterparts to be detained prior to adjudication, they are at greater risk for more serious punitive measures, including confinement, within the juvenile justice system. Besides prior offenses and the seriousness of the current offense(s), other personal and demographic characteristics can influence outcomes. The location of the juvenile court (Kempf-Leonard and Sontheimer, 1995) can make a difference. In some cases, urban courts have been found to be more evenhanded in their processing of minorities than were rural courts (Bridges et al., 1993; Kempf-Leonard and Sontheimer, 1995).

In summary, it is clear, from even a brief review of prior research, that research investigating differential minority processing across various stages of the juvenile justice system has not produced a consistent body of findings, and certainly has not yielded consistent evidence that minority youth are handled differently as a major consequence of race or ethnicity. Some studies find differential handling at certain stages but not at others. Some studies find urban versus rural differentials, while other studies find the reverse. Still other research finds no racial differentials at all, and instead, has determined that youth (regardless of race or ethnicity) proceed further and further through the various stages of the system and receive unfavorable decisions at these stages because of the severity of their present conduct and/or the frequency and severity of their prior delinquent conduct. Despite the view maintained in OJJDP publications to the contrary, "substantial" evidence of systematic racial discrimination is simply not available.

Limitations

Of course, there may be numerous explanations for the inconsistency of prior research. Therefore, a few of the more obvious candidates are offered next by way of suggesting the possibilities for the inconsistent results rather than being an exhaustive discussion.

First, the inconclusiveness of earlier research may be a function of the research design and statistical methodology used. A great deal of the previous research has relied primarily on bivariate statistical techniques and has thereby been restricted to examining associations between race/ethnicity and other variables one by one. Furthermore, the differential handling findings from these studies are very probably confounded by the uncontrolled variance of other key variables. For instance, while researchers could empirically verify racial differences among youth in court dispositions, they were unable to determine whether (1) these differences were attributed to racial bias within the courts; (2) they were due to differences in the severity or the types of offenses that Anglo and non-Anglo youth were accused of; or (3) they collectively represented an artifact of disparities that occurred during earlier stages in juvenile justice processing.

In order to address these and other questions, recent research has incorporated more rigorous statistical techniques, such as multivariate regression analyses, and these more rigorous techniques have allowed researchers to control for a number of critical variables (both offense-related and sociodemographic) and to examine and explain outcomes at individual decision points. However, even though more recent studies have utilized rigorous multivariate techniques, such as logistic regression, multivariate models have not always been used correctly. For example, a paper by Feld (1989, 1995) demonstrates the dangers of using advanced statistical techniques incorrectly. Feld used statewide data for Minnesota from 1986 and selected all cases from the largest county, Hennepin (Minneapolis), as it also had the highest proportion of minority youth according to census data. After presenting a series of the customary bivariate analyses, Feld reports regression analyses of factors influencing the following: (1) appointment of counsel; (2) detention decision; and (3) out-of-home/secure placement. The significant problem with Feld's multivariate analyses is simply that he used ordinary least-squares (OLS) regression analysis with binary dependent variables. It is well known that OLS statistical analysis procedures are totally inappropriate under such circumstances. Among the most significant problems associated with using least-squares regression analysis with binary dependent variables are the following: (1) the assumption of homoskedasticity is untenable; (2) the dependent variable is bounded, that is, between 0 and 1, but the predicted values of *Y* can be greater than 1 or negative; (3) the error terms will not be independent of the *X* values; and (4) deriving estimates of *Y* is complicated further when explanatory variables are themselves categorical (like race). There is every reason to believe, therefore, that Feld's findings are meaningless and are merely an artifact of using inappropriate statistical analyses.

Another prime example of using inadequate, or at least less than robust statistical analyses, is a paper by Austin (1995). (See also Austin, Dimas, and Steinhart, 1991.) Austin collected aggregate data on arrests, dispositions, and confinement data for California, but also collected case-level data, covering the point of arrest through final court disposition, from California's Bureau of Criminal Statistics. Austin's findings from the analysis of aggregate data indicated that minorities, especially African Americans, are overrepresented in California's juvenile justice system (1995: Tables 7.1–7.5). However, of particular relevance here is the fact that the assessment of whether such overrepresentation was legitimate was reported through the use of cell percentage comparisons based on contingency table analysis without any accompanying significance tests or measures of association to assess the quality and strength of the results. Further, Austin used the approach of introducing only one variable at a time in a process of elaboration to explain the relationship between minority status and two key dependent variables (detention status and secure confinement disposition). On the basis of these rudimentary analyses, Austin concluded that African-American youth were disadvantaged at both stages of juvenile processing. The reader learns only in a footnote (Austin, 1995: footnote 4) that a logistic analysis was conducted which showed a "residual ethnic effect" but one for which "the effects of race were clearly diminished." How small was the residual effect? How diminished was the race factor after using a powerful technique, such as logistic regression analysis, compared to the much more limited technique of contingency tables? Which background factors were significant predictors of the processing decisions? These crucial questions are not answered.

Perhaps the best example of research that includes both inadequate measurement and limited statistical analysis is a very recent report by the National Council on Crime and Delinquency (NCCD) (*And Justice for Some,* Poe-Yamagata and Jones, 2000), that was released with much fanfare at the National Press Club on 25 April 2000, and covered extensively by the print media (see for example, *Washington Post,* 26 April 2000; *USA*

Today, 27 April 2000). The NCCD report claims that minority youth are disadvantaged at each and every stage of the juvenile justice system compared to white youth. Although the research was conducted some ten years after the Pope and Feyerherm assessment discussed previously, and although most of the research community has moved beyond mere descriptive analyses, the NCCD study reflects the three most glaring errors of past research. First, the measurement of offense severity is accomplished through a four-category system (i.e., person, property, drugs, and public order). It is clear that these gross offense categories do not permit a sophisticated analysis of just how different and more severe the offenses may be (even within a category). Second, the study makes only a rudimentary effort to control for prior record. The measure used is prior admissions to facilities rather than the necessary measures of number and severity of prior offenses. Third, there are no multivariate analyses included in the study, but rather, only descriptive tables and charts are used. Clearly, this is the type of study that speaks loudly about racism within the juvenile justice system yet offers weak data and inadequate analyses to back up such accusations. It is not possible to demonstrate that the juvenile justice process is racist or discriminatory throughout the various decision points without controlling for crucial variables that affect such decisions. Thus the failure to measure and statistically account for the quantitative severity of the current offense, the frequency and severity of past criminal record, and the number and outcome of past court dispositions is a failure indeed.

Second, previous research has analyzed the administration of juvenile justice only in selected jurisdictions in a particular area (e.g., Kempf et al., 1990), revealing considerable variation among jurisdictions regarding how juvenile justice is administered to minorities. This is a serious limitation. By overlooking important regional and area differences in how juvenile justice cases are processed, the generalizability of these studies has been severely constrained (Bridges et al., 1995). Much of the previous research has thus neglected the broader context within which processing decisions are carried out.

Last, the focus of most prior research has been almost exclusively on the characteristics of cases and their outcomes, without consideration of the views and perceptions of juvenile justice administrators and personnel (Kempf, 1992; Kempf-Leonard et al., 1995; Bridges et al., 1995). Because the views, perceptions, policies, and practices of juvenile justice practitioners may affect the processing of youth accused of offenses, by not explicitly accounting for this information in the research, previous studies are limited to only partially addressing the issue of racial disparity. Bridges and Steen (1998) have recently provided a very persuasive argument in this regard. They note:

> A critical but overlooked concern is how court officials' perceptions of juvenile offenders contribute to racial differences in legal dispositions. Differing perceptions

of youth and their crimes may legitimate racial disparities in official assessments of a youth's dangerousness and risks of future criminal behavior. They also may foster the differential treatment of minority and white offenders in the disposition of criminal cases. (1998: 554)

Although the Bridges and Steen study did not find significant racial differentials, and in fact found that case characteristics mediated the relationship between race and perceived risk, the study is important for developing such an innovative approach to minority overrepresentation research—including practitioner judgments as part of the analysis of outcomes. Further research should endeavor to follow this example. After all, at the various stages of juvenile justice decision making, it is the behavior of court and system officials that research is trying to explain—not the behavior of the juveniles themselves. The present study was conducted prior to the Bridges and Steen article, yet it essentially follows their advice and includes qualitative insights gleaned from a survey of juvenile justice practitioners statewide.

Like others before it, the current study is necessarily selective in scope as it is restricted to three Texas counties. However, the research relied on a combination of data—aggregate arrests, juvenile referral data compiled by state agencies, and survey data—to provide a comprehensive picture of juvenile processing in Texas. Further, this review of the current literature underscores significant gaps in our understanding of the nature and extent of racial disparity and the underlying attitudes and perspectives of the various system personnel that administer the process.

In attending to many of the suggestions and limitations of previous studies, this study reflects an attempt to take these concerns seriously. First, juvenile processing is examined at various stages (detention at intake, referral to the prosecutor, prosecutor's decision, and court disposition). Second, both quantitative data (juvenile archival) and qualitative data (from open-ended responses to survey questions) are included. Third, to ensure that the study covers as wide a range of disparity as possible, it focuses on African-American, Hispanic, and Asian-American minority youth, and females, and varying county types (i.e., two urban and one rural) were selected. Last, multivariate statistical techniques (logistic regression) were used to test for significant correlates of juvenile decision making across the various decision points.

3

Methods

BACKGROUND TO PRESENT RESEARCH

The previous chapters establish the federally promulgated climate surrounding disproportionate minority confinement in the juvenile justice system. Essentially this climate is one in which differential processing data (especially statistics concerning confinement) for minority as opposed to white youth are immediately suspect. The present study was one component of a comprehensive, multi-year effort by the Criminal Justice Division of the state of Texas to fulfill its statutory mandates under the JJDP Act to investigate the processing of juvenile delinquency cases through the various agencies of the juvenile justice system and to analyze the various decision points at which juvenile justice officials determine whether and how juveniles should be handled. The ultimate goal of the research was to utilize this statewide study as a basis to measure disproportionate minority confinement, analyze its correlates, if any, and inform the development of appropriate program initiatives as needed. Thus, this research project was conducted to meet the requirements of the federal mandates, rules and guidelines, as detailed in Chapter 1 concerning disproportionate minority confinement.

Prior to this study, the Criminal Justice Division, through its Juvenile Justice and Delinquency Prevention Advisory Board, and a special subcommittee on Minority Youth in the Juvenile Justice System, had completed an earlier assessment and provided a plan for addressing minority overrepresentation. These issues were addressed in a previous report, *Balancing the*

Scales (Vickers, 1992). After reviewing *Balancing the Scales*, OJJDP determined that Texas was not in full compliance with Section 223(a), (23) of the JJDP Act. OJJDP had determined that the state plan had not provided the required assessment of the differences across minority groups concerning arrest, diversion, court disposition, commitment, and transfer to adult court. Consequently, beginning in August 1994, the Criminal Justice Division engaged in ongoing remedial actions to address the issue of noncompliance. These actions indicate the extent to which the Criminal Justice Division developed strategic initiatives to comply with the OJJDP disproportionate minority confinement guidelines. It is instructive, therefore, to review briefly the history of these efforts.

In September 1994, the Criminal Justice Division contacted the Texas Criminal Justice Policy Council (CJPC), the state agency with a statutory mandate to conduct studies and make recommendations concerning policy issues in the criminal and juvenile justice systems, seeking assistance in conducting research on minority overrepresentation. The Criminal Justice Division was advised that the CJPC was conducting an offender-based study in Dallas County consisting of 1,500 case referrals. In October 1994, the Criminal Justice Division contacted OJJDP to determine if the CJPC study could be supplemented and then replicated statewide to meet OJJDP guidelines. OJJDP officially responded to the Criminal Justice Division in January 1995, advising that the Dallas County study and the Criminal Justice Division's plans for a statewide study were acceptable and further asked for a time-limited plan for the FY 95 formula grant application.

In April 1995, the Criminal Justice Division requested technical assistance of OJJDP through Community Research Associates, Inc. (a national contractor chosen by OJJDP to provide assistance to the states), with respect to anticipated surveys for Phase II of the minority overrepresentation assessment. In May 1995, the Criminal Justice Division, together with the Criminal Justice Policy Council and the Texas Youth Commission, met with representatives of Community Research Associates. The meeting constituted a comprehensive review of the overrepresentation issue and the development of a specific plan for subsequent action, including the formulation of a Request for Applications (RFA) for an outside contractor to conduct required data collection in support of the overrepresentation assessment. Later in May 1995, the Criminal Justice Division advised OJJDP of the meeting with Community Research Associates, Inc., and also submitted a task list and timetable for the revised study of minority overrepresentation.

In late May 1995, the Criminal Justice Division sought approval from the General Counsel to publish the Request for Applications for a minority overrepresentation study in the *Texas Register.* The RFA was subsequently published with a 3 July 1995 submission date. Two applications were received in response to the RFA. The Criminal Justice Division assembled an applications scoring team who subsequently competitively evaluated the two proposals. In late August 1995, the application from the Public Policy Research Institute of Texas A&M University was awarded the grant to conduct the research on minority overrepresentation. In early September 1995, the Criminal Justice Division appointed a Minority Confinement Study Group to meet with the Texas A&M representatives, and thus, provide an advisory mechanism which would ensure that the research would be well planned and monitored in an ongoing fashion.

The ongoing efforts of the Criminal Justice Division have been guided by a single overriding concern—that given the importance of juvenile justice processing, the present research should represent a comprehensive, objective, and scientifically defensible study. The Criminal Justice Division firmly believed that the citizens of Texas, government officials, the press, and other interested parties should expect nothing less than a study as definitive as possible in informing programmatic and policy initiatives. The present research adhered to the principle that this investigation should produce empirical findings that would assist the Criminal Justice Division in responding to the issue of minority overrepresentation in the Texas juvenile justice system and address the attendant OJJDP guidelines. In order to appreciate fully the importance of the research, it is useful to highlight here the design of the research and how the various components of the study fit together to provide a comprehensive assessment of juvenile justice processing in Texas.

The study design called for the selection of three Texas counties for which data collection would occur. The three counties selected represent a useful basis for comparative analyses—two of the large urban counties in the state are included and a small rural county was also chosen. Second, the research collected and analyzed two kinds of juvenile justice system data in the three counties. The first set of data collected and analyzed were aggregate statistics pertaining to arrests of juveniles as recorded by the Texas Department of Public Safety for the period 1990–1994. These arrest statistics were supplemented by a second set of aggregate data from the Texas Juvenile Probation Commission concerning the delinquency cases that were referred to probation departments for further processing. These aggregate counts of arrests and referrals were then merged with population data so that *prevalence rates* across gender, and race/ethnicity categories could be computed and analyzed. Moreover, because these aggregate data cover the period 1990–1994, they comprise a useful baseline period with which to assess the differential involvement of juveniles in various categories of crime. Texas has been experiencing population growth over the past several years, and as of 1994, Texas became the second most populous state after California. It is thus crucially necessary to document the extent to which population growth and the trends in juvenile crime are related.

In addition to aggregate data, the study conducted data collection and analysis on a random sample of offenders in each county using county automated case-management systems. This procedure facilitated the tracking of individual cases through the various processing points of the juvenile justice system. Through the application of multivariate statistical models, the research was able to investigate and determine if particular categories of youth were being processed differently as their cases moved from stage to stage of the juvenile justice system. The use of client tracking data provided two major advantages to the study. First, the assessment could directly calculate differences in the handling of youth with reference to stage-specific transition probabilities as opposed to the imprecise inferences that must be drawn from summary data. Second, client tracking permitted the establishment of relationships between case characteristics (i.e., prior record, instant offense severity) to processing decisions and thereby permitted the determination of whether there are any race or ethnicity biases in these relationships.

A second, and highly important, prong of the research project was the use of survey methodology to conduct a statewide study of juvenile justice practitioners. The surveys address a range of significant issues concerning the processing of delinquency cases, factors related to the genesis of delinquency, and general concerns about delinquency and resources available in the juvenile system to respond to the problem of delinquent behavior. The use of the survey methodology was crucially necessary to tap into the underlying factors that various juvenile justice decision makers may be using in rendering processing decisions as a juvenile moves through the system. Further, the use of a statewide telephone survey to supplement the case-level data collection in the three study counties provided very useful comparative data that enhanced the determination of whether minority overrepresentation occurs and the identification of factors correlated with overrepresentation.

SAMPLE SELECTION

In Texas, juvenile cases are processed at the county level, as juvenile probation departments and courts are organized along county lines. The data for this study were obtained from three Texas counties: two urban, referred to as County-1 and County-2, and one rural, referred to as County-3. These particular counties were chosen because they reflect very different environments (extremely large urban, large urban, and small rural), and thus, constitute very different contexts for the occurrence of delinquent acts in the first place, and different local cultures for the processing of delinquency cases once they happen. In addition, these three counties were selected because each had the following: (1) a representative proportion of racial/ethnic minorities, as compared with the entire state;[1] (2) a sufficient number of annual juvenile referrals; and (3) a computerized database. Furthermore, because each county was easily accessible to the researchers, the data collection process and interaction with local officials were greatly facilitated.

The original plan entailed investigating, in each of the three counties, referrals to the juvenile justice system from 1990 through 1994. However, when researchers learned that County-2 had updated its computer system in late 1992, a revised data collection plan was adopted: Cases in County-1 and County-2 would be sampled from 1993 through 1994, while cases from County-3 would be sampled from 1990 through 1995. The longer data collection period for the rural county was necessary owing to the lower base rate of referrals, as would be expected in a rural area.

Data are reported on the proportion of referrals of offenders who were processed through the juvenile justice system during the time periods indicated previously. A general approach is described and the actual numbers for each county are provided. The first step in selecting a sample for analysis was to determine the number of overall referrals and youth (a juvenile could have multiple referrals) for the specified time period. Each county's management information system contained all referrals, including administrative referrals, in the county for the specified time period. The most serious offense was always listed as the reason for referral. The next step involved selecting youth whose last referrals fell within the indicated time period. This restriction was necessary for two important reasons.

First, the socio-demographic data available were accurate only for the most recent referral. By selecting youth whose last referral occurred during the indicated time period, researchers could be more confident about the accuracy of the socio-demographic data provided in the database. This sampling strategy also precluded the sampling of youth who were in the system during the 1993–1994 period, but who had referrals after 1994. By sampling in this way, all of the final dispositions for cases processed during 1993–1994 were available by the time data collection efforts began in 1995. In County-3, researchers had to access all cases processed during 1990–1995 to obtain a large enough sample.

Second, to avoid any bias created by the presence of a few multiple offenders, researchers allowed only one referral per juvenile in this sample. If a juvenile had multiple referrals during the specified time period, only the last was selected.

From the nonduplicate sample, a sub-sample containing 2,000 youth was created, whenever possible. This sub-sample was restricted to male and female Anglo, African-American, and Hispanic youth who had been referred for a delinquent act, whether a misdemeanor or felony offense. A similar sub-sample was also created for youth who had been referred for status offenses. In this study, a status offender is "a child who was accused and adjudicated for conduct that would not, under state law, be a crime if committed by an adult, including truancy, running away from home . . . and violating a juvenile curfew ordinance or order" (*Texas Family Code,* 3, Section 51.03, 1995). Asian-American youth were analyzed separately.

The sub-samples were randomly generated in the following manner. First, data were sorted by the offender's juvenile number. Second, each juvenile number was assigned a random number produced by using a SAS function, the statistical analysis software used for data analysis. Third, data were sorted by the assigned random numbers. Finally, the first 2,000 youth generated from this sorting procedure were output to a new data set.

Specific descriptions of the data obtained from each county follow. Due to county-specific data definitions and the resultant differences in variable measurements, cross-county comparisons must be made cautiously. These differences among the counties also precluded merging the individual county data sets into one comprehensive data set. However, by maintaining three separate data sets, the richness of data in a particular county could be used in the analyses, rather than a homogenous set of measures common to all three counties.

From the county databases the number of referrals made during the targeted time frame was identified. Due to the possibility of multiple referrals per juvenile, it was necessary to identify the number of youth referred. From these individual referrals, researchers focused on the most recent referral for the time period, for reasons outlined earlier. Finally, researchers identified nonduplicate referrals for misdemeanors and felonies committed during the study period. A sample of 2,000 was drawn from each county. Similar steps were taken to generate 2,000 status offense cases. In the rural county, all referrals from 1990 through 1995 were included to generate an adequate sample.

For County-1, 62,101 referrals were accessed from 35,583 youth, representing 1.8 referrals per juvenile. Researchers identified 27,591 individuals whose last referral occurred between 1993 and 1994. In other words, at the time the study was initiated in 1995, none of these youth had any subsequent referrals, and the most recent referral in 1993 or 1994 appeared as the last entry in the database. From this pool of individuals, 2,000 nonduplicate cases involving felonies and misdemeanors were randomly selected (see Table 3.1).

Another 2,000 nonduplicate cases involving status offenses were also selected. Details on the racial/ethnic and gender composition are provided in Table 3.1. Generally, for misdemeanors and felonies, each racial/ethnic group represented approximately one-third of all juvenile referrals. The majority of cases involved males. For status offenses, however, Anglo youth accounted for about 50% of the cases in the data set. Similar breakdowns are presented for County-2 and County-3.

For County-2, 15,142 referrals were accessed from 7,089 youth, representing 2.1 referrals per juvenile. Researchers identified 4,857 individuals whose last referral occurred between 1993 and 1994. In other words, at the time the study was initiated in 1995, none of these youth had any subsequent referrals, and the most recent referral in 1993 or 1994 appeared as the last entry in the database. From this pool of individuals, 2,000 nonduplicate

TABLE 3.1 Referral Data from the Targeted Counties (1993–1994)

	County-1	County-2	County-3
Number of referrals	**62,101**	**15,142**	**763**
African American, %	33.6	30.4	55.6
Anglo, %	30.5	25.7	27.1
Hispanic, %	34.1	42.7	17.0
Female, %	28.9	24.0	12.5
Male, %	71.1	76.0	53.5
Number of juveniles	**35,583**	**7,089**	**386**
African American, %	31.2	25.6	43.8
Anglo, %	33.9	31.8	33.7
Hispanic, %	32.9	40.8	22.0
Female, %	34.2	31.6	17.9
Male, %	65.8	68.3	82.1
Last referral data			
Nonduplicates—juveniles	**27,591**	**4,857**	**381**
African American, %	29.3	24.3	43.6
Anglo, %	35.8	35.8	33.6
Hispanic, %	32.7	37.8	22.3
Female, %	36.7	34.6	18.1
Male, %	70.1	67.8	82.2
Sample of misdemeanors/felonies			
Nonduplicates—juveniles	**2,000**	**2,000**	**371**
African American, %	34.3	26.5	44.2
Anglo, %	31.3	36.5	33.7
Hispanic, %	34.5	37.0	22.1
Female, %	30.0	32.3	17.8
Male, %	70.1	67.8	82.2
Sample of status offenses			
Nonduplicates—juveniles	**2,000**	**506**	**6**
African American, %	22.0	13.0	16.7
Anglo, %	52.8	48.6	50.0
Hispanic, %	25.3	38.3	33.3
Female, %	66.9	71.3	50.0
Male, %	33.2	28.7	50.0

cases involving felonies and misdemeanors were randomly selected (see Table 3.1). Also, as in County-1, 2,000 nonduplicate cases referred for status offenses were selected.

For County-3, 763 referrals were accessed pertaining to 386 youth, representing 2.0 referrals per juvenile. Due to the much lower number of referrals, all cases in the County-3 database were included in the analyses.

MEASUREMENT OF VARIABLES

The details of the variables that were directly extracted from the three county databases or were developed from archival records are presented next.

Dependent Variables

All relevant data were drawn from county MIS databases. The research staff used the hierarchical data sets developed for administrative purposes to develop a sequential flow of events and were able to identify the following key processing points. Juvenile justice personnel in all three counties were consulted to ensure that our understanding of the process was correct.

One goal was to standardize the analyses in all counties and to create comparable variables, whenever possible. The following dependent (or outcome) variables were analyzed:

1. whether the juvenile was detained at intake;
2. whether the juvenile's case was informally adjusted by the intake juvenile probation officer or was sent to the District Attorney (DA) for possible prosecution;
3. whether a petition to refer the case to court was filed by prosecutors; and
4. whether prosecution resulted in secure placement in a Texas Youth Commission secure facility or some other alternative (e.g., probation, acquittal, dismissal, or administrative order).

In the rural county, staff were unable to obtain information on the activity of the DA. Consequently, the results for County-3 do not include an analysis of the DA's decision to prosecute.

A multivariate analysis was conducted on a random sample of 2,000 youth (African Americans, Hispanics, and Anglos) who committed offenses during 1993–1994 in both County-1 and County-2. For County-3, a multivariate analysis was done on 371 youth who had been processed by the county juvenile probation system from 1990 through 1995. Multivariate analyses were done for each stage of the process mentioned earlier, using logistic regression (SAS version 6.11). Regression models do not necessarily reflect causal relationships. They predict associations or correlations between a set of independent predictor variables and a specified dependent variable. Unlike ordinary least-squares (OLS) regression, logistic regression is designed to handle dichotomous dependent variables. A dichotomous variable is one for which there are only two alternatives. For example, gender is a dichotomous variable because one must either be male or female. At each of the stages described earlier, researchers constructed a dichotomous variable and determined the likelihood of youth moving to the next stage, when all factors were controlled for. As an example of an outcome or decision point, a dependent dichotomous variable was developed where the

DA filed a petition against the juvenile, deferred prosecution, or dropped the case.

Intake. In the County-1 data set, the intake decision category was coded as a unique variable with six categories. Each category represents the job position of the person who made the final decision for that referral. These categories are (1) receiving; (2) intake juvenile probation officer (JPO); (3) legal screening officer/DA (LSO/DA); (4) court JPO; (5) judge; and (6) Texas Youth Commission (TYC). By matching these stages with final dispositions, the study was able to develop a sequence of events within the juvenile justice system in this county. In the County-2 data, all of the final dispositions were coded as one variable and ordered in sequence with the decision process and the codes were numerically organized to reflect stages in the decision process. The higher the final disposition code number, the further into the process the juvenile had advanced. County-3 used the Case-Worker/3 system; key differences between this rural county and the urban counties are discussed next.

In this study, county cases were coded as missing if they were sent to other agencies or to other criminal jurisdictions, were dropped for a lack of evidence, or involved youth who either had escaped or were too old. When a case entailed any kind of "service" at intake, such as counseled and released, that case was coded as an active referral and the disposition was coded as an informal adjustment.

Detention. The first measurable event after a juvenile is referred to the Juvenile Probation Office (JPO) is the decision to detain the juvenile. There are as many as three ways of defining detention. Because *Texas Family Code* statutes require that a probable cause hearing be held within two working days after detention, two kinds of detention data are present in the MIS systems: (1) detentions of less than 48 hours; and (2) court-ordered detentions. In County-1 and County-2, researchers also obtained a computerized record of court-ordered detentions.

In County-3, a proxy for court-ordered detentions was used (i.e., detentions that are more than two days in duration). Here, if a juvenile was detained for more than two days, researchers assumed that a hearing had been held, which resulted in continued detention. This is a highly restrictive definition of detention, as the youth may have been released after a short stay, but since this could not be determined for sure, it was decided to err on the side of overinclusion rather than exclusion.

Informal adjustment/file sent to the DA. The next stage in juvenile processing is the decision whether to make an informal adjustment in the case. That is, a juvenile may be placed in the custody of family/guardian, pay a fine, be diverted to a community service program, or receive counseling. The probation staff usually make the decision to arrange an informal adjustment. Decisions made by anyone other than a probation officer are treated as cases sent to the DA. Some cases were coded as missing because the juveniles involved were (1) too old to be classified as juveniles; (2) sent to other state agencies (such as Child Protective Services); (3) sent to other criminal jurisdictions; or (4) escapees. Also coded as missing were cases involving youth whose value for the final disposition was missing from the original data set.

County-3 used the Texas Juvenile Probation Commission's Case-Worker/3 MIS program, so the operating definition of informal adjustment is somewhat different for this county than that for either County-1 or County-2. In County-3, Case-Worker/3 allowed only two options: (1) adjusted informally or (2) sent to court. The data for County-3 do not indicate who made the informal adjustment; it could have been the DA or the intake JPO. This step was modeled as a yes/no decision. In other words, did the juvenile obtain an informal adjustment, or was the case referred to the DA for prosecution? At this point, some cases were coded as missing for various reasons (e.g., counseled and released, too old, diverted to another agency, escaped, or insufficient evidence). All youth who had their cases decided by the court were coded as having been sent to court.

The DA's decision. If the final outcome of the case was decided by the DA or by the court, that case was coded as having been sent to the DA for review. As mentioned earlier, in the rural county (County-3), the study was unable to obtain information on the activity of the DA. The DA usually decided to arrange deferred prosecution, to drop the case entirely, or to file a petition and prosecute the case. If the case went to court, it was assumed that the DA prosecuted the case. In instances where a petition was filed and the DA moved for a non-suit, the case was coded as having been prosecuted, because it appeared that both the defense and the prosecution made some sort of arrangement, such as a plea bargain, for a less serious offense. If the DA made the final decision about a case that was not prosecuted, the case was coded either as an adjustment or as a dropped case.

In County-2, one variable contained the final disposition for all youth who entered the system. If the case was handled by the DA but not prosecuted, it was coded as an adjustment by the DA. If the DA adjusted or dropped the case, researchers coded it as a case that was not prosecuted. If any kind of court-ordered disposition was reported, researchers treated it as a prosecuted case. If the DA filed a non-suit after filing a petition, or if some court-ordered disposition was found, researchers coded the case as having been prosecuted.

If the intake juvenile probation officer informally adjusted the case, it was coded as missing and not considered in the DA portion of the analysis. If the case was coded as missing for the informal adjustment decision stage (e.g., the juvenile was too old or was sent to another agency or jurisdiction), it was also coded as missing for the DA's decision to prosecute.

The court's decision to place a juvenile in TYC. The court makes a decision regarding each case. If the juvenile is adjudicated delinquent owing to a determination that he/she had committed the alleged offense, the court must then decide if the juvenile is to be given secure placement or some other disposition. If the juvenile was sent to TYC, that juvenile was coded as having been sent to a secure facility. If the juvenile was acquitted or placed on some type of probation, the case was dropped, or the court handed down an administrative order, researchers coded those cases as not having been sent to a secure facility (TYC).

In County-3, only one juvenile received a commitment to TYC. The Case-Worker/3 program coded dispositions of the court into administrative dispositions, probation, or secure placement. An analysis was conducted of the decision to grant probation to youth. If the court's disposition was administrative in nature, it was coded as no probation. If the court's disposition was to order probation or to modify an existing probation order, project staff coded that juvenile as having been placed on probation. If the court ordered secure placement in a TYC facility, project staff coded that juvenile as one who did not receive probation.

Interestingly, a number of youth in both urban counties were coded as having their initial decision made by the TYC. All of these youth were under TYC jurisdiction and had violated parole arrangements. If the juvenile's referral had a petition number and a TYC disposition code, the juvenile was defined as having gone through the county juvenile system. If there was no petition number, it was determined that the juvenile was handed over to TYC and was not processed by the county. In both urban counties, a number of youth were processed by county courts and returned to TYC. In addition, if the court ordered other youth (non-TYC intakes) to TYC, they were coded as having been placed in TYC. All other dispositions of the court, where the DA had filed a petition, were coded as not having been sent to secure placement (TYC).

Independent Variables

Researchers focused on a set of independent variables present in all three counties. Each county defined some of these variables in a unique fashion. In addition, each county has its own unique independent variables. A description of the independent variables present in all three data sets follows, as well as how they were defined and operationalized. Descriptive statistics for the sample from the three counties are presented in Table 3.2.

Race/ethnicity. Two dichotomous variables were established for race/ethnicity. The first variable, comparing African-American and Anglo youth, coded *African American* yes, whereas all others were coded no. For a comparison of Hispanic and Anglo juveniles, *Hispanic* was coded yes,

TABLE 3.2 Descriptive Statistics of Samples from Targeted Counties (Felonies and Misdemeanors)

	County-1	County-2	County-3
African American, %	34.0	26.5	44.2
Anglo, %	31.0	36.5	22.1
Hispanic, %	35.0	37.0	33.7
Male, %	70.0	67.8	82.2
School, %	45.0	32.2	87.1
Parents married, %	11.0	9.4	N/A
Living with two parents, %	12.2	N/A	27.5
Gangs, %	N/A	10.5	9.4
Mean age	15.3	15.3	14.9
(std. deviation)	(1.6)	(1.7)	(1.6)
Mean severity of current offense	2.4	2.8	3.3
(std. deviation)	(1.6)	(1.7)	(1.8)
Average severity of past offenses	0.9	1.1	1.3
(std. deviation)	(1.7)	(1.8)	(2.2)
Average number of previous referrals	1.3	1.5	1.4
(std. deviation)	(3.1)	(3.2)	(3.2)
N	**2,000**	**2,000**	**371**

N/A = not applicable

whereas all others were coded no. The comparison or reference category was always *Anglo/white.*

Gender. Females were coded 1; males were coded 0.

Age. The age of an individual was calculated by subtracting the year of his or her birth from the year of the referral being analyzed. *Age* is the number of years in whole numbers, ranging in value from 10 to 17 years.

School enrollment. If a juvenile was enrolled in school, then, *School,* a dummy variable, was coded yes, whereas all others were coded no. In the County-1 data, *School* was coded 1 (yes) if a juvenile was attending school, was enrolled but not attending, was held back, or had irregular attendance. In County-2 and County-3, the only information available was whether the juvenile was enrolled in school; no data were available on attendance.

Family characteristics. Data collection was not able to produce consistent information on family characteristics across all three counties. In County-1, a dummy variable was constructed, where 1 indicated that the juvenile lived with two parents and 0 indicated other situations. Additionally, parental marital status was coded 1 when parents were married and 0 when they were not. In County-2, the marital status of the juvenile's parents was easy to determine. However, determining with whom the juvenile lived was problematic. After reviewing the coding provided by county staff, the decision was made to use only the marital status of the juvenile's parents. In County-3, the marital status of the parents was not available. Therefore, researchers conducted the analysis with a dummy variable, where 1 meant that the juvenile lived with both parents and 0 denoted other situations.

Severity of the last offense. Following Frazier and Bishop (1995), a six-point scale was adopted to measure the severity of the offense. Because a juvenile can have multiple referrals, each of which can, in turn, involve multiple offenses, only the most severe charge of the referral was included in the analysis. If the offense was a felony committed against a person, it was given a value of 6. If the offense was a felony committed against property, it was given a value of 5. If the offense was a felony of any other type (drugs, public order), it was given a value of 4. If the offense was a misdemeanor committed against a person, it was coded 3. If the offense was a misdemeanor committed against property, it was coded 2. If the offense was a misdemeanor of any other type (drugs, public order), it was coded 1. Status offenses were also given a value of 1.

Criminal history. Two variables were constructed to capture prior criminal history. First, the frequency of previous offenses was used to capture the extent of prior delinquency. Second, in order to capture the nature of prior delinquency, all prior delinquent offenses were coded for severity using the six-point scale described previously. The severity scores across all prior offenses were summed and the total divided by the number of referrals (scores ranged from 1 to 15). This measure is thus the average severity of past delinquent offenses. The average severity score had a correlation of .60 with the frequency of past offenses in County-1. In County-2 and County-3, the correlation was .50, and possible multicollinearity was investigated, but it was determined that it would not be a factor in the analyses.

Other variables of interest. Some of the counties had additional variables of interest to the project. In the County-2 data set, there is a unique variable *(gang)* that identifies the gang with which a juvenile might be affiliated. If the *gang* variable was not missing, *gang* was coded 1, whereas all others were coded 0. Approximately 10% of the offender sample in County-2 and County-3 were identified as gang members. In County-3, the Case-Worker/3 program provided information on the level of gang activity. A variable in the County-3 data set was coded for the following information: (1) if the juvenile is currently a gang member; (2) if the juvenile was previously a gang member; or (3) if the juvenile wants to be a gang member. Also, the Case-Worker/3 program provided a yes/no variable indicating whether the last offense was gang related. Researchers developed a dummy variable, where 1 meant the offense was gang related or the juvenile was in a gang, and 0 denoted other situations.

Interaction terms. The role of two-way interactions, particularly those involving race/ethnicity and measures of criminal behavior, was also examined. Interaction terms enable researchers to determine if the relationship between main effects, such as race/ethnicity and an outcome, is conditioned or mediated by a third factor, such as the number of prior referrals. After preliminary analyses, it was determined that the interaction between race/ethnicity and the number of prior referrals had a significant impact on a limited number of outcomes and improved the overall fit of the models being tested (e.g., Table 5.3). Interaction models were tested where a main race/ethnicity effect was evident, and the results are discussed only when including these interaction terms improved the fit of the models in question.

Measurement Problems

In large data sets maintained for administrative purposes, it is not uncommon for problems to arise when using archival information to develop substantive variables. The validity and reliability of the data are often questionable. The study obviously had no control over how and when information was collected and stored in the county databases. Researchers attempted to minimize measurement errors by selecting youth whose last referral occurred during 1993–1994, because many background variables were updated at the time of the last referral. Of primary concern was the measurement of "social background" variables (i.e., the education level of youth, with whom they lived, their parents' marital status, and their gang affiliation). First, there was the issue of missing values. It was unclear whether the information on youth had been obtained from the source in the first place, or whether the information was simply omitted from the database. Second, it was unclear who had supplied the information (the juvenile, a parent, or someone else), because, in many instances, staff in probation departments often contacted someone other than the juvenile for the information. The likelihood of probation department staff verifying information about a juvenile increases as a juvenile traverses further through the system. In other words, when a juvenile appears in court, it is quite likely that at least one probation officer, probably a court-based juvenile probation officer, will have verified his/her background and made a report to the judge. This is not likely to occur in the case of a juvenile brought in for a minor offense and sent home immediately.

It is thus impossible to discern which methods were used to gather information on a particular juvenile. Furthermore, the reliability of the information that was gathered is unclear. Nevertheless, the variables were included in the models because there were theoretically valid reasons to use them, and they improved the understanding of the juvenile probation process. In logistic regression models, the models fit better when these variables were included. However, in the multivariate analyses, some of the social variables in the models had counterintuitive signs, which the researchers feel may be due in part to the measurement problems.

Sample Selection Bias

When modeling the juvenile justice system, one must view the system as a series of distinct stages in a sequential process. In the first stage, some youth are arrested, while others are not. There are at least three other stages in the juvenile justice process within the three counties: (1) receiving an informal adjustment; (2) having a case sent to the DA and the case being subsequently prosecuted; and (3) a court adjudication with a disposition ordering a secure placement. At each of these four stages (arrest, informal adjustment, prosecution, and secure placement), the characteristics of the juvenile population are significantly and qualitatively different from the preceding stage. This often leads to a situation called "sample selection bias." The demographic changes in the juveniles as they move through these stages in the three targeted counties are outlined in Figures 5.1, 6.1, and 7.1.

Some researchers have argued that the sample selection bias imposed on the data by this multistage process should be corrected with an econometric method called the Heckman (1979) procedure (Kempf-Leonard and Sontheimer, 1995). Heckman developed the procedure to correct for the sample selection bias inherent in two-stage data sets. His sample was composed of two groups: (1) women who were working and (2) women who were not working. The two stages of his model were that some women chose to work, while others did not, two qualitatively distinct groups. Heckman was able to make statements about women who worked and women who chose not to work. In addition, based on data collected from the group of working women, Heckman could predict the wages of working women, overall. However, he could not predict how much a non-working woman would earn. In order to predict how much a non-working woman would earn in the workplace, Heckman needed to correct for the sample selection bias. This procedure became known as the Heckman correction procedure.

In theory, the Heckman technique is only applicable for two-stage processes. However, Kempf-Leonard and Sontheimer (1995) argue that even though the juvenile justice process entails more than two stages, the Heckman procedure is necessary to correct for the selection bias inherent in the decision-making system. In the current study, researchers have data to model three distinct stages. Furthermore, the study could not make the kind of corrections necessary to generalize the findings to the entire population of juveniles, because data were not available for the first stage (i.e., for those juveniles who were not arrested). It would seem highly unlikely that any study of juvenile justice decision making would have available a comparable sample of at-risk youth who had been criminally active yet who had not been arrested for these activities.

Additionally, in order for the Heckman procedure to work correctly, two assumptions must be made about the selection bias in the data. The first assumption is that there were some juveniles who did not get prosecuted (or detained or placed in TYC), but who could (should) have been. Since the current study entailed examining the possibility of race/ethnicity effects in the prosecution of juveniles, among other things, researchers recognized the distinct possibility that juveniles of one race/ethnicity may be less likely to be prosecuted (or other outcomes) than are juveniles of another race/ethnicity. The second key assumption is that only those juveniles who should have been prosecuted were, in fact, prosecuted. Given the information available in the current literature, researchers for this study could not make the assumption that if a juvenile was prosecuted in court, there was no alternative outcome for that juvenile. The inability to meet these two fundamental assumptions underlies the problem with using the Heckman correction in this study. Thus, after a thorough review of the literature and consultations with statisticians, researchers felt that it was inappropriate to use a Heckman correction procedure on the models used in this study.

NOTE

1. According to the 1990 Census, the proportions of African Americans and Hispanics respectively are as follows: (1) statewide: 11.9% and 25.5%; (2) County-1: 19.2% and 22.4%; (3) County-2: 11.9% and 25.3%; and (4) County-3: 27.5% and 11.9%.

4

Minority Overrepresentation: Aggregate Measures

Texas, like all states that receive federal funds awarded under the provisions of the Juvenile Justice and Delinquency Prevention Act (42 U.S.C. 5601 et seq.), as a condition of participation must fulfill two essential provisions. First, states must fulfill an *identification* provision by documenting whether minority juveniles are disproportionately detained or confined in secure detention and correctional facilities in relation to their proportion of the state juvenile population. Under the Act, minorities are juveniles who may be classified as African American, Hispanic American, Asian American, or Native American. The second process involves fulfilling an *assessment* provision by explaining differences that may exist in arrest, diversion, and adjudication rates; court dispositions other than incarceration; rates and periods of pre-hearing detention in, and dispositional commitments to, secure facilities of minority youth in the juvenile justice system; and transfers to adult court.

In this chapter, the basic parameters are established surrounding differential minority processing in the juvenile justice system in the three Texas counties included in the research. These data will provide a descriptive context for the processing of juveniles in Texas and they represent a necessary prerequisite to the multivariate analyses that were performed for each county separately and will be reported on in Chapters 5, 6, and 7.

AGGREGATE DATA

Data were collected from the Texas Data Center concerning the at-risk youth population (i.e., ages 10–16) statewide, and in the three specific counties, for the years 1990–1994, by gender and race/ethnicity (Table 4.1). Basic archival data were collected concerning the incidence of delinquency from two official sources. First, data were collected pertaining to the frequency of crime arrests from the Texas Department of Public Safety (DPS) which uses the Uniform Crime Reports (UCR) classification system of the Federal Bureau of Investigation. Second, data were collected on the frequency of juvenile referrals for serious crimes from the Texas Juvenile Probation Commission (TJPC) reports. The two data sets reflect different dimensions of delinquency. The DPS arrest data contain all persons who were arrested for a juvenile offense regardless of what may have occurred in subsequent processing stages. The juvenile probation data pertain to cases that move beyond the arrest stage and are referred to juvenile intake for further processing (i.e., further penetration into the system). Each of the measures of delinquency incidence was broken down by race/ethnicity and gender for the period 1990–1994. The population data were used, together with the DPS and TJPC frequency data, to calculate arrest/referral rates for delinquent offenses (index, violent, property, drug, and weapon offenses) by race/ethnicity and gender across the five-year period. The arrest/referral rates, grouped by race/ethnicity and gender, for each county and for the entire state were calculated using the following formula:

$$\frac{\text{Frequency of offense type by race} \div \text{Ethnic group by gender}}{\text{Population of ethnic group by gender}} \times 1{,}000$$

Arrest/Referral Ratios

The purpose here is to go beyond the mere calculation of arrest or referral rates to identify minority differentials in delinquency by examining pairwise arrest or referral rates by race/ethnic group. A convenient way to display these data is to calculate the ratio of arrest and referral rates for the various pair-wise race/ethnic group combinations (i.e., African American versus Hispanic; African American versus Anglo; and Hispanic versus Anglo). The first consideration is the ratios for the arrest rates. These results are shown in Tables 4.2 to 4.6.

Index arrests. The data in Table 4.2 indicate that the rates of index offense arrests are much higher for African Americans compared to either Hispanics or Anglos. The data further indicate that the African-American rates are higher for all youth, as well as for both genders separately. In County-1 for example, the rates for African-American males are between 1.4 to 1.7 times as high as those for Hispanic males, and about 2.5 to 3.3 times

TABLE 4.1 Juvenile Population in Targeted Counties and Statewide (Texas Data Center, 1990–1994)

County	Year	Total	Male	Female	Anglo	Ang Male	Ang Fem	A.Am	A.Am Male	A.Am Fem	Hispanic	His Male	His Fem
County-1	1990	288,208	147,106	141,102	130,671	66,664	64,007	62,158	31,423	30,735	82,539	42,290	40,249
County-3	1990	1,696	905	791	836	454	382	564	283	281	294	167	127
County-2	1990	46,757	23,800	22,957	24,860	12,700	12,160	7,159	3,567	3,592	13,611	6,956	6,655
Statewide	1990	1,788,434	915,476	872,958	913,140	468,871	444,269	238,141	120,742	117,399	597,118	305,223	291,895
County-1	1991	298,662	152,539	146,123	134,424	68,751	65,673	63,652	32,241	31,411	87,399	44,702	42,697
County-3	1991	1,715	907	808	838	442	396	581	298	283	292	165	127
County-2	1991	49,231	25,082	24,149	26,401	13,559	12,842	7,304	3,639	3,665	14,311	7,250	7,061
Statewide	1991	1,847,262	945,309	901,953	946,022	485,944	460,078	244,848	124,119	120,729	614,755	313,836	300,919
County-1	1992	305,998	156,224	149,774	136,888	69,986	66,902	64,242	32,477	31,765	91,288	46,740	44,548
County-3	1992	1,737	922	815	851	448	403	588	304	284	294	168	126
County-2	1992	51,369	26,202	25,167	27,651	14,210	13,441	7,411	3,703	3,708	14,978	7,586	7,392
Statewide	1992	1,883,294	963,885	919,409	964,999	495,798	469,201	248,963	126,221	122,742	626,417	319,788	306,629
County-1	1993	314,834	160,722	154,112	139,983	71,552	68,431	65,205	33,019	32,186	95,524	48,906	46,618
County-3	1993	1,760	929	831	860	450	410	582	298	284	312	179	133
County-2	1993	54,841	27,940	26,901	29,667	15,251	14,416	7,624	3,791	3,833	16,022	8,093	7,929
Statewide	1993	1,938,230	991,960	946,270	993,143	510,170	482,973	254,618	129,097	125,521	645,376	329,532	315,844
County-1	1994	319,550	163,056	156,494	142,466	72,816	69,650	65,843	33,319	32,524	97,166	49,701	47,465
County-3	1994	1,691	876	815	814	416	398	549	279	270	320	178	142
County-2	1994	60,049	30,643	29,406	32,659	16,839	15,820	7,973	3,970	4,003	17,485	8,813	8,672
Statewide	1994	1,978,746	1,012,544	966,202	1,014,228	520,815	493,413	258,301	131,084	127,217	659,946	336,890	323,056

TABLE 4.2 Arrest Rate Ratios for Index Offenses in Targeted Counties and Statewide, Grouped by Year (DPS)

		All			Males			Females		
County	Year	AA/His	AA/Ang	His/Ang	AA/His	AA/Ang	His/Ang	AA/His	AA/Ang	His/Ang
County-1	1990	1.68	2.45	1.46	1.72	2.53	1.48	1.59	2.20	1.39
County-1	1991	1.41	2.51	1.77	1.45	2.59	1.78	1.30	2.26	1.73
County-1	1992	1.31	2.59	1.98	1.35	2.66	1.97	1.20	2.38	1.98
County-1	1993	1.38	3.10	2.24	1.44	3.22	2.24	1.22	2.74	2.24
County-1	1994	1.52	3.11	2.04	1.58	3.31	2.09	1.37	2.57	1.88
County-2	1990	1.60	4.82	3.01	1.61	5.17	3.21	1.67	4.03	2.41
County-2	1991	1.43	4.20	2.93	1.45	4.47	3.08	1.43	3.66	2.57
County-2	1992	1.24	3.86	3.12	1.27	4.22	3.33	1.18	3.14	2.66
County-2	1993	1.60	4.19	2.62	1.66	4.54	2.74	1.47	3.50	2.39
County-2	1994	1.61	4.95	3.07	1.65	5.38	3.26	1.55	4.21	2.72
County-3	1990	1.55	3.98	2.56	1.53	4.17	2.72	2.25	4.02	1.79
County-3	1991	3.19	3.64	1.14	3.32	4.09	1.23	3.95	2.51	.64
County-3	1992	1.64	6.61	4.04	1.94	6.87	3.55	1.06	5.84	5.50
County-3	1993	1.20	2.73	2.26	1.36	2.81	2.07	1.00	2.44	2.45
County-3	1994	1.98	3.20	1.62	1.83	3.17	1.73	14.38	3.45	.24
Statewide	1990	1.53	2.54	1.66	1.54	2.60	1.69	1.55	2.40	1.55
Statewide	1991	1.67	2.82	1.69	1.68	2.90	1.73	1.65	2.61	1.59
Statewide	1992	1.66	2.81	1.69	1.69	2.89	1.71	1.58	2.60	1.64
Statewide	1993	1.69	2.98	1.76	1.71	3.05	1.79	1.66	2.82	1.70
Statewide	1994	1.70	2.91	1.71	1.71	2.97	1.74	1.69	2.77	1.64

higher than among Anglo males. The differential for Hispanics versus Anglos is smaller and falls between the previous sets of rates (about a factor of 1.5 to 2.2). In County-2, African-American males again have rates that are from 1.2 to 1.6 times greater than those for Hispanic males, and have a substantial differential compared to Anglos (between 4.2 and 5.3 times greater). In County-2, generally, the rates for Hispanic males versus Anglos is also substantial as the ratio ranges between 2.7 and 3.2. In County-3, these differentials are similar. African-American males have an arrest rate for index offenses that is from 1.3 to 3.3 times higher than the rate for Hispanics, and substantially higher than for Anglo males (2.8 to 6.8). Among females, across all three counties and statewide, the arrest rate for African-American girls exceeds the rates of her Hispanic and Anglo counterparts, but the differentials are not as substantial as her African-American male counterpart.

Violent arrests. In Table 4.3 it can be seen that, when the violent character of the offense is considered, African Americans predominate substantially. Compared to Anglo males, African-American youth have an arrest rate for violent index crimes (homicide, rape, robbery, and aggravated assault) that is generally from 4 to 10 times higher, and even reaches ratios of 14, 16, and 20 to 1 in a few instances. The difference between African-American and Hispanic youth is less substantial, but still generally ranges between 2 and 4 times higher for African Americans. The Hispanic versus Anglo comparison is also substantial as the former predominate in violent arrests by factors ranging from 2.6 to 10.5. These differentials are repeated when gender is considered. African-American girls have substantially higher violent arrest rates than Anglos (4.4 to 20.8) and higher rates but with lower differentials compared to Hispanics (1.8 to 3.8). Hispanic girls have higher rates than Anglos.

Property arrests. Table 4.4 shows that the differentials for property index offense arrest rates are much smaller than was the case for total or violent index crimes. African-American boys and girls generally have rates that are less than twice as high for property offenses compared to Hispanics, while they generally have between two and four times higher arrest rates than Anglos. Nonetheless, the data do indicate a significantly greater involvement in property offenses for African Americans, regardless of county, statewide location, or year.

Drug arrests. Drug offenses by juveniles have received increased scrutiny in recent years as society attempts to divert youth away from such troubling conduct which carries an associated risk of other delinquent conduct and even subsequent criminal involvement. Thus, the drug arrest data presented in Table 4.5 are important and clearly indicate that African Americans have substantially higher rates for drug offenses than either Hispanic or Anglo

TABLE 4.3 Arrest Rate Ratios for Violent Offenses in Targeted Counties and Statewide, Grouped by Year (DPS)

		All			Males			Females		
County	Year	AA/His	AA/Ang	His/Ang	AA/His	AA/Ang	His/Ang	AA/His	AA/Ang	His/Ang
County-1	1990	3.44	9.71	2.82	3.54	10.18	2.87	2.81	6.50	2.31
County-1	1991	3.31	9.68	2.93	3.43	10.08	2.94	2.60	7.42	2.85
County-1	1992	2.70	8.03	2.97	2.77	8.25	2.98	2.45	7.03	2.87
County-1	1993	2.43	8.96	3.69	2.52	9.27	3.67	1.92	7.19	3.75
County-1	1994	2.14	10.43	4.88	2.20	10.91	4.95	1.80	8.00	4.44
County-2	1990	1.94	13.91	7.18	2.01	14.51	7.21	1.66	11.52	6.94
County-2	1991	1.78	11.99	6.74	1.80	12.07	6.72	1.83	13.86	7.59
County-2	1992	4.21	12.99	3.09	4.31	13.40	3.11	3.89	12.40	3.19
County-2	1993	4.50	15.71	3.49	4.76	16.33	3.43	3.34	14.52	4.35
County-2	1994	2.74	19.97	7.30	2.79	20.35	7.30	2.63	20.82	7.91
County-3	1990	.73	6.92	9.48	.75	7.91	10.51	.90	5.44	6.02
County-3	1991	5.48	5.69	1.04	6.04	5.86	.97	N/A	N/A	N/A
County-3	1992	1.41	4.46	3.16	1.48	4.52	3.06	1.77	4.51	2.54
County-3	1993	1.41	4.46	3.16	1.48	4.52	3.06	1.77	4.51	2.54
County-3	1994	N/A	2.47	N/A	N/A	2.24	N/A	N/A	4.42	N/A
Statewide	1990	2.66	7.47	2.81	2.66	7.67	2.88	2.79	6.71	2.40
Statewide	1991	2.99	7.56	2.53	2.99	7.83	2.62	3.10	6.37	2.05
Statewide	1992	3.06	7.15	2.33	3.13	7.42	2.37	2.75	5.94	2.16
Statewide	1993	2.69	7.18	2.67	2.67	7.44	2.79	2.97	6.13	2.07
Statewide	1994	2.53	7.24	2.86	2.54	7.45	2.93	2.53	6.50	2.57

N/A = not applicable

TABLE 4.4 Arrest Rate Ratios for Property Offenses in Targeted Counties and Statewide, Grouped by Year (DPS)

		All			Males			Females		
County	Year	AA/His	AA/Ang	His/Ang	AA/His	AA/Ang	His/Ang	AA/His	AA/Ang	His/Ang
County-1	1990	1.47	2.04	1.38	1.47	2.04	1.39	1.53	2.08	1.36
County-1	1991	1.17	1.97	1.69	1.17	1.97	1.69	1.21	2.03	1.68
County-1	1992	1.17	1.97	1.69	1.17	1.97	1.69	1.21	2.03	1.68
County-1	1993	1.17	1.97	1.69	1.17	1.97	1.69	1.21	2.03	1.68
County-1	1994	1.35	2.35	1.75	1.37	2.39	1.74	1.31	2.29	1.75
County-2	1990	1.57	4.51	2.87	1.57	4.80	3.04	1.67	3.93	2.35
County-2	1991	1.40	3.93	2.80	1.42	4.15	2.92	1.41	3.50	2.49
County-2	1992	1.14	3.54	3.12	1.15	3.84	3.33	1.12	2.96	2.65
County-2	1993	1.40	3.60	2.58	1.41	3.81	2.70	1.39	3.27	2.35
County-2	1994	1.48	4.26	2.87	1.50	4.56	3.04	1.47	3.80	2.59
County-3	1990	1.66	3.89	2.34	1.63	4.05	2.48	2.44	3.97	1.63
County-3	1991	3.07	3.53	1.15	3.16	3.96	1.25	3.95	2.51	.64
County-3	1992	1.67	6.99	4.19	1.99	7.36	3.70	1.06	5.84	5.50
County-3	1993	1.17	2.54	2.17	1.34	2.65	1.98	.82	2.00	2.43
County-3	1994	1.67	3.39	2.04	1.55	3.43	2.21	11.75	3.29	.28
Statewide	1990	1.41	2.24	1.59	1.40	2.26	1.61	1.48	2.24	1.51
Statewide	1991	1.52	2.48	1.63	1.52	2.52	1.66	1.56	2.45	1.57
Statewide	1992	1.49	2.43	1.63	1.49	2.45	1.64	1.50	2.42	1.62
Statewide	1993	1.54	2.57	1.67	1.54	2.58	1.68	1.57	2.62	1.67
Statewide	1994	1.57	2.53	1.61	1.57	2.53	1.62	1.62	2.58	1.60

TABLE 4.5 Arrest Rate Ratios for Drug Offenses in Targeted Counties and Statewide, Grouped by Year (DPS)

		All			Males			Females		
County	Year	AA/His	AA/Ang	His/Ang	AA/His	AA/Ang	His/Ang	AA/His	AA/Ang	His/Ang
County-1	1990	3.90	7.14	1.83	4.05	7.39	1.82	3.04	5.55	1.82
County-1	1991	3.90	7.14	1.83	4.05	7.39	1.82	3.04	5.55	1.82
County-1	1992	3.90	7.14	1.83	4.05	7.39	1.82	3.04	5.55	1.82
County-1	1993	2.60	6.09	2.35	2.64	6.23	2.36	2.44	5.40	2.22
County-1	1994	2.89	6.36	2.20	3.01	6.71	2.23	2.17	4.38	2.02
County-2	1990	3.22	8.14	2.53	3.29	8.36	2.54	3.27	7.88	2.41
County-2	1991	7.44	21.24	2.85	8.63	24.14	2.80	2.51	8.44	3.36
County-2	1992	5.55	13.15	2.37	6.13	14.49	2.36	2.63	6.85	2.60
County-2	1993	3.45	6.29	1.82	3.80	6.62	1.74	2.06	5.30	2.57
County-2	1994	2.32	5.90	2.55	2.34	6.22	2.66	2.32	5.15	2.22
County-3	1990	N/A	N/A	N/A	N/A	N/A	N/A	N/A	N/A	N/A
County-3	1991	N/A	2.16	N/A	N/A	1.48	N/A	N/A	N/A	N/A
County-3	1992	4.50	N/A	N/A	4.97	N/A	N/A	N/A	N/A	N/A
County-3	1993	N/A	42.66	N/A	N/A	43.59	N/A	N/A	N/A	N/A
County-3	1994	N/A	65.24	N/A	N/A	65.61	N/A	N/A	N/A	N/A
Statewide	1990	2.50	4.91	1.96	2.56	5.25	2.05	2.21	3.38	1.53
Statewide	1991	3.14	7.26	2.31	3.28	7.66	2.34	2.27	4.99	2.20
Statewide	1992	2.69	6.95	2.59	2.83	7.54	2.67	1.86	4.11	2.22
Statewide	1993	2.16	5.12	2.37	2.22	5.43	2.44	1.80	3.71	2.06
Statewide	1994	1.90	4.36	2.29	1.96	4.64	2.37	1.56	3.07	1.97

juveniles. The African-American arrest rate for drugs is between two and eight times higher for Hispanic males and 1.5 to 3.2 times higher for Hispanic females. Compared to Anglos, the drug differential for African Americans is even more substantial, as the African-American arrest rate for drugs is between 4.6 and 24.1 times higher for Anglo males and 3.0 to 8.4 times higher for Anglo females. Hispanics also demonstrate a higher drug involvement than Anglos with a rate that falls between 1.7 to 2.8 times higher than the rate for Anglo males and between 1.5 to 3.3 times higher than the rate for Anglo females.

Weapon offenses. Similar to drug offenses, weapon offenses, as a group, began to receive increased juvenile justice system concern as rates of juvenile violence escalated across America throughout the late 1980s and early years of the 1990s. The results shown in Table 4.6 reveal that African-American youth had substantially higher rates of arrest for weapon offenses than their Hispanic and Anglo counterparts. The African-American arrest rates for weapons are generally higher than the rates for Hispanic males (from about the same to 2.9 times higher) and for Hispanic females (from about the same to 2.7 times higher). The involvement in weapon offenses among African-American youth is even more substantial when compared to Anglo males (1.4 to 9.4) and Anglo females (3.1 to 8.8). As with all the prior offenses, Hispanics exceed Anglos in weapon offenses, but show differences that are less substantial than the other two race/ethnic pairings but still of concern nonetheless (range from 1.8 to 3.8 for males and range from 1.7 to 3.8 for females).

The DPS arrest rate data suggest that minority youth are arrested for, or are associated with, more severe criminal activities than are Anglo youth. Based on statewide data, the inter-racial/ethnic differences between Anglo and African-American youth are particularly pronounced for violent, drug, and weapon arrests. Statewide, between 1990 and 1994, African-American youth were 5.7 times more likely than Anglo youth to be arrested for drug offenses and were 7.3 times more likely than Anglos to be arrested for violent offenses. The African-American/Anglo differences within the targeted counties were even larger, whereas the differences between Anglos and Hispanics were generally smaller. For example, based on average rates over the five-year period statewide, Hispanic youth were 2.6 times more likely than Anglo youth to be associated with violent offenses. In County-1 and, to a certain extent, in County-2 violent index arrest rates of African-American males climbed steadily during the period under study, whereas index arrest rates of Anglo and Hispanic males declined. Drug arrests for all males in County-1 and County-2 increased between 1990 and 1995. Weapon arrests of African-American and Anglo youth declined in both urban counties during the same time period.

TABLE 4.6 Arrest Rate Ratios for Weapon Offenses in Targeted Counties and Statewide, Grouped by Year (DPS)

		All			Males			Females		
County	Year	AA/His	AA/Ang	His/Ang	AA/His	AA/Ang	His/Ang	AA/His	AA/Ang	His/Ang
County-1	1990	2.41	7.35	3.04	2.45	7.41	3.03	2.38	7.28	3.06
County-1	1991	2.30	7.38	3.21	2.33	7.45	3.21	2.28	7.31	3.21
County-1	1992	1.90	5.03	2.65	1.92	5.09	2.65	1.87	4.97	2.65
County-1	1993	1.48	5.69	3.85	1.49	5.74	3.84	1.46	5.63	3.85
County-1	1994	1.07	4.04	3.78	1.08	4.09	3.78	1.06	4.00	3.78
County-2	1990	1.47	4.83	3.30	1.50	4.95	3.29	1.43	4.71	3.30
County-2	1991	2.54	9.18	3.62	2.58	9.46	3.67	2.49	8.89	3.57
County-2	1992	2.80	5.04	1.80	2.84	5.18	1.83	2.76	4.89	1.77
County-2	1993	1.99	6.31	3.18	2.02	6.53	3.24	1.95	6.10	3.12
County-2	1994	1.05	3.28	3.11	1.07	3.39	3.18	1.04	3.16	3.04
County-3	1990	2.61	7.41	2.84	2.95	8.02	2.72	N/A	N/A	N/A
County-3	1991	N/A	1.44	N/A	N/A	1.48	0	N/A	N/A	N/A
County-3	1992	2.00	5.79	2.89	2.21	5.89	2.67	1.77	5.68	3.20
County-3	1993	1.88	7.76	4.13	2.10	7.93	3.77	N/A	N/A	N/A
County-3	1994	N/A	1.98	N/A	N/A	1.99	N/A	N/A	N/A	N/A
Statewide	1990	1.80	4.61	2.56	1.80	4.67	2.60	2.05	4.52	2.21
Statewide	1991	2.05	4.73	2.30	2.06	4.75	2.31	2.18	5.26	2.41
Statewide	1992	1.98	4.27	2.16	1.96	4.29	2.20	2.46	4.61	1.87
Statewide	1993	1.78	4.54	2.55	1.80	4.64	2.57	1.62	4.11	2.53
Statewide	1994	1.54	3.66	2.38	1.56	3.72	2.39	1.42	3.46	2.43

Arrests of female youth occur at much lower rates than those of male youth. Among offenses, index and property crimes have the highest incidence among females. Minority female youth have higher arrest rates than do Anglo female youth, but the inter-racial/ethnic differences are generally smaller than those for males. Finally, arrest rates for offenses among females involving drug possession and violence increased among all three ethnic groups in County-1 and County-2. Similar to the trend observed for males, weapon arrests for females declined in the two urban counties.

Texas Juvenile Probation Commission (TJPC) Referral Data

The TJPC data are quite consistent with the UCR data. County-2 generally has higher referral rates for minorities than either of the other two counties. County-1 generally mirrors the statewide data very well. The referral rates in County-3 vary a great deal from year to year, due in large part to the low baseline population. The TJPC data are shown in Tables 4.7 to 4.11.

The TJPC data show the same trends previously discussed with respect to arrests (and also previously documented in Vickers, 1992). That is, the data indicate that African-American youth were referred at higher rates than their Anglo and Hispanic peers. This particular trend is especially apparent with respect to violence, drugs, and weapon offenses for which the African-American-to-Anglo referral ratios are substantial. Like the DPS data, the TJPC data show that the number of drug and violent offense referrals has risen over the last five years. Referrals of female youth occur at lower rates than those for males. Minority females have higher referrals than Anglo females, but the interracial/ethnic differences are generally smaller than those for males. Finally, females generally commit more index offenses involving property as compared to violence, and fewer drug or weapon crimes. However, although current incidence rates are low compared to males, statewide referrals for drug and violent offenses among all three ethnic groups increased during the 1990–1994 time period.

Disproportionate Representation Index (DRI)

Using the DPS arrest statistics and the TJPC referral data, a Disproportionate Representation Index (DRI) was calculated similar to that used in Vickers (1992). The DRI was calculated as follows:

$$\frac{\text{Frequency of offenses by race/ethnic group by gender} \div \text{Frequency of offenses by gender}}{\text{Population of race/ethnic group by gender} \div \text{Total gender-specific population}}$$

TABLE 4.7 Referral Rate Ratios for Index Offenses in Targeted Counties and Statewide, Grouped by Year (TJPC)

		All			Males			Females		
County	Year	AA/His	AA/Ang	His/Ang	AA/His	AA/Ang	His/Ang	AA/His	AA/Ang	His/Ang
County-1	1990	1.65	2.83	1.72	1.63	3.14	1.93	1.89	1.89	1.00
County-1	1991	1.61	2.86	1.78	1.58	3.03	1.92	1.90	2.24	1.18
County-1	1992	1.47	2.63	1.78	1.49	2.70	1.81	1.45	2.35	1.61
County-1	1993	1.48	3.14	2.12	1.47	3.38	2.29	1.62	2.23	1.38
County-1	1994	1.73	3.43	1.98	1.67	3.66	2.19	2.23	2.71	1.21
County-2	1990	1.64	5.87	3.58	1.75	6.70	3.82	1.30	3.67	2.81
County-2	1991	1.40	4.72	3.37	1.52	5.01	3.30	1.07	4.02	3.77
County-2	1992	1.10	4.41	4.03	1.18	4.90	4.16	.87	3.26	3.74
County-2	1993	1.67	4.75	2.85	1.68	4.85	2.88	1.67	4.80	2.87
County-2	1994	1.55	5.05	3.26	1.62	5.37	3.31	1.37	4.46	3.27
County-3	1990	1.19	2.53	2.13	1.01	2.58	2.57	5.42	2.72	.50
County-3	1991	3.06	2.76	.90	2.77	3.71	1.34	N/A	1.29	N/A
County-3	1992	2.28	6.59	2.89	2.35	7.16	3.05	3.11	4.97	1.60
County-3	1993	1.07	3.58	3.34	1.26	3.34	2.65	.62	N/A	N/A
County-3	1994	1.07	3.58	3.34	1.26	3.34	2.65	.62	N/A	N/A
Statewide	1990	1.73	2.84	1.64	1.72	2.95	1.71	1.83	2.51	1.37
Statewide	1991	1.92	3.03	1.58	1.91	3.12	1.63	2.03	2.80	1.38
Statewide	1992	1.82	3.02	1.66	1.83	3.12	1.70	1.78	2.74	1.54
Statewide	1993	1.82	3.29	1.81	1.83	3.39	1.85	1.81	3.01	1.66
Statewide	1994	1.86	3.18	1.71	1.85	3.22	1.74	1.95	3.11	1.59

TABLE 4.8 Referral Rate Ratios for Violent Offenses in Targeted Counties and Statewide, Grouped by Year (TJPC)

		All			Males			Females		
County	Year	AA/His	AA/Ang	His/Ang	AA/His	AA/Ang	His/Ang	AA/His	AA/Ang	His/Ang
County-1	1990	3.26	6.26	1.92	3.24	6.35	1.96	4.26	5.80	1.36
County-1	1991	3.13	7.21	2.30	3.16	7.48	2.37	3.08	5.61	1.82
County-1	1992	2.57	6.64	2.58	2.54	6.43	2.53	3.17	10.06	3.17
County-1	1993	2.41	6.56	2.73	2.36	6.80	2.89	3.60	5.12	1.42
County-1	1994	2.25	6.34	2.82	2.09	6.28	3.00	5.00	7.14	1.43
County-2	1990	1.85	10.90	5.89	1.88	11.57	6.16	2.08	7.62	3.65
County-2	1991	1.73	8.52	4.92	1.82	9.12	5.02	1.16	5.26	4.55
County-2	1992	3.47	7.33	2.11	3.98	7.60	1.91	1.50	6.52	4.36
County-2	1993	3.07	8.84	2.88	2.96	9.91	3.35	5.61	5.10	.91
County-2	1994	2.30	12.23	5.32	2.31	12.09	5.22	2.33	16.37	7.04
County-3	1990	1.04	1.48	1.42	.59	.80	1.36	N/A	N/A	N/A
County-3	1991	1.26	7.21	5.74	1.38	7.42	5.36	N/A	N/A	N/A
County-3	1992	N/A	N/A	N/A	N/A	N/A	N/A	N/A	N/A	N/A
County-3	1993	2.41	3.32	1.38	2.10	2.64	1.26	N/A	N/A	N/A
County-3	1994	2.91	1.48	.51	3.19	1.49	.47	N/A	N/A	N/A
Statewide	1990	2.96	6.35	2.15	2.84	6.34	2.24	4.91	7.04	1.43
Statewide	1991	3.27	6.37	1.95	3.19	6.60	2.07	4.50	5.27	1.17
Statewide	1992	3.23	5.95	1.84	3.14	5.96	1.89	4.23	6.42	1.52
Statewide	1993	2.79	6.31	2.27	2.68	6.38	2.38	4.29	6.35	1.48
Statewide	1994	2.60	6.14	2.36	2.48	5.97	2.41	3.90	8.02	2.06

TABLE 4.9 Referral Rate Ratios for Property Offenses in Targeted Counties and Statewide, Grouped by Year (TJPC)

		All			Males			Females		
County	Year	AA/His	AA/Ang	His/Ang	AA/His	AA/Ang	His/Ang	AA/His	AA/Ang	His/Ang
County-1	1990	1.45	2.46	1.70	1.41	2.72	1.93	1.77	1.76	.99
County-1	1991	1.39	2.39	1.72	1.34	2.50	1.87	1.79	2.04	1.14
County-1	1992	1.23	2.05	1.67	1.24	2.11	1.70	1.22	1.85	1.51
County-1	1993	1.22	2.43	1.99	1.20	2.59	2.15	1.40	1.91	1.37
County-1	1994	1.56	2.82	1.80	1.52	3.02	1.99	1.87	2.23	1.19
County-2	1990	1.61	5.49	3.40	1.73	6.26	3.61	1.27	3.53	2.78
County-2	1991	1.36	4.41	3.24	1.47	4.63	3.14	1.06	3.97	3.74
County-2	1992	.97	4.09	4.24	1.01	4.53	4.47	.85	3.15	3.72
County-2	1993	1.49	4.26	2.85	1.49	4.19	2.82	1.56	4.77	3.05
County-2	1994	1.42	4.34	3.06	1.48	4.56	3.08	1.28	4.00	3.12
County-3	1990	1.20	2.63	2.20	1.03	2.81	2.72	4.97	2.49	.50
County-3	1991	3.46	2.63	.76	3.08	3.53	1.15	N/A	1.29	N/A
County-3	1992	2.06	5.95	2.89	2.07	6.32	3.05	3.11	4.97	1.60
County-3	1993	.94	3.64	3.86	1.17	3.52	3.02	.31	N/A	N/A
County-3	1994	1.12	3.09	2.76	.88	2.98	3.38	N/A	3.44	N/A
Statewide	1990	1.58	2.52	1.60	1.56	2.60	1.66	1.68	2.30	1.37
Statewide	1991	1.73	2.67	1.54	1.71	2.70	1.58	1.88	2.63	1.40
Statewide	1992	1.59	2.60	1.64	1.60	2.67	1.67	1.58	2.43	1.54
Statewide	1993	1.63	2.83	1.74	1.63	2.88	1.76	1.63	2.73	1.67
Statewide	1994	1.70	2.74	1.61	1.69	2.76	1.63	1.76	2.75	1.56

TABLE 4.10 Referral Rate Ratios for Drug Offenses in Targeted Counties and Statewide, Grouped by Year (TJPC)

		All			Males			Females		
County	Year	AA/His	AA/Ang	His/Ang	AA/His	AA/Ang	His/Ang	AA/His	AA/Ang	His/Ang
County-1	1990	4.10	6.60	1.61	4.76	7.85	1.65	1.21	1.72	1.43
County-1	1991	3.53	8.18	2.32	3.66	10.44	2.85	2.43	1.82	.75
County-1	1992	2.70	6.67	2.47	2.72	8.54	3.14	2.83	1.85	.66
County-1	1993	2.28	4.64	2.04	2.40	5.19	2.16	1.43	1.94	1.35
County-1	1994	2.82	5.82	2.06	2.94	6.85	2.33	1.86	1.70	.91
County-2	1990	4.04	11.48	2.84	4.25	14.24	3.35	3.09	4.21	1.36
County-2	1991	8.06	26.41	3.28	9.09	30.19	3.32	3.03	9.68	3.19
County-2	1992	6.21	15.22	2.45	7.01	19.41	2.77	2.00	3.03	1.52
County-2	1993	3.63	7.74	2.14	3.83	8.72	2.28	2.54	4.01	1.58
County-2	1994	2.61	6.43	2.46	2.99	7.90	2.64	.96	1.91	1.99
County-3	1990	N/A	N/A	N/A	N/A	N/A	N/A	N/A	N/A	N/A
County-3	1991	N/A	2.88	N/A	N/A	2.23	N/A	N/A	N/A	N/A
County-3	1992	2.00	N/A	N/A	2.21	N/A	N/A	N/A	N/A	N/A
County-3	1993	N/A	N/A	N/A	N/A	N/A	N/A	N/A	N/A	N/A
County-3	1994	N/A	N/A	N/A	N/A	N/A	N/A	N/A	N/A	N/A
Statewide	1990	2.73	5.77	2.11	3.03	7.05	2.33	1.34	1.98	1.48
Statewide	1991	3.24	8.31	2.56	3.43	9.88	2.88	1.98	2.91	1.47
Statewide	1992	2.83	8.02	2.83	3.05	9.58	3.15	1.52	2.54	1.67
Statewide	1993	2.33	5.72	2.45	2.43	6.66	2.74	1.66	2.47	1.48
Statewide	1994	1.81	4.59	2.54	1.96	5.42	2.76	.93	1.63	1.75

TABLE 4.11 Referral Rate Ratios for Weapon Offenses in Targeted Counties and Statewide, Grouped by Year (TJPC)

		All			Males			Females		
County	Year	AA/His	AA/Ang	His/Ang	AA/His	AA/Ang	His/Ang	AA/His	AA/Ang	His/Ang
County-1	1990	2.43	4.77	1.96	2.34	4.67	2.00	7.20	7.64	1.06
County-1	1991	2.05	5.95	2.90	1.89	5.44	2.87	21.75	N/A	N/A
County-1	1992	1.84	4.54	2.46	1.72	4.56	2.64	11.22	4.81	.43
County-1	1993	1.24	4.24	3.43	1.18	4.22	3.56	2.90	4.96	1.71
County-1	1994	1.32	4.15	3.15	1.30	4.46	3.43	2.08	2.14	1.03
County-2	1990	1.21	5.72	4.73	1.13	5.93	5.23	5.56	5.08	.91
County-2	1991	2.10	15.49	7.38	2.15	16.77	7.79	1.93	10.51	5.46
County-2	1992	2.24	8.90	3.98	2.12	8.27	3.89	5.98	N/A	N/A
County-2	1993	1.70	7.94	4.67	1.69	8.21	4.87	4.14	7.52	1.82
County-2	1994	1.42	2.99	2.10	1.34	2.89	2.15	6.50	11.86	1.82
County-3	1990	1.04	N/A	N/A	1.18	N/A	N/A	N/A	N/A	N/A
County-3	1991	N/A	N/A	N/A	N/A	N/A	N/A	N/A	N/A	N/A
County-3	1992	N/A	N/A	N/A	N/A	N/A	N/A	N/A	N/A	N/A
County-3	1993	1.47	5.42	3.68	1.65	5.54	3.35	N/A	N/A	N/A
County-3	1994	N/A	2.97	N/A	N/A	2.98	N/A	N/A	N/A	N/A
Statewide	1990	1.42	4.06	2.85	1.40	4.06	2.89	1.93	4.79	2.49
Statewide	1991	1.79	4.68	2.61	1.75	4.60	2.62	2.88	7.79	2.71
Statewide	1992	1.77	4.02	2.27	1.74	4.01	2.31	2.95	5.17	1.76
Statewide	1993	1.83	5.01	2.74	1.74	4.90	2.81	3.80	7.60	2.00
Statewide	1994	1.43	4.04	2.83	1.40	4.07	2.89	1.90	4.26	2.25

As illustrated by the formula, the DRI is a comparison, in ratio format, of the proportion of a specific racial or ethnic youth group, processed at a certain point in the juvenile justice system, of the total cases processed, compared to the proportion of this group in the at-risk youth population. For example, if 10% of the 10- to 16-year-old population is represented by African Americans, and yet they account for 25% of the arrests for an offense group (e.g., property offenses), the index would have a value of 2.5 (or 25% divided by 10%), indicating that this race group is 2.5 times more likely, than their numbers in the population would suggest, to be represented among those arrested for property offenses.

The DRI ratio was chosen because of its simplicity and ease of interpretation. The value 1 represents parity, which means that members of a racial/ethnic or gender group commit a particular offense at a rate that is consistent with that group's proportion of the population. Numbers less than 1 reflect underrepresentation, whereas numbers greater than 1 indicate overrepresentation.

Tables 4.12 and 4.13 provide the DRI results for the DPS arrest data and the TJPC referral data. The results are based on the average number of arrests or referrals for offenses committed in the targeted counties (County-1, County-2, and County-3) and statewide over the five-year period (1990–1994).

In every instance, the DRI results in Table 4.12 show that Anglos have a DRI of less than 1 for both males and females. Anglos of either gender are underrepresented for all five offense types, for all three targeted counties, and for statewide data as well. The opposite is the case for African Americans. African-American youth have the highest DRIs, and they are all greater than 1, for all offense types and for all locations. Whether male or female, African-American youth are disproportionately arrested for all offenses, particularly those involving violence and drug and weapons charges. Hispanics fall between the Anglos at the low end and African Americans at the high end, and generally have DRIs greater than 1.2. However, there are cases where Hispanics are underrepresented. For example, in County-3, Hispanic males are underrepresented for all offense types, with the exception of index property crimes for which they are at parity. Similarly, Hispanic females in County-3 are underrepresented for violent and property crimes and only slightly overrepresented for total index crime (1.14).

The inter-ethnic differentials are greatest between African-American and Anglo youth. Excluding drug offenses, the DRIs for Hispanic youth are generally larger than 1.0. However, the DRIs for Hispanic female youth are greater than 1 across the state and in both urban counties, but not in the rural county (County-3). Too few females were arrested for drug and weapons offenses in County-3 for DRIs to be calculated. Hispanic male and female overrepresentation is highest for offenses involving weapons possession. Generally, the Hispanic/Anglo differential is smaller than the

TABLE 4.12 Disproportionate Representation Index (DRI) for UCR Data by Offense, Gender, Race/Ethnicity, and County (1990–1994)

Offense categories for males		County-1	County-2	County-3	Statewide
Index	A. American	1.73	2.24	1.83	1.95
	Anglo	.61	.47	.46	.68
	Hispanic	1.16	1.47	.98	1.17
Violent	A. American	2.75	3.61	1.83	3.13
	Anglo	.29	.24	.47	.41
	Hispanic	.97	1.26	.99	1.12
Property	A. American	1.48	2.09	1.78	1.77
	Anglo	.70	.49	.46	.72
	Hispanic	1.20	1.49	1.00	1.18
Drugs	A. American	2.73	3.80	2.71	2.87
	Anglo	.39	.38	.31	.48
	Hispanic	.85	.88	.31	1.13
Weapons	A. American	2.18	2.53	1.93	2.32
	Anglo	.37	.45	.56	.53
	Hispanic	1.23	1.34	.53	1.27
Offense categories for females		**County-1**	**County-2**	**County-3**	**Statewide**
Index	A. American	1.57	2.01	1.75	1.87
	Anglo	.65	.54	.52	.71
	Hispanic	1.19	1.39	1.14	1.19
Violent	A. American	2.45	3.32	1.14	3.00
	Anglo	.34	.23	.24	.47
	Hispanic	1.08	1.33	.56	1.06
Property	A. American	1.49	1.95	1.71	1.78
	Anglo	.68	.37	.54	.72
	Hispanic	1.32	1.39	.91	1.15
Drugs	A. American	2.40	2.89	N/A	2.26
	Anglo	.47	.45	N/A	.60
	Hispanic	.93	1.14	N/A	1.18
Weapons	A. American	2.14	2.42	N/A	2.35
	Anglo	.37	.46	N/A	.54
	Hispanic	1.24	1.32	N/A	1.23

N/A = not applicable

Source: 1990–1994 Texas Uniform Crime Reports. Population estimates are from the State Data Center at Texas A&M.

TABLE 4.13 Disproportionate Representation Index (DRI) for TJPC Data by Offense, Gender, Race/Ethnicity, and County (1990–1994)

Offense categories for males		County-1	County-2	County-3	Statewide
Index	A. American	1.80	2.30	1.69	2.06
	Anglo	.57	.43	.48	.65
	Hispanic	1.15	1.49	1.13	1.13
Violent	A. American	2.53	3.17	1.77	2.99
	Anglo	.38	.33	.57	.48
	Hispanic	.96	1.30	.79	1.05
Property	A. American	1.60	2.16	1.68	1.87
	Anglo	.62	.45	.46	.69
	Hispanic	1.19	1.52	1.20	1.14
Drugs	A. American	2.71	4.16	2.74	3.08
	Anglo	.36	.31	.16	.41
	Hispanic	.86	.85	.22	1.13
Weapons	A. American	2.01	2.52	1.83	2.16
	Anglo	.43	.37	.62	.50
	Hispanic	1.23	1.51	.59	1.35
Offense categories for females		**County-1**	**County-2**	**County-3**	**Statewide**
Index	A. American	1.68	1.93	1.79	2.00
	Anglo	.74	.48	.55	.71
	Hispanic	.94	1.56	.73	1.07
Violent	A. American	2.74	2.73	1.15	3.45
	Anglo	.43	.39	N/A	.53
	Hispanic	.74	1.32	N/A	.80
Property	A. American	1.53	1.87	1.68	1.86
	Anglo	.78	.48	.55	.73
	Hispanic	.97	1.58	.95	1.09
Drugs	A. American	1.60	2.39	N/A	1.70
	Anglo	.89	.60	N/A	.74
	Hispanic	.88	1.09	N/A	1.17
Weapons	A. American	2.93	3.81	N/A	2.83
	Anglo	.46	1.74	N/A	.49
	Hispanic	.52	.88	N/A	1.09

Source: 1990–1994 Texas Juvenile Probation Statistical Reports. Population estimates are from the State Data Center at Texas A&M.

African-American/Anglo differential. Finally, except for violent and weapon offenses, the DRIs for African-American and Hispanic males are higher in the urban counties than they are in the rural county. Another noteworthy finding featured in Table 4.12 is that the DRIs for African-American youth are lower than the state average in both County-1 and County-2.

The TJPC data presented in Table 4.13 pertain to referrals made to juvenile probation departments during the 1990–1994 period. Based on the average rates for the five-year period, the DRIs are remarkably consistent in both the UCR and TJPC data. The Pearson correlation between the two data measures is .99. Moreover, the inter-ethnic and other differences reported for the UCR data also hold true for the TJPC data.

LIMITATIONS OF AGGREGATE DATA

At this juncture, an extremely important issue needs to be raised and its implications thoroughly explored. That is, while interesting and important in their own way, the aggregate data, that are often used to demonstrate overrepresentation statistically, are actually of very limited usefulness. Clearly, the ability to analyze properly, and thereby fully document and subsequently explain, minority overrepresentation is greatly compromised when sole reliance is placed on aggregate data and summary tables. The use of summary data as opposed to case-level, offender-based data substantially reduces the usefulness of measurements of overrepresentation and precludes determination of its causes, or at least its statistical correlates.

The limitations surrounding aggregate data are exemplified in the report, *Balancing the Scales* (Vickers, 1992), which was conducted during Governor Ann Richards' administration and which necessitated the present study. A few of the more significant problems with the Vickers' study are detailed next.

Vickers has indicated that "Initial research into the question of overrepresentation of minority youth in the Texas juvenile justice system showed that there is indeed a problem" (1992: 3). Vickers concluded this because the research supposedly indicated that, while 59% of the juvenile arrests in Texas in 1989 involved minority youth, 73% of all detained youth and 74% of all Texas Youth Commission (TYC) commitments were members of minority groups. Overrepresentation differed by specific ethnic groups, however. Hispanic youth were only slightly overrepresented, black youth were more highly overrepresented, and white youth were underrepresented.

It is necessary to discuss here the data upon which Vickers based his determination that minorities were overrepresented. These data are contained in two main tables in Appendix A of the report. There is a Phase One table which documents five specific OJJDP items (i.e., juveniles: detained; confined; confined in adult jails/lockups; arrested; and transferred to adult court), by ethnic groups; and a Phase Two table which documents specific steps in the processing of juveniles in the system. These two tables are supported by documentation concerning the varying samples of the at-risk youth population in Texas that were used as the basis for the computation of overrepresentation.

There is a significant problem with the population data that were used to represent the at-risk youth population. That is, instead of using a standardized and consistent set of age-specific figures showing the distribution, by ethnic groups, for the population of juveniles at risk, *Balancing the Scales* uses four different population tallies which vary in terms of the percentage of the total youth population that are covered and the specific age categories that are included. Thus, population data are given which represent either 100%, 61.7%, 54.5%, or 44% of the youth population. These data are further compromised by the fact that the tallies not only do not cover the same percent of the youth population but they also cover different age ranges—either ages 10–16 or the population under age 18.

The consequence of using differing representations of the at-risk youth population, whether in terms of the sample percentage or the age range included, is that it is impossible to generate a consistent set of estimates of overrepresentation by the specific data items included in the phase one and two tables. Simply, the underlying percentage of African-American, Hispanic, Anglo, and other youth differs from sample to sample and from age group to age group, thus producing a differing and inconsistent figure for overrepresentation.

In addition to these population data, *Balancing the Scales* also includes further documentation which is designed to indicate graphically various summary descriptive measures for juvenile arrests, charges, dispositions, and so on. The problem with these summary data is that they are neither calculated correctly nor are they presented or displayed analytically enough so that they could be useful in understanding either the amount of overrepresentation, or more importantly, the possible correlates of the overrepresentation that was evident. *Balancing the Scales* does include a number of caveats and disclaimers concerning the adequacy of the statistical data that were used in the report. At one point early in the report, the data deficiencies were indicated as follows:

> In gathering the statistics for this report, it was found that there are gaps in reporting in the area of juvenile justice. Many of the samples used for this report are not statewide and the nature of the system would not allow random sampling. (Vickers, 1992: 5)

Similarly, later in the report the following statement is offered:

> The state was able to document overrepresentation of minority youth in the juvenile justice system through the use of several different samples. Unfortunately, the *differences in sample size* do not allow for comparison between the different points in

the system. Therefore it is impossible to accurately identify the reasons why overrepresentation is occurring. (Vickers, 1992: 23, emphasis added)

Finally, on the first page of both Appendix A and B, *Balancing the Scales* offers the following highlighted "important note": "Since there is no statewide reporting system for juvenile justice information, the samples provided here are limited" (Vickers, 1992: 29, 37).

The important point here that needs to be clearly indicated is that the sampling used for the assessment of overrepresentation *and* the summary data presented in the appendices to demonstrate overrepresentation statistically are of limited usefulness. Vickers admits this. However, the problem is not just that the sample sizes differ, nor that the differing sample sizes compromise the ability to identify the causes of overrepresentation. The more important and crucial point is that, because the samples are not random, and because the sample sizes differ throughout the Phase One and Phase Two measures, the representativeness of the data in *Balancing the Scales* is severely limited thus reducing the generalizability of the assessment. But, more important, and more to the point, the inability to analyze and thereby fully document and subsequently explain overrepresentation is *not due* to the fact that the sample sizes differ as incorrectly suggested by Vickers. On the contrary, this inability is caused by the use of aggregate data and summary tables. The use of summary data as opposed to case-level, offender-based data substantially restricts the usefulness of *Balancing the Scales* to either measure and document overrepresentation, or to subsequently determine its correlates.

The limitations inherent in the use of summary data like those in the Vickers' study have been well documented by Community Research Associates, Inc. (CRA). CRA is a federal contractor entrusted by OJJDP with the responsibility to provide technical assistance to the states under the Act. CRA (1992) has provided technical assistance materials which indicate the possible sources of minority overrepresentation. CRA has recognized that a client tracking system provides analytical approaches which permit the identification of problem areas with greater precision than is possible with "summary" types of data.

For example, CRA has shown that one of the major drawbacks of the summary system of data collection is that the cases reported in disposition cells of summary tables may actually reflect arrest cases from prior years. CRA has indicated a second major drawback to the use of summary measures—the inability to relate client characteristics to the client outcome in ways which then allow an examination of the effects of indirect relationships or decision-making variables at various points along the juvenile justice case processing dynamic. In particular, CRA has noted that a state with only summary statistics places the planner or analyst in an undesirable situation in describing the reasons for minority overrepresentation.

In contrast to summary measures, the availability of client tracking data provides two major advantages. First, the assessment can directly calculate differences in the handling of youth with reference to stage-specific transition probabilities as opposed to the imprecise inferences that must be drawn from summary data. Second, client tracking permits the establishment of relationships between case characteristics (e.g., prior record, instant offense, and severity) to processing decisions and thereby permits the determination of whether there are any race or ethnicity biases in these relationships.

In light of the preceding commentary concerning the inadequacy surrounding aggregate measures of juvenile justice system processing, and the inherent dangers present in the use of such data to document either the extent or the correlates of minority overrepresentation, the next four chapters turn to the results of individual case-level analyses and a statewide survey of practitioners.

5

Decision Making in County-1

Two thousand felony and misdemeanor delinquency cases that had been processed in County-1 from 1993 through 1994 were selected for analysis (as detailed in Chapter 3). Figure 5.1 provides a flow chart with descriptive counts of the various stages of juvenile justice processing in County-1 and the attrition of cases as they move from stage to stage. This study was able to highlight a number of different stages within the juvenile system which involved decision making to handle cases one way or another: (1) decision to detain at intake; (2) decision to refer a case to the DA; (3) decision to file a petition; and (4) decision to place a juvenile in secure custody at a Texas Youth Commission facility (TYC).

Figure 5.1 indicates that at intake, the race/ethnic breakdown of the cases was almost perfectly even: 34.3% African American, 34.5% Hispanic, and 31.3% Anglo. These data indicate the appropriateness of the sampling technique used in the study as no race or ethnic group is differentially represented (i.e., selection bias) at the intake stage. About 68% of the cases were handled at the initial intake stage with no further processing. Of the 2,000 cases, only 641 (32%) were referred to the DA for further processing. There is an indication that African Americans were slightly more likely to have their case referred to the DA, as opposed to being handled informally, as African Americans comprise a slightly higher percentage of the referred cases compared to intake (37.1% versus 34.3%). On the other hand, the percentage of Hispanics declined (31.3% versus 34.5%) and the concentration of Anglos was almost identical (31.6% versus 31.3%).

FIGURE 5.1 Juvenile Justice Process in County-1

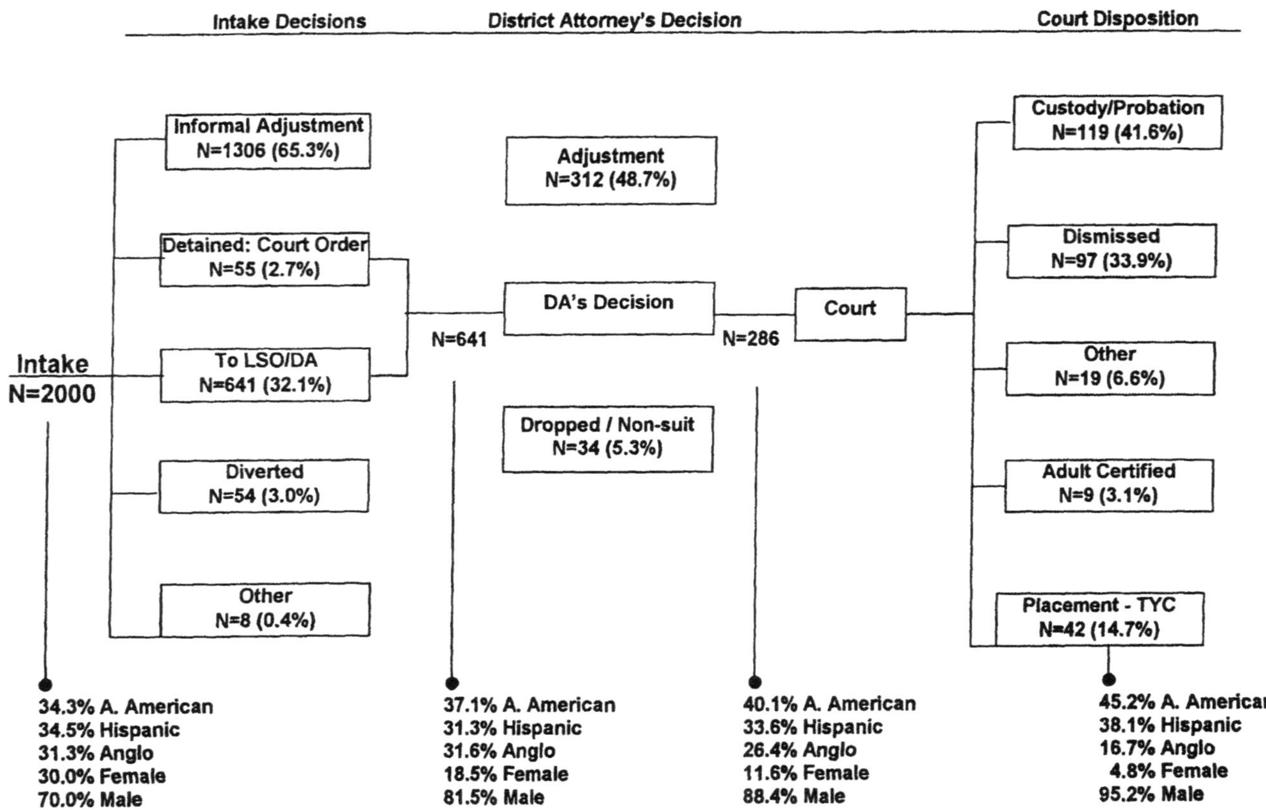

Of the 641 cases referred to the DA for further processing, 286 (44.6%) had petitions filed against them by the DA. At this stage, African Americans (40.1% versus 34.3% at intake) are slightly overrepresented, while Hispanics (33.6% versus 34.5% at intake) and Anglos (26.4% versus, 31.3% at intake) were slightly underrepresented. Among the 286 youth who were petitioned to court, 97 (34%) of the cases were dismissed or the individuals were found not guilty; another 9 cases (3.1%) were certified as adults; 19 cases (3.1% received some other type of court disposition); and 42 (14.7%) were sent to TYC for secure placement. The racial/ethnic profile of the cases which received a secure disposition indicates that, compared to their initial percentage at intake, African Americans (45.2%) and Hispanic youth (38.1%) were overrepresented, while Anglos (16.7%) were substantially underrepresented.

Thus, Figure 5.1 provides the race/ethnicity and gender characteristics of youth as they are processed through the juvenile justice stages in County-1. Comparisons made between the demographic profile at intake and at subsequent stages indicate that African Americans are consistently overrepresented, Anglos are consistently underrepresented, and Hispanics vary between these positions. The fundamental question, however, is whether these differences that arise stage by stage are legitimate and can be explained by permissible legal criteria, or whether, in the absence of such criteria, the race/ethnic differentials are representative of differential selection of minority youth for "harsher" handling by juvenile justice authorities. Thus, in this chapter, statistical analyses are reported that were conducted to determine if differences due to race/ethnicity and gender persist among youth facing similar charges in the juvenile system in County-1, once background factors, especially prior delinquency history, are held constant.

DETENTION DECISIONS

In Texas, a juvenile may be held in detention (pre-adjudication incarceration) after intake for up to two working days before being brought before a judge. If a child is brought before the court or delivered to a detention facility as authorized by Sections 51.12(a)(3) and (4) of the *Texas Family Code,* the intake or other authorized officer of the court shall immediately make an investigation and shall release the child unless it appears that his detention is warranted under subsection (b). When a child is brought before an intake worker, a judge or some other referee, at least one of five statutory criteria must be met to detain him/her for a longer period of time. According to Section 53.02, subsection (b), *Texas Family Code,* a child taken into custody may be detained prior to hearing on the petition only if:

a. he is likely to abscond or be removed from the jurisdiction of the court;

b. suitable supervision, care, or protection for him is not being provided by a parent, guardian, custodian, or other person;

c. he has no parent, guardian, custodian, or other person able to return him to the court when required;

d. he may be dangerous to himself or he may threaten the safety of the public if released; or

e. he has previously been found to be a delinquent child or has previously been convicted of a penal offense punishable by a term in jail or prison and is likely to commit an offense if released.

In County-1, detention data were measured in three ways: (1) ever detained; (2) detained for longer than two days; and (3) detained by order of a judge or referee. Two hundred and forty-four (12.2%) youth were detained at intake. Of these youth, 101 (5.1%) were detained for more than two days. Fifty-six youth (2.8%) were detained after a court hearing. The last measurement of detention turned out to be the most accurate. The variable "detained for more than two days" corresponds with court-ordered detention approximately 75% of the time. The reasons for detention were not available on computer records in County-1; therefore, researchers conducted a separate analysis of the reasons for detention. The effect of each of the following factors in detention decisions was examined: (1) being African American; (2) being Hispanic; (3) being female; (4) age; (5) school enrollment; (6) parents' marital status; (7) living with both parents; (8) severity of the alleged criminal offense; (9) severity of past offenses; and (10) number of previous offenses.

Table 5.1 presents the results of logistic regression modeling of the decision to detain a juvenile at intake. Like a usual regression result table, Table 5.1 lists the unstandardized coefficients (b) and the standard error (s.e.), which allow readers to determine the significance of the relationships.[1] Usually, a positive coefficient means that the factor is associated with a more severe outcome at a particular decision point. The importance of the variables in the model is based on the maximum predicted effect (MPE) of the independent variable on the probability of being in one category of the dependent variable.[2] For dummy variables, for example, race/ethnicity, it is the maximum predicted effect of being of that race versus the baseline (Anglo). For continuous variables (e.g., severity of the offense), the MPE is the maximum predicted effect of a two-standard-deviation shift in that variable on the probability of being in the category of the dependent variable indicating presence of the particular trait or status being studied. The MPE can be interpreted as a percentage. The MPE percentages are reported only when a significant racial, ethnic, or gender effect is identified. The sample size and the goodness-of-fit statistic are also provided for each model. Results are presented for models with all cases in the sample, for male offenders only, and for female offenders only (where applicable).

TABLE 5.1 Factors in the Detention Decision

	All cases	Males
	Unstandardized coefficient (s.e.)	Unstandardized coefficient (s.e.)
African American	.35	.44
	(.46)	(.49)
Hispanic	.90*	1.03*
	(.46)	(.48)
Female	−1.3	N/A
	(.74)	N/A
Age	.10	.08
	(.12)	(.12)
School enrollment	.15	.04
	(.35)	(.37)
Parental marital status	.08	.09
	(.24)	(.24)
Live with both parents	.08	.08
	(.22)	(.23)
Offense severity	.87**	.90**
	(.12)	(.13)
Severity of past offenses	.13*	.14*
	(.07)	(.07)
Number of past offenses	.12*	.12**
	(.02)	(.03)
Intercept	−9.6	−9.5
	(.20)	(2.1)
N	1,992	1,394
−2Log L	189.7	161.9
(df)	(10)	(9)

N/A = not applicable
*$p < .05$ **$p < .01$

All Cases

Table 5.1 provides the logistic regression results for court-ordered detention status and the group of predictor variables. The strongest correlate of court-ordered detention status is the "severity of the alleged criminal offense." In addition to the severity of the presenting offense, significant coefficients were obtained for the following: (1) number of past offenses; (2) severity of past offenses; and (3) Hispanic status. Each of these factors has a positive and significant impact on detention status. If the juvenile is alleged to have committed a severe offense, has more rather than fewer past offenses, has relatively serious past offenses, and is Hispanic (rather than Anglo), that particular juvenile is more likely to be detained. In terms of the Maximum Predicated Effect scores, Hispanics are 24% more likely than Anglos to be detained, once all factors are held constant. In contrast, a two-standard-deviation shift in offense severity produces a 44% shift in the dependent variable. None of the other factors were significantly related to court-ordered detention. In particular, African Americans were not more likely than whites to be detained.

Males

A similar regression model was estimated with only the male delinquents. In this model, two of the three offense-related measures (severity of the presenting offense and the number of past offenses) have the strongest predictive power concerning whether the juvenile was detained. In addition, two other variables have significant (but at a less significant level) effects on detention status. These measures are (1) severity of past offenses and (2) being a Hispanic offender. Thus, if a male who is alleged to have committed a relatively severe current offense and has committed a higher frequency of offenses previously, he has significantly greater odds of being placed in detention. Based on the MPE, a two-standard-deviation shift in offense severity produces a 46% shift in the dependent variable. To a lesser extent, but significant also, if the male also has a relatively serious prior offense career and is Hispanic, he has significantly higher odds of being placed in detention (Hispanics are 26% more likely than Anglos to be detained, once all factors are held constant).

Females

In the female-only model, only two females in the sample were detained with a court order. These are not a sufficient number of cases to conduct multivariate analyses.

Conclusion

In County-1, three legally permissible offense measures are significant correlates of definition decisions: (1) severity of the current alleged offense; (2) number of prior delinquent acts; and (3) severity of prior delinquent acts. All of these factors meet the detention eligibility criteria shown previously. In addition, after offense conduct measures are controlled, Hispanic males are significantly more likely than Anglo males to be detained. It must be noted in addition, that African-American status was not significant in either the total case or the male-only regression models. This signifies that

African-American youth, when the severity of past and current conduct, and the number of prior referrals are controlled in the equation, do not receive detention more often merely as a consequence of their minority status.

Parenthetically (and only speculatively, of course), it is suspected that gang membership/activity is a likely candidate that is responsible for the significant effect of Hispanic status. County-1 has a significant delinquent gang problem and Hispanic gangs are very active in the county. However, data collection in County-1 did not provide a measure that would allow the effect of gang membership to be controlled in the County-1 analysis. This was due to a lack of reliable gang information in the county database.[3] It is believed, however, that if gang membership had been included in the models, it likely would have mitigated the impact of being Hispanic, or at least reduced the disparity between Hispanic and Anglo youth.

FORWARD A CASE TO THE DISTRICT ATTORNEY

An informal adjustment is a means of resolving a juvenile's case through community service, counseling, or release under parental supervision, among other possibilities. Some delinquency cases are deemed more serious and are not accorded an informal adjustment and are forwarded to the prosecutors for further decision making. The analysis examined the role of each of the following factors in the decision to refer delinquency cases to prosecutors: (1) being African American; (2) being Hispanic; (3) being female; (4) age; (5) school enrollment; (6) parents' marital status; (7) living with both parents; (8) severity of the alleged criminal offense; (9) severity of past offenses; and (10) number of previous offenses. The results are presented in Table 5.2.

All Cases

On the basis of the regression analysis, the factors that are predictive of the decision to forward a case to the DA for possible prosecution are these (in order of importance): (1) severity of the alleged offense; (2) number of previous offenses; (3) school enrollment; (4) being female; and (5) living with both parents. All these variables, except for gender, increase the likelihood of the case being sent to the DA. Female youth are less likely to have their cases sent to the DA (MPE = 7%). Committing serious offenses, having more prior offenses, not living with two parents, and school status are factors which ensure that the case is reviewed by the DA for possible prosecution. The coefficients for African-American and Hispanic youth were not significant. Thus, neither race nor ethnicity was associated with a decision to forego informal proceedings and send the case to the DA for further processing. In effect, African-American, Hispanic, and Anglo youth had statistically similar chances of such action.

TABLE 5.2 Factors in the Decision to Send a Case to the DA

	All cases	Males	Females
	Unstandardized coefficient (s.e.)	Unstandardized coefficient (s.e.)	Unstandardized coefficient (s.e.)
African American	.03	.19	.35
	(.16)	(.19)	(.29)
Hispanic	–.16	.21	–1.2**
	(.16)	(.19)	(.33)
Female	–.30**	N/A	N/A
	(.15)	N/A	N/A
Age	–.06	.06	.08
	(.04)	(.05)	(.09)
School enrollment	.40**	.48**	.34
	(.13)	(.16)	(.27)
Parental marital status	.19	.20	.05
	(.11)	(.12)	(.99)
Live with both parents	.28*	.24	1.9
	(.11)	(.12)	(1.2)
Offense severity	.94**	.98**	.83**
	(.04)	(.05)	(.10)
Severity of past offenses	.06	.08	–.06
	(.05)	(.05)	(.13)
Number of past offenses	.08**	.07**	.22*
	(.03)	(.02)	(.10)
Intercept	–4.5	–4.7	4.5
	(.67)	(.76)	(1.5)
N	1,921	1,348	573
–2Log L	854.4	700.9	143.0
(df)	(10)	(9)	(9)

*$p < .05$ **$p < .01$

Males

In the male-only model, the factors that are correlated with the decision to forward a case to the DA for possible prosecution, as opposed to obtaining an informal adjustment at intake, are these: (1) severity of the alleged offense; (2) number of previous offenses; and (3) school enrollment. Each of these components is positively correlated with the decision to refer a case to the DA for possible prosecution. Again, neither race nor ethnicity is significantly associated with this decision.

It might be surprising, and even counterintuitive, that school enrollment would have a positive impact on the odds that the case would be referred to the DA. However, this variable was coded 1 if any of the following was true: (1) juvenile was attending school; (2) juvenile was enrolled but not attending; (3) juvenile had been held back; or (4) juvenile had irregular attendance. Since the file was available to the intake workers, it would be likely that criteria 2, 3, and 4, if present, could possibly lead to a referral decision.

Females

In the female-only model, the factors that are correlated with the decision to refer a juvenile's case to the DA for possible prosecution, as opposed to obtaining an informal adjustment at intake, are these: (1) severity of the alleged criminal offense; (2) being Hispanic; and (3) the number of prior offenses. Being Hispanic, as opposed to being Anglo, has a negative influence. In other words, Hispanic females are less likely than Anglo females to be referred to the DA's office (MPE = 27%). Youth who have committed relatively serious offenses and who have prior referrals are more likely to have their cases sent to the DA. Interaction terms were not significant for this model.

Conclusion

The severity of the current offense, a factor which is not only legally permissible, but also, obviously highly determinative of a need to refer a case for prosecution, is the most important factor in all three models, although the number of prior offenses and school enrollment also play significant roles at this decision point. Generally, females, particularly Hispanic females, are less likely to have their cases referred to the DA. Most important, there is no evidence, whatsoever, that minority youth receive unfavorable referral decisions. African-American and Hispanic offenders are treated the same as Anglo delinquents, unless the youth is a female and Hispanic. In the latter case, the treatment is significantly more likely to be favorable (i.e., fewer cases are referred for prosecution).

DA'S DECISION TO PROSECUTE A CASE

The DA's decision to prosecute a case was modeled as a simple yes/no dichotomy. The DA chooses either to prosecute a case, or to follow another course of action, such as deferring prosecution and authorizing an informal adjustment, or even dropping the case altogether.

The analysis examined the role of each of the following factors correlated with the decision to prosecute a case: (1) being African American; (2) being Hispanic; (3) being female; (4) age; (5) school enrollment; (6) parents' marital status; (7) living with two parents; (8) severity of the alleged criminal

TABLE 5.3 Factors in the Decision to Prosecute a Case

	All cases	Males	Males
	Unstandardized coefficient (s.e.)	Unstandardized coefficient (s.e.)	Unstandardized coefficient (s.e.)
African American	.41	.52*	.94**
	(.22)	(.24)	(.27)
Hispanic	.36	.51*	–.63**
	(.22)	(.25)	(.28)
Female	–.60**	N/A	N/A
	(.24)	N/A	N/A
Age	.07	.05	.04
	(.06)	(.06)	(.06)
School enrollment	.70**	.66**	.67**
	(.19)	(.21)	(.21)
Parental marital status	.23	.20	.68
	(.11)	(.13)	(.41)
Live with both parents	.001	.04	–.08
	(.11)	(.12)	(.43)
Offense severity	.20**	.19**	.21**
	(.05)	(.05)	(.06)
Severity of past offenses	.04	.04	–.01
	(.05)	(.05)	(.05)
Number of past offenses	.01	.007	.30
	(.02)	(.03)	(.12)
Number of prior offenses,			–.33**
*A. American	N/A	N/A	(.12)
Number of prior offenses,			–.22**
*Hispanic	N/A	N/A	(.12)
Intercept	–2.8	–2.6	–2.4
	(.94)	(.99)	(5.1)
N	616	502	502
–2Log L	78.5	49.8	60.6
(df)	(9)	(9)	(11)

*$p < .05$ **$p < .01$

offense; (9) severity of past offenses; and (10) number of previous offenses. The results are presented in Table 5.3.

All Cases

The factors that are significantly associated with the DA's decision to prosecute a case, rather than to defer prosecution, are as follows: (1) severity of the alleged offense; (2) school enrollment; and (3) being male. Youth who are alleged to have committed serious offenses, are enrolled in school, and are male are more likely to have petitions filed by the DA. There are no race or ethnicity effects.

Males

In the male-only model, the factors that are significantly associated with the DA's decision to prosecute a case, rather than to defer prosecution, are these: (1) severity of the offense; (2) school enrollment;[4] (3) being African American; and (4) being Hispanic. All of these factors are positively correlated with the DA's decision to prosecute. Compared to similarly situated Anglo males, African-American (MPE = 13%) and Hispanic (MPE = 12%) youth are more likely to be prosecuted. A model was then developed to determine if the relationship between race/ethnicity and the DA's decision to prosecute might be conditioned on the number of prior referrals a juvenile has in his delinquency career. Thus, an interaction effect was introduced consisting of the interaction between race/ethnicity and the number of prior referrals. These interactions (one each for African Americans and Hispanics) are included in the model in column three of Table 5.3. Previously, the number of priors was not significant, but the interaction terms for this measure for both African Americans and Hispanics attain significance. Thus, the differential number of prior referrals for these groups compared to Anglos has a critical effect in the DA's decision to prosecute.

Females

In the female-only data, only 31 cases were prosecuted. The logistic model did converge.[5] However, due to the small sample size, the results should be interpreted with caution. The only factor that is correlated with the DA's decision to prosecute a case, rather than to defer prosecution, is the severity of the alleged criminal offense. Race/ethnicity is not correlated with the decision to file a petition or to prosecute the case.

Conclusion

The severity of the offense and school status are the strongest correlates of the decision to file a petition. When the variables in the model are taken into account, there is a correlation between being an African-American or Hispanic male and the decision to prosecute in the male-only model. This relationship between race/ethnicity and the decision to prosecute appears to be conditioned by the number of prior referrals. As noted previously, the absence of a gang variable may also be a critical factor, since it may mitigate the race/ethnicity effect reported here. Gender is also correlated with this decision; fewer females have petitions filed against them.

PLACEMENT BY THE COURT

Of course, the ultimate issue which confronts us in this research concerns whether, upon adjudication, minority youth are disproportionately (and selectively) sentenced to a secure placement in a juvenile facility. Given the range of options available to the court, secure placement would represent the harshest possible disposition. In this study, placement was generally considered to be any kind of court-ordered relocation of a juvenile to a "new" environment. In the context of this report, placement means being sentenced to the Texas Youth Commission (TYC). The decision for court-ordered placement is modeled as an either/or decision (two alternatives). Thus, either the juvenile is placed in the custody of TYC or another disposition is handed out. The latter possibility includes probation, community service, acquittal, dismissal, or an administrative order.

The analysis examined the role of each of the following factors in the decision to place youth in TYC facilities: (1) being African American; (2) being Hispanic; (3) being female; (4) age; (5) school enrollment; (6) having parents who are married; (7) living with two parents; (8) severity of the alleged criminal offense; (9) severity of past offenses; and (10) number of previous offenses. The results are presented in Table 5.4.

All Cases

The factors that are a statistically significant component influencing whether the juvenile court orders placement in a facility are these: (1) number of previous offenses; and (2) severity of the alleged criminal offense. Each of these components of the judicial decision has a substantial positive impact on the odds that the youth will be incarcerated. A juvenile with more past offenses who has committed a serious current offense is likely to be committed to a TYC facility. Moreover, each of these two factors is not only legally permissible, but each is exactly the type of delinquency factor that a court would be expected to utilize in its decision making. Further, and most important, neither of the race/ethnicity factors was associated with secure confinement decisions—neither African-American nor Hispanic status, compared to Anglo delinquent status, significantly influenced the court in rendering an out-of-home placement decision.

Males

Likewise, in the male-only data, the variables that were significant correlates of the decision to order placement were (1) number of previous offenses and (2) severity of the alleged criminal offense. The findings are identical to those for all cases. In County-1, there is no racial impact at this confinement stage of juvenile processing.

TABLE 5.4 Factors in Placement to Texas Youth Commission

	All cases	Males
	Unstandardized coefficient (s.e.)	Unstandardized coefficient (s.e.)
African American	.13	.26
	(.53)	(.57)
Hispanic	–.07	.11
	(.57)	(.60)
Female	.63	N/A
	(.81)	N/A
Age	.20	.21
	(.18)	(.19)
School enrollment	–.10	.02
	(.46)	(.48)
Parental marital status	.19	.24
	(.25)	(.26)
Live with both parents	–.12	–.14
	(.25)	(.25)
Offense severity	.38**	.43**
	(.14)	(.15)
Severity of past offenses	.07	.08
	(.10)	(.10)
Number of past offenses	.25**	.24**
	(.06)	(.06)
Intercept	–7.6	–8.3
	(3.0)	(3.1)
N	271	240
–2Log L	55.9	50.8
(df)	(10)	(9)

**$p < .01$

Females

In the female-only data, only two females were sent to TYC. Consequently, no multivariate analyses could be conducted.

Conclusion

The number of previous offenses and the severity of new offenses are the most important components of the court's decision to place a juvenile in a TYC facility. There is no significant effect attributable to the race or ethnicity of the delinquent.

SUPPLEMENTARY ANALYSIS: DETENTION RECORDS

In addition to conducting analyses based on MIS data, data collection also examined detention orders for youth so that the research could investigate the specific reasons why the offenders had been detained. Reasons for detention were not available from the MIS in all counties. Using records of individuals who had ever been detained, the data collection attempted to obtain paper detention orders. Of the 125 randomly selected records, 103 records were tracked (e.g., where offense characteristics matched detention orders). In the remaining cases, records had been deleted or misplaced. The sample of 103 records consisted of 51% African Americans, 36% Hispanics, and 13% Anglos, proportions similar to the overall 1993–1994 detention trends in County-1 (see Table 5.5).

As noted, in Texas, there are five statutory reasons why juveniles may be detained at intake. In the sample, the overwhelming reason (82%) for detaining youth was "lack of suitable supervision, care, or protection for the youth." The next most frequently stated reason (8%) was that the juvenile had committed a felony offense and would be a danger to himself/herself or to the community if released. Thirty-four of the detention orders indicated more than one reason for detention. In 74% of the cases, the secondary reason was that the juvenile had serious past offenses. For these cases, 76% of the records documented a "lack of suitable supervision" as the first reason. In this sample of 103 cases, there were no significant differences by race/ethnicity.

In the survey conducted as part of this study, researchers were able to identify unique issues that juvenile justice practitioners dealt with in working with minority youth. The analyses of these key issues, presented in Chapter 9, should clarify some of the findings reported here.

STATUS OFFENSES

A separate analysis was conducted on 2,000 randomly selected individuals in County-1 who committed status offenses. In this study, a status offender is "a child who is accused or adjudicated for conduct that would not, under state law, be a crime if committed by an adult, including truancy,

TABLE 5.5 Detentions in County-1

	A. American (%)	Hispanic (%)	Anglo (%)	N
All detentions, 1993–1994	49.4	38.1	12.5	512
Detention study sample	51.0	36.3	12.8	103

running away from home . . . and violating a juvenile curfew ordinance or order" (*Texas Family Code,* 3, Section 51.03, 1995). Of the 2,000 status cases, only one was detained by court order. Researchers examined the probability of a juvenile being processed by the DA's office, as opposed to receiving an informal adjustment at intake. Only 62 cases were forwarded to the DA's office. The logistic regression results for this stage are given in Table 5.6. The factors that are correlated with the decision to send the case to the DA are these: (1) age; (2) school enrollment; and (3) number of previous offenses. Older youth with more previous offenses who were not enrolled in school were more likely to have their cases referred to the DA. Race/ethnicity and gender are not correlated with the decision to send a case to the prosecutor. Subsequently, only one case was sent to court. The remaining cases were settled by the DA.

TABLE 5.6 Factors in the Decision to Send Status Offense Cases to the DA

	All cases Unstandardized coefficient (s.e.)
African American	.23 (.32)
Hispanic	.09 (.33)
Female	−.32 (.27)
Age	.25* (.110)
School enrollment	−.73* (.36)
Parental marital status	.19 (.14)
Live with both parents	.10 (.13)
Severity of past offenses	.04 (.06)
Number of past offenses	.11* (.05)
Intercept	−7.2 (1.8)
N	1,989
−2Log L (df)	33.1 (9)

*$p < .05$

The results clearly indicate that in County-1, although the DA scrutinizes the files of youth with prior offenses, only one petition was filed, and obviously, race/ethnic differentials were not observed.

OFFENSES COMMITTED BY ASIAN-AMERICAN YOUTH

The main analyses reported previously were restricted to Anglo, African-American, and Hispanic youth. In County-1, only 582 Asian-American youth were referred to the county probation department during the 1993–1994 period. Of these, only 9 (1.5%) youth were detained after a hearing. In addition, only 25% of the youth had prior delinquency records, thus constraining the variance and the predictability of the independent variables. Thus, separate analyses were conducted on Asian-American youth to determine what factors might be associated with their processing decisions. One hundred and fifty-five cases were sent to the DA. Another 62 cases were prosecuted by the DA. The role of each of the following factors in the decision to refer cases to the DA/prosecutors was studied: (1) being female; (2) age; (3) school enrollment; (4) parents' marital status; (5) living with two parents; (6) severity of the alleged criminal offense; (7) severity of past offenses; and (8) number of previous offenses. The results are presented in Table 5.7. The statistically significant correlates of the decision to refer a case to the DA's office are these (in order of their importance): (1) severity of the alleged criminal offense; (2) parents' marital status; and (3) being female. With the exception of being female, each component is positively correlated with detention. The MPE for females is 18%.

The factors that are correlated with the DA's decision to prosecute are these (in order of their importance): (1) number of previous offenses and (2) school enrollment. Each component mentioned is positively correlated with the DA's decision to prosecute. If the Asian-American juvenile has relatively more previous offenses and is enrolled in school, he/she will be detained. There were only a few cases of Asian-American youth sent to TYC; consequently, no analyses were conducted.

In both models, some of the statistically significant variables that account for how Asian-American youth were processed in County-1 were also significant correlates of the outcomes for other racial/ethnic groups. The severity of offenses, gender (in referral to the DA model), and the number of previous offenses in the model for petitions filed were also important for African-American, Hispanic, and Anglo youth. These results provide convergent evidence for the robustness of the models and the factors which have been identified as important criteria in decision making as cases move through the various stages.

TABLE 5.7 Factors in the Processing of Asian-American Cases in County-1

	Case sent to the DA	DA files petition
	Unstandardized coefficient (s.e.)	Unstandardized coefficient (s.e.)
Female	–.75*	–.38
	(.32)	(.60)
Age	.16	.25
	(.10)	(.15)
School enrollment	–.06	1.5**
	(.29)	(.45)
Parental marital status	.80**	–.49
	(.24)	(.36)
Live with both parents	–.02	.26
	(.22)	(.34)
Offense severity	1.1**	.15
	(.10)	(.10)
Severity of past offenses	.15	–.13
	(.14)	(.12)
Number of past offenses	–.09	.32**
	(.09)	(.12)
Intercept	–5.6	–6.1
	(1.5)	(2.5)
N	570	155
–2Log L	29.3	35.7
(df)	(8)	(8)

$^{*}p < .05$ $^{**}p < .01$

COUNTY-1 SUMMARY

Table 5.8 summarizes the multivariate analyses conducted for the County-1 juvenile processing data. It is readily apparent that the severity of the current offense is consistently the strongest factor in the various juvenile justice stages for all cases, males, and females. In addition, in most instances, other criminal history variables, such as severity of prior record and/or number of prior offenses were also found to be significant correlates of processing decisions. However, in addition to these offense-related measures, the County-1 analyses indicate that there are five instances where race/ethnicity is a significant correlate in processing decisions—four of the instances disfavor minority males, while one instance favors minority females. Otherwise, race/ethnicity does not play a significant role in any of

TABLE 5.8 Significant Factors in Decision Making

	Race/ethnicity	Offense data (past/present)	Other variables
All cases			
Detention	Hispanic	Offense severity	None
	Unfavorable	Severity of priors No. of priors	
Refer case to DA	None	Offense severity No. of priors	Female School
Refer case to court	None	Offense severity No. of priors	Female School
Sentence to secure facility	None	Offense severity No. of priors	None
Males			
Detention	Hispanic	Offense severity	None
	Unfavorable	Severity of priors No. of priors	
Refer case to DA	None	Offense severity No. of priors	School
Refer case to court	A. American Unfavorable	Offense severity No. of priors* A. American[†]	School
	Hispanic Unfavorable	No. of priors* Hispanic[†]	
Sentence to secure facility	None	Offense severity No. of priors	None
Females			
Detention	Not applicable	Not applicable	Not applicable
Refer case to DA	Hispanic Unfavorable	Offense severity No. of priors	None
Refer case to court	None	Offense severity	None
Sentence to secure facility	Not available	Not available	Not available

[†] Asterisks (*) signify two-way interaction effect.

the other stages in County-1. Thus, out of a possible 13 decision stage analyses, it was found that there are four occasions, or about 30%, when minority youth were handled differentially by the juvenile justice process. Importantly, however, none of these instances involved the penultimate stage of commitment to a secure facility. The unfavorable decisions are as follows.

First, Hispanic youth, both overall and for males, are significantly *more likely* than their Anglo peers to be detained at intake. For this decision point, being Hispanic is the second strongest correlate of the detention decision, after the severity of the offense.

Second, African-American and Hispanic males are significantly more likely than Anglo males to have their case referred by the DA to court for adjudication. However, the relationship between race/ethnicity and the prosecutor's decision is conditioned by another predictor variable—the number of prior referrals. That is, in addition to the main effects of Hispanic and African-American status, it was found that Hispanic and African-American status interacted with number of prior offenses and had a significant impact on the decision to refer a case to court for adjudication.

Last, Hispanic females are significantly *less likely* than Anglo females to have their cases referred to the DA. The status of being a Hispanic female is the second strongest correlate of this decision, after the severity of the offense.

These analyses suggest that race/ethnicity does matter at two decision points in the male-only case data: detention and court referral. It is nonetheless possible that the race/ethnicity effects for Hispanic and African-American males may be mitigated by controlling for gang membership. However, no reliable data on gang membership were available in the County-1 data for the 1993–1994 period. Moreover, as will be discussed in Chapters 8 and 9, statewide survey respondents report that other factors, such as the juvenile's demeanor or attitude at his/her hearing, are correlated with outcomes or decisions. Survey findings also indicate that there are significant communication-related issues between juvenile justice staff and parents of minority youth that could explain actions taken against minority youth, particularly at the intake stage when detention is determined. Nevertheless, County-1 does have a differential minority processing issue that should be remedied. This and other issues will receive more thorough discussion in subsequent chapters.

Finally, females receive less severe dispositions at two of the decision points. However, changes in the *Texas Family Code,* introduced in January 1996, are likely to have resulted in recent decisions that are more gender neutral (Tracy and Kempf-Leonard, 1998). That is, Texas now uses a system of Progressive Sanction Guidelines which require the judiciary to follow recommended sanctions, or provide on the record the rationale for any departure from the recommended sanctions.

NOTES

1. An asterisk denotes a significant relationship between the variable or factor and the outcome. Variables that are not asterisked are neither statistically significant nor direct correlates of the outcome measure.

2. MPE = (1/(1 + exp(–b*standard deviation)))–.5, where MPE is the maximum predicted effect, and b is the unstandardized coefficient (standard deviations of continuous variables are presented in Table 5.1). The MPE is interpretable as a percentage.

3. In a victim data set that we coded from police reports, it was determined that 35% of the Hispanic offenders were alleged to have gang affiliations, as opposed to 6.4% of African Americans and 13.2% of Anglo juveniles. This provides some support for the hypothesis that Hispanic delinquents are more likely to be involved with gangs.

4. There are a number of instances where the findings are counterintuitive. As reported earlier, these cases may be attributes of measurement issues over which the researchers had no control. Dropping these variables did not change the findings.

5. In this process, the SAS program estimates the coefficients through maximum likelihood estimations. If the available information is insufficient, the procedure stops. With small samples, the estimated coefficients that are generated are not robust.

6

Decision Making in County-2

Two thousand felony and misdemeanor cases processed in County-2 from 1993 through 1994 were selected as described in Chapter 3. Figure 6.1 shows the various stages of juvenile justice processing in County-2 and the case flow characteristics by race/ethnicity and gender. As with County-1, it was possible to highlight four different stages within the juvenile system in County-2: (1) decision to detain at intake; (2) decision to refer a case to the DA; (3) decision to file a petition; and (4) decision to place a juvenile in TYC.

At the intake stage, the gender characteristics of the youth show that about two-thirds of the cases were male, while a little less than one-third were female. In terms of the race/ethnicity of the youth, 26.6% were African Americans, 37% were Hispanic, and 36.5% were Anglo delinquents. About 36% of the cases were resolved at intake with no further processing. Of the 2,000 cases, 1,286 (64.3%) youth were referred to the DA. Compared to County-1, the referral rate in County-2 is approximately twice as high (64.3% versus 32.1%). The profile of the cases referred to the DA is almost exactly the same as the profile at the starting point (27.1%, African American; 37.2%, Hispanic; and 35.7%, Anglo). Of the 1,286 cases referred to the DA, in turn, 128 (9.9%) had petitions filed by the DA for subsequent court processing. At this processing point, the percentage of African Americans has increased by about 5.5 percentage points from the initial intake stage (32.0% versus 26.5%), Hispanics have slightly increased (38.8% versus 37.9%), and Anglos have become underrepresented (29.7% versus 36.5%).

FIGURE 6.1 Juvenile Justice Process in County-2

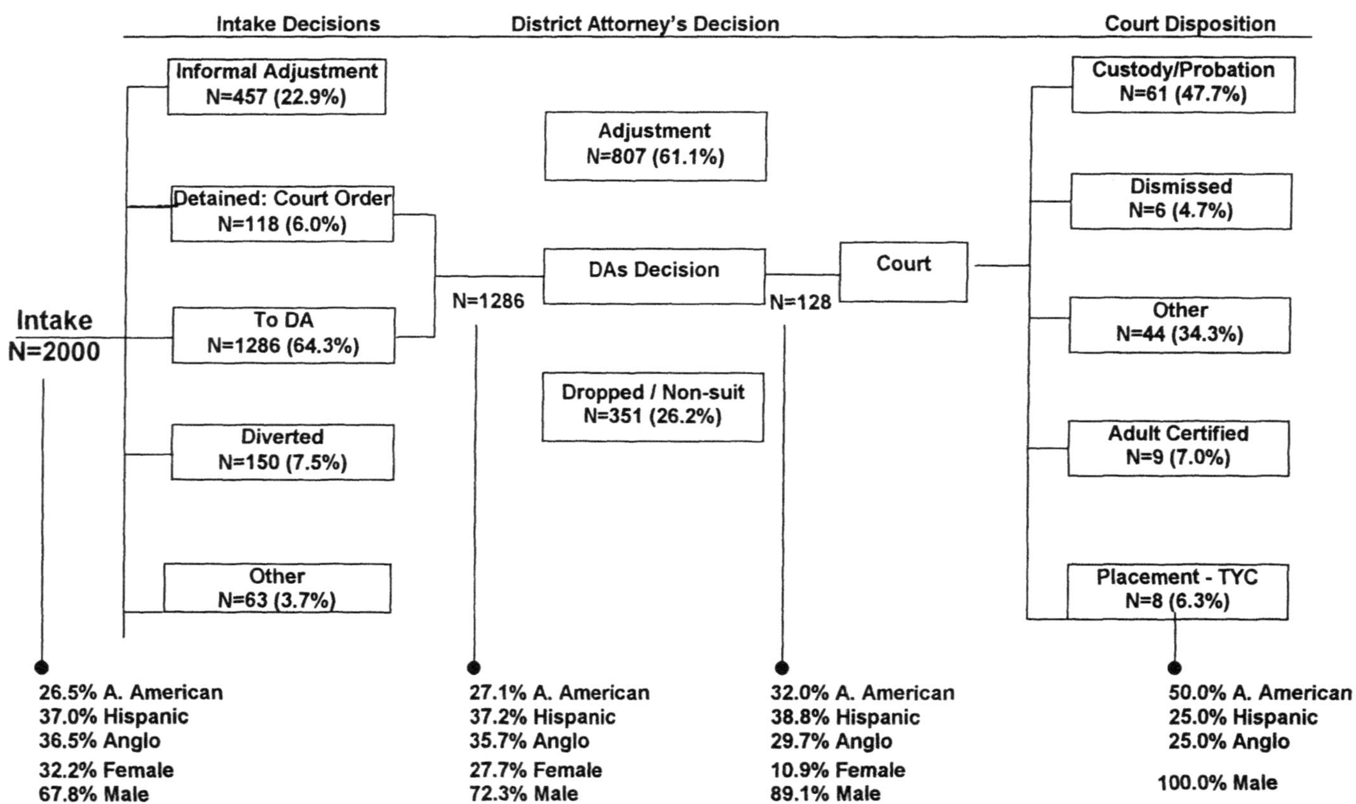

Of the 128 youth who were petitioned to court, 6 (4.6%) of the cases were dismissed or found not guilty, 9 (7%) were certified as adults, and 8 (6.3%) were sent to TYC. The remainder received some kind of disposition, such as probation (61, 47.7%), or other disposition categories that were clearly not probation or TYC placements (34%). Because there were just eight cases where the court ordered a placement to TYC, the relative percentages by race/ethnicity should be viewed with caution, as they represent just .4% of the original cases at intake. Nevertheless, African Americans had twice as many of the referrals (4, 50%), as compared to both Hispanics and Anglos (2, 25%).

Thus, although the confinement cases are not sufficiently numerous to permit as rigorous (and reliable) an analysis as was possible with County-1, the analyses of the other three decision points will still determine if differences due to race/ethnicity and gender are apparent among youth at the other decision points in the juvenile justice process in County-2.

DETENTION DECISIONS

In the County-2 data, detention status was measured in three ways: (1) never detained; (2) detained for more than two days; and (3) detained after a hearing. Two hundred and thirty-five (11.8%) youth were never detained at intake, 120 (6.0%) were detained for more than two days, and 117 (5.9%) of these youth were detained after a hearing. The correlation between the latter two measurements of detention is .85. The analyses investigated the role of each of the following factors in the detention decisions: (1) being African American; (2) being Hispanic; (3) being female; (4) age; (5) school enrollment; (6) parents' marital status; (7) severity of past offenses; (8) number of previous offenses; and (9) severity of the alleged criminal offense.

The results of the logistic regression, used to model the decision to detain a juvenile at intake, are presented in Table 6.1. Like the other regression tables, this one lists the unstandardized coefficients (b) and the standard error (s.e.), which allow the reader to determine the significance of the relationships. Usually, a positive coefficient means that the factor is associated with a more severe outcome at a particular decision point. The importance of the variables in the model is gauged by the maximum predicted effect (MPE) of the independent variable on the probability of being in one category of the dependent variable. For dummy variables, for example, race/ethnicity, it is the maximum predicted effect of being of that race versus the baseline (i.e., Anglo). For continuous variables (e.g., severity of the offense), the MPE is the maximum predicted effect of a two-standard-deviation shift in that variable on the probability of being in one category of the dependent variable. (Refer to Chapter 3 for definitions of these variables.) The MPE is interpretable as a percentage. As in Chapter 5, MPE percentages are reported

TABLE 6.1 Factors in the Detention Decision

	All cases	Males	Females
	Unstandardized coefficient (s.e.)	Unstandardized coefficient (s.e.)	Unstandardized coefficient (s.e.)
African American	.40	.93**	–1.89**
	(.27)	(.32)	(.70)
Hispanic	.09	.43	–1.93**
	(.26)	(.32)	(.73)
Female	–.24	N/A	N/A
	(.15)	N/A	N/A
Age	.15	–.25**	–.49
	(.08)	(.09)	(.20)
School enrollment	–.66**	–.46	–1.61**
	(.25)	(.29)	(.59)
Parental marital status	–.67	–.85	–.31
	(.49)	(.61)	(.99)
Offense severity	.39**	.37*	.45**
	(.06)	(.07)	(.15)
Severity of past offenses	.10**	.09	.47**
	(.05)	(.04)	(.13)
Number of past offenses	.14**	.12**	.26**
	(.02)	(.02)	(.07)
Intercept	6.54	8.4	3.7
	(1.3)	(1.5)	(3.1)
N	1,835	1,242	595
–2Log L	195.6	154.4	62.4
(df)	(9)	(8)	(8)

N/A = not applicable
$^{*}p < .05$ $^{**}p < .01$

only when a significant racial/ethnic or gender finding is apparent. The sample size and the goodness-of-fit statistic are also provided for each model. Results are presented for models for all cases, for males only, and for females only (where applicable).

All Cases

The factors that are associated with the decision to detain a juvenile after a hearing are as follows: (1) severity of the alleged criminal offense; (2) number of previous offenses; (3) school enrollment; and (4) severity of past offenses. Excluding school enrollment, each component is positively correlated with detention. If the juvenile is alleged to have committed a severe offense, has committed more prior offenses, is not enrolled in school, and has been involved in serious past offenses, he/she has a significantly greater chance of being detained.

As was the case for County-1, the regression results do not indicate that either race or ethnicity was significantly associated with a decision to detain the delinquent prior to the delinquency hearing.

Males

In the model with only male offenders, the variables that are associated with detention are these: (1) severity of the alleged criminal offense; (2) age; (3) being African American; and (4) number of previous offenses. Each component is positively predictive with a male juvenile's detention status. If the male juvenile is alleged to have committed a serious offense, has committed previous offenses, is an African American (as opposed to an Anglo), and is relatively younger, he will probably be placed in detention. Based on the MPE, African Americans are 22% more likely to be detained than are Anglos. A statistical control for gang membership does not substantially mitigate the effect of being African American: African-American youth are still 21% more likely to be detained than are their Anglo peers. In an effort to determine whether interaction terms might influence the effects, alternate models were estimated, but these effects were not significant.

Females

In the female-only data, just 21 females were detained. The logistic model did converge. However, due to the small sample size, caution must be exercised in interpreting the results. That is, because of small numbers of detainees, the coefficients are relatively unstable, and a small change in numbers could change the size and direction of the coefficients owing to the higher standard errors. The factors associated with the detention decision are these: (1) age; (2) being Hispanic; (3) being African American; (4) severity of the alleged criminal offense; (5) severity of past offenses; (6) number of previous offenses; and (7) school enrollment. It is noteworthy, that African-American (MPE = 37%) and Hispanic (MPE = 28%) females are *less likely* than Anglo females to be detained at intake. The severity of the alleged criminal offense and the number and severity of past offenses are positively associated with the decision to detain females.

Conclusion

Two predictors reflecting offense-related conduct, the severity of the alleged criminal offense and the number of past offenses, are the strongest predictors of the detention decision. However, all other factors being equal,

African-American males are 22% more likely than their Anglo peers to be detained. Similarly, but in the opposite direction, minority females (both Hispanics and African-Americans) are less likely than Anglo female youth to be detained at intake. It also appears that age (the older a juvenile offender is, the more likely a decision to detain) and school enrollment have a significant influence on the decision to detain girls.

DECISION TO FORWARD A CASE TO THE DA

This stage in the juvenile justice system is modeled as a yes/no decision. Once the juvenile has been brought in by the police, does he/she receive an information adjustment, or is his/her case referred to the DA for possible prosecution? At this point, some cases are dropped for various reasons (e.g., too old, diverted to another agency, escaped, not enough evidence). These dropped cases were coded as missing and were not included in the analysis.

The reasons for a case being referred to the DA or being given an informal adjustment were modeled with the following: (1) being African American; (2) being Hispanic; (3) being female; (4) age; (5) school enrollment; (6) parents' marital status; (7) severity of the alleged criminal offense; (8) severity of past offenses; and (9) number of previous offenses. Results from the logistic regression models are presented in Table 6.2.

All Cases

The factors associated with sending a case to the DA for possible prosecution, as opposed to obtaining an informal adjustment at the intake screening stage, are as follows: (1) severity of the alleged criminal offense; (2) parents' marital status; (3) number of previous offenses; and (4) being female. Except for the last factor, "being female," each of the components is positively correlated with the decision to refer a case to the DA for possible prosecution. Based on the MPE, females were 12% less likely to have their cases forwarded to the DA. There were no significant race or ethnic differences in the decision to refer.

Males

In the male-only data, the factors that are correlated with sending a juvenile's case to the DA for possible prosecution, as opposed to obtaining an informal adjustment are (1) severity of the alleged criminal offense and (2) parents' marital status.[1] Each of these factors is significantly and positively associated with the decision to refer a case to the DA for possible prosecution. If a male juvenile is alleged to have committed a relatively serious offense and has parents who are married, his case will probably be referred to the DA for possible prosecution. As with the models for all delinquent cases, there were no significant race or ethnicity effects.

TABLE 6.2 Factors in the Decision to Send a Case to the DA

	All cases	Males	Females
	Unstandardized coefficient (s.e.)	Unstandardized coefficient (s.e.)	Unstandardized coefficient (s.e.)
African American	–.02	.15	–.12
	(.16)	(.21)	(.25)
Hispanic	–.02	–.18	.45
	(.14)	(.17)	(.25)
Female	–.51**	N/A	N/A
	(.12)	N/A	N/A
Age	.03	–.003	.18**
	(.04)	(.05)	(.06)
School enrollment	.07	.05	.17
	(.19)	(.23)	(.33)
Parental marital status	.74**	.69*	.92*
	(.23)	(.28)	(.42)
Offense severity	.55**	.47**	.84**
	(.05)	(.05)	(.12)
Severity of past offenses	.08	.06	.17
	(.03)	(.05)	(.11)
Number of past offenses	.09**	.05	.19**
	(.03)	(.04)	(.09)
Intercept	–.93	–.14	–4.6
	(.62)	(.77)	(1.2)
N	1,666	1,102	530
–2Log L	254.3	123.7	125.9
(df)	(9)	(8)	(8)

*$p < .05$ **$p < .01$

Females

In the female-only model, the variables that are correlated with sending a juvenile's case to the DA for possible prosecution, as opposed to obtaining an informal adjustment, are these: (1) severity of the alleged criminal offense; (2) number of previous offenses; (3) age; and (4) having married parents. Without exception, all of these components are positively correlated with the decision to refer a case to the DA for possible prosecution. If a female juvenile is alleged to have committed a relatively serious offense, has more previous offenses, is comparatively older, and has married parents, her case will probably be referred to the DA for possible prosecution. As with the models for all delinquent cases and males, there were no significant race or ethnicity effects.

Conclusion

The strongest correlate of the decision to send a file to the prosecutor is the severity of the alleged criminal offense. This particular factor was significant in all three models. This factor is not only legally permissible, but should, in fact, constitute the predominant factor used at intake to determine if the case requires screening by the DA's office. Similarly, the number of prior offenses was significant for all cases and for females cases. Females are less likely to be referred to the DA at this stage. The marital status of the juvenile's parents is another significant factor in this decision. Race/ethnicity does not significantly affect decisions made at this stage of the process in County-2.

DA'S DECISION TO PROSECUTE A CASE

The DA's decision to prosecute is modeled as a simple yes/no question. The DA chooses one of two options: (1) to prosecute the case or (2) to pursue another course of action such as defer prosecution, authorize an informal adjustment, or drop the case altogether. These dropped cases were coded as missing only when final disposition codes were not available. The regression models test the role of each of the following factors in the decision to prosecute in court: (1) being African American; (2) being Hispanic; (3) being female; (4) age; (5) school enrollment; (6) parents' marital status; (7) severity of the alleged criminal offense; (8) severity of past offenses; and (9) number of previous offenses. Table 6.3 presents a summary of the logistic regression analyses for these factors.

All Cases

The factors that are correlated with the DA's decision to prosecute a case, rather than to defer prosecution are these: (1) severity of the alleged criminal offense; (2) number of previous offenses; (3) severity of past offenses; and (4) being female. All of these components are significantly associated with increased odds that the DA will decide to prosecute. However, being female has a negative correlation with the DA's decision. If a juvenile is alleged to have committed a relatively severe offense, has committed previous offenses, has comparatively serious past offenses, and is male, that juvenile has significantly greater chances of being prosecuted. All factors being constant, females are 26% less likely to be prosecuted; however, only 14 females in the sample were prosecuted. These results, therefore, should be treated with caution. There were no significant race or ethnicity effects.

TABLE 6.3 Factors in the Decision to Prosecute a Case

	All cases	Males	Females
	Unstandardized coefficient (s.e.)	Unstandardized coefficient (s.e.)	Unstandardized coefficient (s.e.)
African American	.08	.17	–.33
	(1.2)	(.27)	(.82)
Hispanic	–.02	–.02	.05
	(.26)	(.26)	(.80)
Female	–.99**	N/A	N/A
	(.30)	N/A	N/A
Age	.10	.10	.16
	(.07)	(.08)	(.26)
School enrollment	.04	–.07	1.22
	(.28)	(.30)	(.97)
Parental marital status	.07	.08	.17
	(.33)	(.36)	(.87)
Offense severity	.38**	.38**	.47**
	(.06)	(.06)	(.19)
Severity of past offenses	.17**	.14**	.44**
	(.06)	(.06)	(.16)
Number of past offenses	.08**	.06*	.20**
	(.03)	(.03)	(.08)
Intercept	–5.43	–5.23	.06
	(1.2)	(1.26)	(.02)
N	1,284	846	338
–2Log L	117.2	73.8	29.0
(df)	(9)	(8)	(8)

*$p < .05$ **$p < .01$

Males

In the male-only data, the only factors that are correlated with the DA's decision to prosecute a case, rather than to defer prosecution, are the offense-related measures: (1) severity of the alleged criminal offense; (2) severity of past offenses; and (3) number of previous offenses. All of these components are positively correlated with the DA's decision to prosecute. If a male has committed a relatively severe offense and has prior offenses that are more serious, he will probably be prosecuted. There were no significant race or ethnicity effects.

Females

In the female-only model, only 14 cases were forwarded for prosecution. The logistic model did converge. However, due to the small sample size, interpretation of the results must be made with great caution. The factors predicting the filing of a petition are, as with males, the legal factors: (1) severity of the alleged criminal offense; (2) severity of past offenses; and (3) number of previous offenses. All three are positively correlated to the DA's decision to file a petition. There were no significant race or ethnicity effects.

Conclusion

The severity of the offense, the severity of prior offenses, the frequency of past offenses, and gender are the most significant predictors of the decision to file a petition. Race/ethnicity is not correlated with the decision to file a petition or to prosecute the case.

PLACEMENT BY THE COURT

In this study placement refers to being sentenced to TYC. Only eight cases were sent to TYC. Consequently, no multivariate analyses could be conducted. All eight of the cases sent to TYC involved males.

STATUS OFFENSES

As was done for County-1, a separate analysis was conducted on the 438 youth brought in for status offense violations in County-2. Of these youth, none were detained for more than two days. One hundred and fifty-five cases were referred to the DA. The probability of the case being sent to the DA's office, as opposed to being informally adjusted at intake, was examined with the following predictors: (1) being African American; (2) being Hispanic; (3) being female; (4) age; (5) school enrollment; (6) parental marital status; (7) number of past offenses; (8) number of prior offenses (African American); and (9) number of prior offenses (Hispanic). Table 6.4 presents a summary of the logistic regression analyses for the model.

The factors that are correlated with the decision to send status offense cases to the DA are these: (1) being Hispanic; (2) being African American; (3) school enrollment; and (4) severity of past offenses. Each component is positively correlated with the decision to send the case to the DA. If the juvenile is Hispanic or African American (as opposed to Anglo), has committed more serious offenses in the past, and is enrolled in school, he/she will probably be referred to the DA. Based on the MPE, Hispanics and African Americans are 27% and 26% more likely to be referred to the prosecutors, respectively. Controls for gang membership and interaction

TABLE 6.4 Factors in the Decision to Send Status Offense Cases to the DA

	All cases
	Unstandardized coefficient (s.e.)
African American	1.20**
	(.39)
Hispanic	1.41**
	(.27)
Female	–.16
	(.20)
Age	–.06
	(.08)
School enrollment	1.06*
	(.37)
Parental marital status	–.20
	(.48)
Number of past offenses	.15
	(.12)
Number of prior offenses (A. American)	–.08
	(.16)
Number of prior offenses (Hispanic)	–.14
	(.14)
Intercept	–1.60
	(1.34)
N	438
–2Log L	63.2
(df)	(10)

*$p < .05$ **$p < .01$

between race/ethnicity and the number of prior offenses did not change these findings. None of the status offense cases were sent to court; all were settled at the DA level.

OFFENSES COMMITTED BY ASIAN-AMERICAN YOUTH

Only 47 Asian-American youth were processed by County-2 probation authorities during the 1993–1994 period. Of these, only one was detained for more than two days. Thirty-seven had no prior referrals. The number of Asian-American youth was too small to conduct multivariate analyses.

COUNTY-2 SUMMARY

Table 6.5 provides a listing of the significant factors which emerged in the regression models concerning decision making through the juvenile justice process in County-2. The multivariate analyses conducted here were designed with controls for background variables, such as criminal antecedents and the severity of the current offense, as well as demographic factors, such as the presence of married parents and gender. As in County-1, there are thirteen possible decision points at which differential processing by race or ethnicity could take place. There are only three occurrences of such differential handling. First, at the detention stage there is a finding that African-American males in County-2 are significantly *more likely* than Anglo males to be detained at intake. Being African American is the third strongest correlate of the detention decision, after the severity of the current offense and age of the juvenile. However, minority females are also less likely to be detained. It is noteworthy that African-American (MPE = 37%) and Hispanic (MPE = 28%) females are appreciably *less likely* than Anglo females to be detained at intake. Second, among status offenders, both African-American and Hispanic youth are more likely to have their case forwarded to the DA's office. However, given that at only one major decision point, there was only one instance of unfavorable treatment (African-American males), the analyses indicate quite strongly that race/ethnicity is generally not a factor in decisions made at later stages of juvenile processing. Thus, there appears to be only a limited and isolated race/ethnicity effect in County-2.

Gender is an important correlate of many outcomes in County-2, where female youth receive less severe outcomes at two of the decision points. While this may have been true during the 1993–1994 time period, County-2 staff and others contacted through the survey indicate that the implementation of the new *Texas Family Code* provisions, effective January 1, 1996, has resulted in more equal treatment of female and male youth. The results of a survey that touch upon these and other issues are discussed in detail in Chapters 8 and 9.

The results for County-2 indicate, unequivocally, that legally permissible and substantively meaningful factors represent the operative criteria upon which juvenile justice officials make their decisions. Consistently, severity of current offense, severity of prior offenses, and number of prior delinquent acts emerged as significant correlates of decision making for all cases and for males and females.

TABLE 6.5 Significant Factors in Decision Making in County-2

	Race/ethnicity	Offense data (past/present)	Other variables
All cases			
Detention	None	Offense severity Severity of priors No. of priors	School
Refer case to DA	None	Offense severity No. of priors	Female Parents' marital status
Refer case to court	None	Offense severity Severity of priors No. of priors	Female
Sentence to secure facility	None	Offense severity No. of priors	None
Males			
Detention	A. American Unfavorable	Offense severity No. of priors	Age
Refer case to DA	None	Offense severity	Parents' marital status
Refer case to court	None	Offense severity Severity of priors No. of priors	None
Sentence to secure facility	None	Offense severity No. of priors	None
Females			
Detention	Hispanic Favorable A. American Favorable	Offense severity Severity of priors No. of priors	School
Refer case to DA	None	Offense severity No. of priors	Age
Refer case to court	None	Offense severity Severity of priors No. of priors	None
Sentence to secure facility	None	None	None

NOTE

1. There were a number of instances where the findings of the regressions were counterintuitive. As reported previously, these instances may be a function of measurement error in the county databases.

7

Decision Making in County-3

County-3 is a small rural county. From 1990 to 1994, the youth population was approximately 1,700 persons aged 10 to 17 (see Table 4.1). About one-half of the youth were Anglo (49%), while 33% were African American and 17% were Hispanic. As a consequence of being a small urban county, there were substantially fewer referrals to the juvenile justice system as compared to the two urban counties (see Table 3.1). The study was not able to sample cases In County-3 as was done in the other two counties; there were just not enough cases from which a sample could be drawn. In fact, compared to the other counties, the study had to use a slightly longer baseline period (1990–1995, compared to 1993–1994). Simply, a longer collection period for the rural county was necessary owing to the lower base rate of referrals, as was expected in a rural area. In County-3, all the cases processed during 1990–1995 were accessed to obtain a large enough sample. This procedure produced 371 cases processed through the juvenile justice system.

Figure 7.1 displays data concerning the various stages of juvenile justice processing in County-3, and these basic counts serve to highlight the restricted range of delinquency processing that occurred in this county. As mentioned in Chapter 3, because of constraints within the Case-Worker/3 management information system, it was not possible to highlight the DA stage in County-3. Thus, focus is on the intake stage, referral to court, and court disposition. Of the 371 youth in the county, few cases, only 17 (4.6%), were detained for more than two days. The vast majority of

FIGURE 7.1 Juvenile Justice Process in County-3

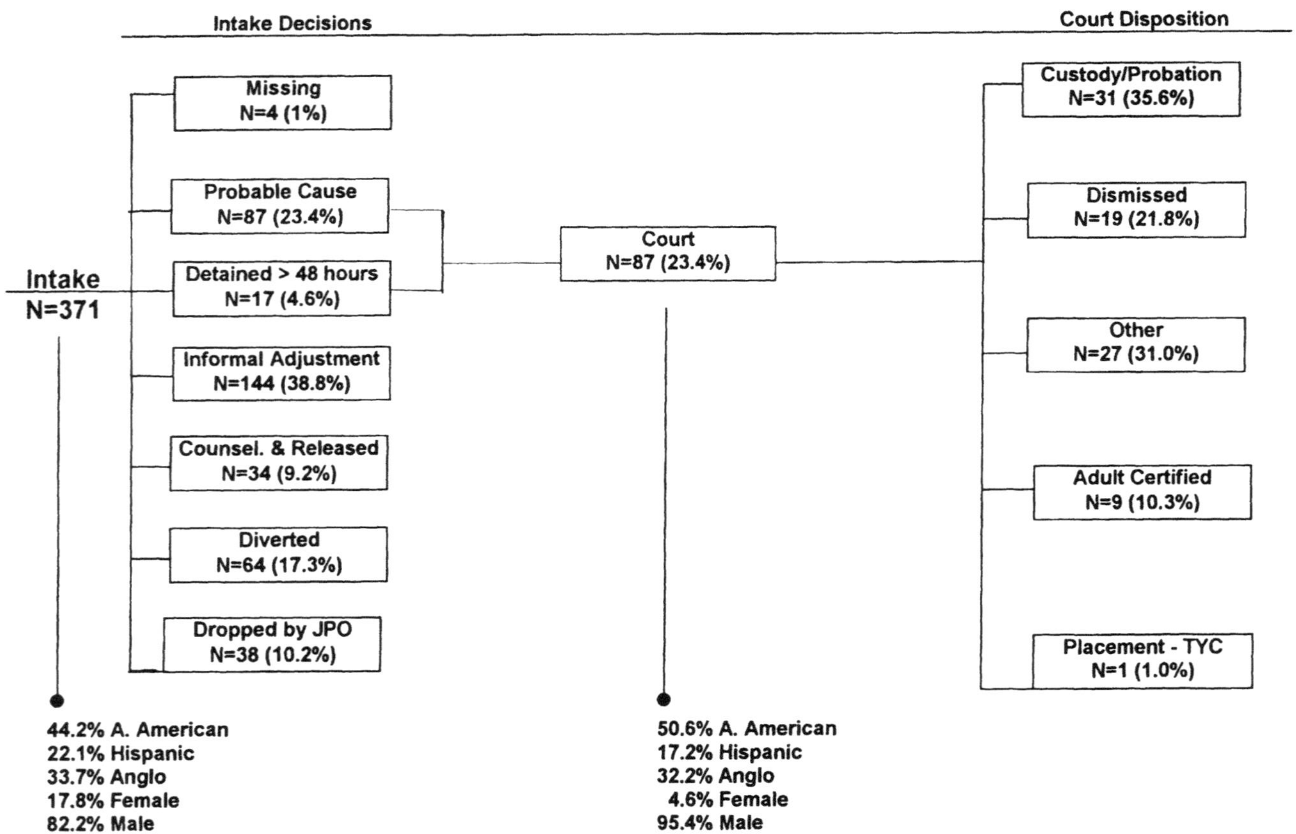

cases, about 77%, were handled at intake. Informal dispositions predominated at the intake stage as 242 cases, or 65.2%, were disposed of at intake. The Informal processing involved the following: adjustment—144 cases (38.8%); diversion—64 cases (17.3%); and counseling—34 cases (9.2%). About 10% of the cases were dropped, and another 23.4% were referred to court. At the intake stage, 44.2% of the cases were African American, 22.1% were Hispanic, and 33.7% were Anglo.

At the court hearing stage, the 87 cases were handled as follows. First, 19 cases, 21.8%, were dismissed, while another 27, 31.0%, received an unspecified, informal disposition. The modal disposition was probation, for which there was 31 cases, or 35.6% of all court dispositions. Nine cases were referred to adult court, and only one juvenile was sent to TYC. At the court hearing stage, the data show overrepresentation for African Americans (50.6% versus 44% at intake), underrepresentation for Hispanics (17% versus 22% at intake), and parity for Anglos (32% versus 33% at intake).

As noted, there are only three decision points available for analysis in County-3: (1) detention at intake; (2) whether the case was sent to court; and (3) adjudication probation decisions.

DETENTION DECISIONS

Computerized records of court-ordered detentions were unavailable in County-3. Therefore, detention status could be measured in only two ways: (1) ever detained and (2) being detained for longer than two days.

Due to the relatively few cases processed in County-3, a smaller number of independent variables were included in the model. The analyses focused on the role of each of the following factors in the decision to detain a juvenile for more than two days: (1) being African American; (2) being Hispanic; (3) being female; (4) severity of the alleged criminal offense; (5) severity of past offenses; and (6) number of past offenses. Table 7.1 presents the results of the logistic regression, modeling the decision to detain a juvenile at intake. Like all the regression tables, this one lists the unstandardized coefficients (b) and the standard error (s.e.), which allow readers to determine the significance of the relationships. Usually, a positive coefficient means that that factor is associated with a more severe outcome at a particular decision point. The importance of the variables in the model is based on the maximum predicted effect (MPE) of the independent variable on the probability of being in one category of the dependent variable. For dummy variables, for example, race/ethnicity, it is the maximum predicted effect of being of that race versus the baseline, Anglo. For continuous variables (e.g., the severity of the offense), the MPE is the maximum predicted effect of a two-standard-deviation shift in that variable on the probability of being in one category of the dependent variable. The MPE is interpretable as a percentage. The MPE percentages are shown only when a significant racial/ethnic or gender finding

TABLE 7.1 Factors in the Detention Decision

	All cases	Males
	Unstandardized coefficient (s.e.)	Unstandardized coefficient (s.e.)
African American	.06	.26
	(.59)	(.64)
Hispanic	–.13	.02
	(.75)	(.78)
Female	–.34	N/A
	(.79)	N/A
Offense severity	.09	.12
	(.15)	(.15)
Severity of past offenses	.21**	.15
	(.10)	(.10)
Number of past offenses	.02	.02
	(.06)	(.06)
Intercept	3.8	–3.8
	(.71)	(.77)
N	371	305
–2Log L	8.44	4.4
(df)	(6)	(5)

N/A = not applicable
**$p < .01$

is apparent. The sample size and goodness-of-fit statistic are also provided for each model. Results are presented for all cases and for males only.

ALL CASES

Only 17 offenders (15 males and 2 females) were detained for more than two days. Although the logistic regression model did converge, interpretation should be made with caution. Only one predictor variable made a significant impact on detention: the severity of past offenses. Thus, an offender with relatively serious past offenses is more likely to be detained at the intake stage. There were no significant race or ethnicity effects surrounding the detention decision, and thus, no disproportionate minority confinement was evident in County-3.

Males

A similar regression model was applied with the male-only data set, lacking only the control variable for being female. Only 15 males were detained for more than two days. Again, interpretations should be made with caution.

There were no significant effects associated with the detention decision for male offenders.

Females

In the female-only data set, four females were ever detained and two females were detained for more than two days. No multivariate analyses were conducted.

Conclusion

The race/ethnicity of the juvenile has no effect on detention decisions made at intake. The only factor that influenced detention decisions was severity of past offenses.

DECISION TO REFER CASE TO COURT

This stage in the juvenile justice system was modeled as a yes/no decision. As mentioned earlier, in County-3, it was not possible to distinguish an intake decision made by a probation officer from that made by prosecutor. Once a juvenile has been brought in by police or other agencies, does he/she receive an informal adjustment at intake, or is his/her case referred to court? At this point, some cases are dropped for various reasons (e.g., too old, diverted to another agency, escaped, not enough evidence). These dropped cases were coded as missing, and they were not included in the analysis.

Models were tested on the role of each of the following factors in the decision to refer cases to court: (1) being African American; (2) being Hispanic; (3) being female; (4) severity of the alleged criminal offense; (5) severity of past offenses; and (6) number of previous offenses (see Table 7.2).

All Cases

The factors that are correlated with the decision to forward a juvenile's case to the next level of processing, as opposed to being informally adjusted, are these (in order of importance): (1) number of previous offenses and (2) being female. If a juvenile has had numerous previous offenses, his case is more likely to be referred for prosecution, but, if the offender is female, she is less likely to be prosecuted. The race/ethnicity of the juvenile is not correlated with this decision.

Males

In the male-only data, there was but one factor correlated with the decision to send a juvenile's case to court for prosecution, as opposed to obtaining an informal

TABLE 7.2 Factors in the Decision to Send a Case to the DA

	All cases	Males
	Unstandardized coefficient (s.e.)	Unstandardized coefficient (s.e.)
African American	.16	.04
	(.35)	(.37)
Hispanic	–.09	–.18
	(.42)	(.43)
Female	–1.8**	N/A
	(.58)	N/A
Offense severity	–.04	–.03
	(.09)	(.09)
Severity of past offenses	.13	.14
	(.09)	(.09)
Number of past offenses	.24**	.25**
	(.11)	(.12)
Intercept	–.77	–.73
	(.40)	N/A
N	222	182
–2Log L	46.4	27.3
(df)	(6)	(5)

**$p < .01$

adjustment: the number of previous offenses. If a male juvenile has committed a relatively higher number of offenses in the past, his case will be referred for prosecution. Race/ethnicity is not correlated with this decision.

Females

In the female-only model, only four females were prosecuted in County-3. Consequently, no multivariate analyses were conducted.

Conclusion

The number of previous offenses and gender are important correlates of the decision to send a case to the DA or court. Race/ethnicity is not a factor in the decision.

PLACEMENT BY THE COURT

In County-3, only one individual was sent to TYC and no private placements were reported. Thus, as an alternative, it was decided to model the principal punitive disposition used by the juvenile court in County-3: adjudicated probation. "Adjudicated probation" means that the court ordered probation for a juvenile or modified his/her status (one case in County-3) to include probation as a part of the sentence. The decision for court-ordered probation was modeled as an either/or decision. Either the juvenile is (1) placed on probation; (2) the case is dismissed; or (3) the juvenile is found not guilty. Other dispositions of the court (administrative) were coded as missing; they were not included in this analysis.

The role of each of the following factors in court-ordered probation decisions were examined: (1) being African American; (2) being Hispanic; (3) being female; (4) severity of past offenses; (5) number of previous offenses; and (6) severity of the alleged criminal offense. Initial models that used these variables showed a significant effect for African-American youth. At this stage, the fuller model, which included both age and whether the juvenile lived in a two-parent household, was tested, and the results are shown in Table 7.3. The variables included here are similar to those used in the models run for the other two counties. The number of juveniles involved at this stage of juvenile processing was quite low. Consequently, interpretations should be made with caution.

All Cases

Being African American is the only significant predictor of this outcome. Based on the MPE, African Americans are 32% more likely to receive adjudicated probation. However, because only 29 youth received this type of adjudication, the results should be interpreted with caution.

Males

In the male-only model, no factor is significantly correlated with the court's decision to order probation. Controlling for current offense, prior offense severity, frequency of prior offenses, age, with whom the juvenile lives, and gang affiliation mitigate the impact of being a minority juvenile at this stage of the decision-making process.

Females

The female-only data contained too few individuals to conduct a meaningful statistical analysis on probation decisions.

Conclusion

Once all background factors are controlled for, there is no direct impact of race/ethnicity evident at this stage. In the male-only model, no factors significantly predict the decision to place a juvenile on probation.

TABLE 7.3 Factors in the Adjudicated Probation Decision

	All cases	Males
	Unstandardized coefficient (s.e.)	Unstandardized coefficient (s.e.)
African American	1.5*	1.5
	(.79)	(.73)
Hispanic	1.7	1.7
	(.95)	(.94)
Female	−1.8	N/A
	(.13)	N/A
Age	.21	.25
	(.22)	(.22)
Live with both parents	−1.0	−.98
	(.79)	(.78)
Gang offense	.43	.44
	(.87)	(.86)
Offense severity	.19	.13
	(.15)	(.18)
Severity of past offenses	−.23	−.19
	(.15)	(.15)
Number of past offenses	−.18	−.20
	(.12)	(.13)
Intercept	4.06	4.3
	(3.3)	(3.4)
N	66	62
−2Log L	19.4	17.2
(df)	(9)	(8)

*$p < .05$

STATUS OFFENSES

During the 1990–1995 time period, fewer than ten cases were recorded as status offenses in the Case-Worker/3 MIS of County-3. Consequently, no multivariate analyses were conducted.

SUMMARY

Table 7.4 provides a listing of the significant effects in predicting processing decisions in County-3. The most important finding concerns the fact that neither race nor ethnicity was a significant factor for the two decision points in County-3 (detention and case referral to the court). Once statistical controls were introduced, no race/ethnicity effect was evident for court

TABLE 7.4 Significant Factors in Decision Making in County-3

	Race/ethnicity	Offense data (past/present)	Other variables
All cases			
Detention	None	Severity of priors	None
Refer case to DA			
Refer case to court	None	No. of priors	Female
Sentence to secure facility			
Males			
Detention	None	None	None
Refer case to DA			
Refer case to court	None	No. of priors	None
Sentence to secure facility			

probation. Females were less likely to be prosecuted, but since only a few females were involved, the impact of gender preferences in favor of girls is not a substantial problem.

The data for County-3 were sparse as compared to the other two counties. There were fewer cases available for analysis overall, and an insufficient number of cases to even analyze some decision points. The rural county results have still been reported because they enhance the generalizability of the study overall and prevent the study from adopting an urban bias which could distort the study and diminish the overall value of the research.

8

Survey of Juvenile Justice Practitioners

This chapter describes the results of the second phase of the research—the views and perceptions of juvenile justice practitioners in Texas. A statewide sample of practitioners was employed and comprehensive telephone interviews were used to solicit practitioner attitudes and opinions concerning various aspects of the juvenile justice system. For example, respondents were asked about the overrepresentation of African-American and Hispanic youth, the strengths and weaknesses of the juvenile justice system and its possible improvement, and the policies and practices that may influence different decision-making stages.

METHODS

Sample Selection

A proportional stratified random sample was drawn of judges, district or county attorneys, probation officers, Texas Youth Commission (TYC) staff, law enforcement personnel, and private attorneys to be interviewed. The sample was drawn as follows. The names of judges and probation officers were obtained from a directory compiled by the Texas Juvenile Probation Commission (TJPC). The juvenile probation directory for 1995 contained names of about 400 judges assigned to juvenile courts. The study was not able to contact 94 (23.5%) randomly selected judges listed in the directory. These 94 individuals had jurisdictions covering 99 counties: a number of judges were listed as juvenile judges in two or more counties (e.g., Falls,

Milam, and Robertson counties), and they provided multiple counties of jurisdiction. The TJPC directory also listed the names of 1,445 juvenile probation officers (JPO). Every tenth name on the list was chosen. Preliminary investigations revealed that larger counties were more likely to have an intake detention department with officers dealing specifically with intake detention issues. To ensure that an adequate number of probation officers with intake experience were included in the sample, staff from the larger juvenile probation departments were over-sampled. Eventually, the study was able to contact 151 (10.4%) respondents, representing 44 separate juvenile departments statewide.

The names of district and county attorneys were obtained from the Texas District and County Attorneys Association. This list was sorted by county of jurisdiction. Interviewers initially tried to contact the DA directly but this was often unsuccessful. After some initial trial and error, survey staff decided to contact prosecutors handling juvenile cases in each county, because, in many counties, prosecutors on the DA's staff and county attorneys handled all juvenile prosecutions. Staff at county seats directed interviewers to prosecutors who were experienced in juvenile cases. This resulted in complete interviews with prosecutors located in 104 counties (41% of the total number statewide). Some prosecutors had multiple county jurisdictions (e.g., Burleson and Washington counties). In nine counties, interviewers obtained more than one interview; these interviews were kept in the data. In all, 118 interviews with prosecutors were conducted.

The names of private attorneys were obtained from the list of members of the Texas Bar Association who specialize in juvenile issues. The list contained 810 names, 50 of which were randomly selected for the interviews. Forty-eight interviews (6.0% of 810) were completed.

Obtaining names of police and other law enforcement personnel was more problematic. No state agency lists the names and contact information of certified police officers in the state. Individual police departments do not usually release names of officers because of security concerns. Staff members established contact with 25 police and law enforcement departments around the state and solicited names of officers who dealt with juvenile issues. Eventually, 17 departments provided names and contact numbers. In some instances, the names were provided after almost eight weeks of negotiation with various police department personnel. The law enforcement officers interviewed represented a sample of 84 officers selected from an estimated 450 (18.6%) officers assigned to juvenile units in approximately 25 police departments in Texas.

TYC has approximately 1,900 staff providing services to youth. After further consultations with TYC staff, the names of caseworkers and others who deal with orientations and assessments at the TYC Marlin facility, where approximately 50 direct service personnel were located were gathered. All TYC commitments are initially processed at Marlin before being

FIGURE 8.1 Occupational Strata of Survey Respondents

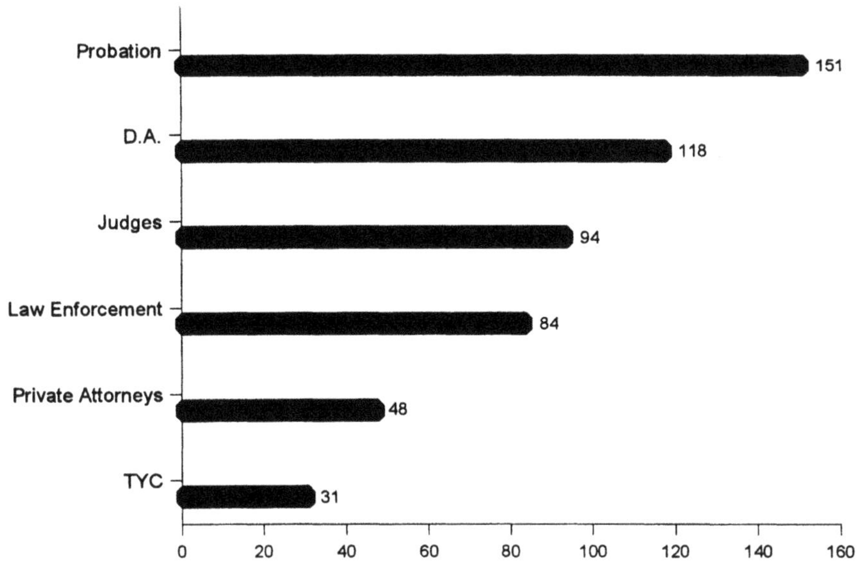

sent to other TYC facilities. Thirty-one individuals (60%) at Marlin were randomly selected and interviewed.

Of the initial sample of 600 juvenile justice practitioners, 526 completed interviews, for an 87.5% completion rate.[1] Figure 8.1 provides a pictorial representation of the following distribution of respondents' occupational strata: (1) 151 probation officers; (2) 118 district and county attorneys; (3) 94 judges; (4) 84 law enforcement personnel; (5) 48 private attorneys; and (6) 31 Texas Youth Commission (TYC) workers.

In each of these six occupation strata, at least 70% of the targeted respondents completed interviews. Since the occupational strata were sampled at different rates, the sample was weighted prior to conducting the analyses. The weighted totals for occupational strata are shown in Table 8.1. Standard statistical packages assume a simple random sample design. Since the survey sample was weighted, researchers used SUDAAN (version 7.11), a statistical package that produces more reliable standard error estimates, to conduct the analyses of the survey data.

Sample Demographics

The socio-demographic characteristics of the sample were as follows. Sixty-eight percent of the sample was male. The average age of the respondent was 42.4 years. Approximately 50% had graduate degrees, 37.5% held bachelor's degrees, 10.3% had received some college education, and 2.5% were high school graduates. As Figure 8.2 illustrates, 70.7% of the sample were Anglo; 16.7% were Hispanic; 10.6% were African American; and 2% were Asian American/American Indian. Only the views of the three most highly represented racial/ethnic groups have been included in this report.

While the job duties of judges, prosecutors, police officers, and attorneys were readily identifiable, probation officers in this sample handled a variety of duties, including assessments, intake functions, court duties, field supervision, and case management. A majority (52.7%) of the sample reported that they supervised staff; 47.3% reported not having supervisory responsibilities.

Respondents in approximately 175 counties in the state of Texas were contacted for the survey. Respondents were proportionately distributed across large metropolitan areas, smaller urban areas, and rural locations so that all areas of Texas would be covered by the survey. The respondents' departments were fairly evenly divided among four location categories: 29.5% were in large metropolitan areas with over a half-million people; 22.8% were in cities with populations between 100,000 and 500,000; 25.7% were in towns or cities with between 15,000 and 100,000 people; and 21.7% were in rural locations and towns with fewer than 15,000 people.

Table 8.2 presents data on the age and experience of respondents across occupational strata. The views presented in the following chapters generally

TABLE 8.1 Weighted Totals for Survey Sample Occupational Strata

	Number in				
Occupational strata	**Population strata (*PS*)**	**Population total for all strata (*PT*)**	**Sample strata (*SS*)**	**Sample total for all strata (*ST*)**	**Weighted total (*WT*)†**
Judges	400	3,421	94	526	.65
Prosecutors	260	3,421	118	526	.34
Probation	1,445	3,421	151	526	1.47
Attorneys	811	3,421	48	526	2.60
Police	450	3,421	84	526	.82
TYC	55	3,421	31	526	.27

†Weighted totals for each occupational strata were calculated using the following formula:

$$WT = \frac{PS}{PT} \times \frac{ST}{SS}$$

come from respondents who have about 12 years (overall experience) in the juvenile justice system and at least 7.5 years (overall experience) in their current positions.

FIGURE 8.2 Race/Ethnicity of Survey Respondents

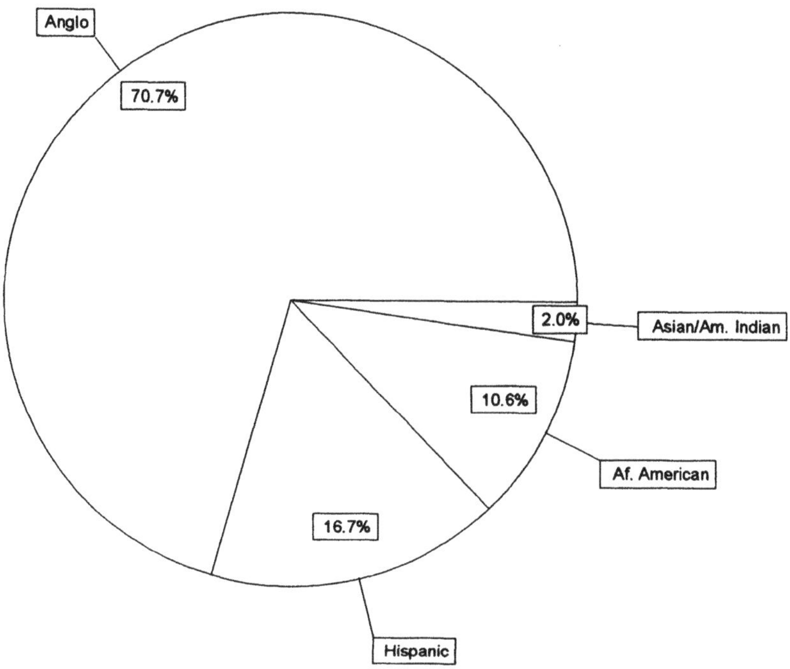

TABLE 8.2 Age and Experience of Respondents, by Occupation (Unweighted)

Occupation	Mean age (years)	Mean years (experience in juvenile justice system)	Mean years (experience in current position)
Judges	51.9	15.9	8.7
Prosecutors	44.1	11.9	7.7
Attorneys	43.6	9.2	9.5
Juenile probation	36.9	9.8	6.0
Police officers	40.8	12.4	7.4
TYC staff	37.4	9.3	5.9

SURVEY RESULTS

The juvenile justice practitioner survey and the attitudes and opinions expressed by the juvenile justice system professionals comprise the focus of this chapter. The results are grouped in three substantive sections. The first section contains findings which primarily concern "Minority Overrepresentation in the Juvenile Justice System." In the second section an effort is made to try to place these respondents' views on overrepresentation within the context of practitioner attitudes and opinions concerning "the Juvenile Justice System in Texas" and "General Views on Delinquency." Finally, as a means of testing the manifest versus latent attitudes and opinions of respondents toward minorities and juvenile justice processing, results are provided for the "Case Scenario Evaluations," which involved testing the effects of race/ethnicity on decision making under conditions when the offense characteristics and the race/ethnicity of the offender were provided directly compared to imputed characteristics by the respondent.

Minorities in the Juvenile Justice System

The survey instrument provided respondents with a series of questions concerning the possible overrepresentation of African-American and Hispanic youth in the juvenile justice system. Specifically, respondents were asked to indicate the extent to which they agreed or disagreed with the following statement, "African-American [and in a separate question, Hispanic] youth are represented at a higher percentage in the juvenile system than their percentage in the general population in Texas." Responses ranged from scores of 1–5 (i.e., from "strongly disagree" to "strongly agree"). The reported scores were re-coded such that values 1–2 reflected "disagreement," 3 referred to "neither agree/disagree," and 4–5 comprised "agreement."

The responses to the question varied with the practitioners' racial/ethnic profile, but generally were the same across occupational strata. As indicated in Table 8.3, among the African-American juvenile justice practitioners surveyed, 78% agreed that African-American youth are overrepresented in the system. A smaller proportion of Anglo (59%) and Hispanic (49%) respondents shared this level of agreement. The race/ethnicity effect was significant ($p < .01$). Overall, 59.6% of all respondents agreed with the statement. Across the six occupational strata, prosecutors were most likely to agree that African-American youth are overrepresented (62.8%), whereas the least likely to think so were police officers (54.9%). The analysis indicates that this difference is not statistically significant. However, the majority of respondents from each occupation agreed with the statement.

Respondents were also asked to identify the three primary reasons for the perceived overrepresentation of African-American youth in the Texas juvenile

TABLE 8.3 Agreement/Disagreement with the Statement on African-American Overrepresentation, by Race/Ethnicity and Occupation of Respondents (%)

	Disagree	Neither agree/disagree	Agree	Weighted N
Race/ethnicity				
African American	15.4	6.6	78.0	55
Anglo	31.1	10.1	58.9	357
Hispanic	29.0	22.0	48.9	80
			χ^2 14.4 (4); $p < .01$	
Occupation				
Judges	30.4	8.7	60.9	60
Prosecutors	32.4	4.9	62.8	35
Attorneys	27.5	12.0	60.6	114
Juvenile probation	25.0	15.9	59.1	209
Police officers	35.4	9.8	54.9	67
TYC staff	20.0	16.7	63.3	8
			χ^2 16.6 (10); $p < .01$	

justice system. Individuals provided 605 open-ended responses (many individuals gave multiple responses), which were grouped into the following categories: (1) family matters; (2) socio-economic matters; (3) youth's environment; (4) system unfair to minorities; (5) lack of personal responsibility; and (6) other.

As shown in Figure 8.3, the most frequently stated response was "family background." Just under one-third (30.7%) of the responses listed the weakening of the family unit, single-parent households, absence of a father, lack of parental role models, or dysfunctional families. Socio-economic issues ranked a close second, as 29.6% of the respondents listed lack of employment opportunities, lack of educational attainment, and welfare dependence as factors critical to this issue. Factors related to the juvenile's environment ranked third: 22.3% of the responses listed high-crime neighborhoods and gang activities as crucial to the overrepresentation of African-American youth. A small percentage of respondents mentioned that the juvenile justice system has problems and/or is unfair to minorities (6.4%). Similarly, another small component (4.8%) suggested a lack of responsibility on the part of accused youth. Six percent of the respondents mentioned other reasons, such as the influence of the media, which were combined into an "other" category.

Table 8.4 lists factors influencing the overrepresentation of African-American youth across respondents' racial/ethnic and occupational strata. Where possible, the analysis tested for differences in responses among the

FIGURE 8.3 Factors Most Frequently Associated with the Overrepresentation of African-American Youth in the Juvenile Justice System

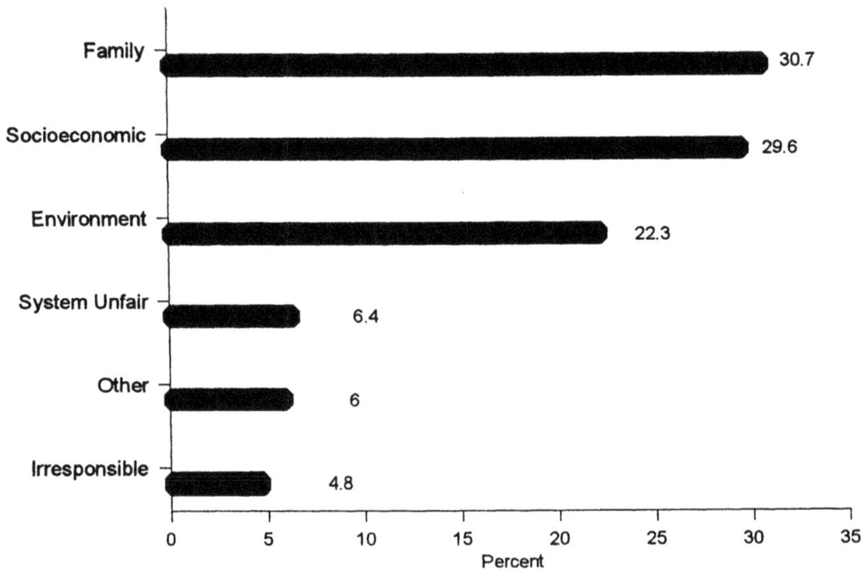

TABLE 8.4 Factors Related to the Overrepresentation of African-American Youth, by Race/Ethnicity and Occupation of Respondents (%)

	Family	Socio-economic	Juvenile's environment	Unfair system	Other	Weighted N
Race/ethnicity						
African American	26.4	26.4	21.4	9.2	16.6	85
Anglo	30.9	27.3	22.2	4.5	15.0	493
Hispanic	20.4	31.8	13.6	11.4	23.0	77
Occupation						
Judges	28.3	28.3	16.6	8.3	19.0	115
Prosecutors	34.5	25.0	23.0	2.0	15.5	134
Attorneys	28.8	27.3	18.1	12.1	13.7	168
Juvenile probation	25.4	31.5	18.2	5.0	19.9	60
Police officers	30.0	20.5	26.7	2.2	21.6	86
TYC staff	23.1	20.5	30.8	18.0	7.6	39

racial/ethnic and occupational categories in the sample population. However, in a number of instances, the sample size was too small to permit valid statistical comparisons among these groups. Therefore, in the following series of analyses, goodness-of-fit and significance levels are reported only when the sample size is adequate. In so doing, the temptation is resisted to

FIGURE 8.4 Suggested Solutions for the Overrepresentation of African-American Youth

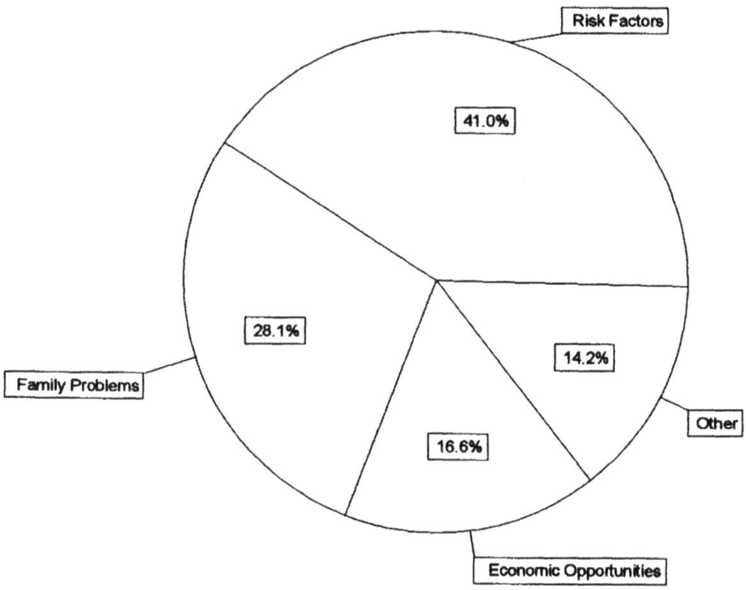

make too much out of the findings, which result from small sample sizes and which render statistical tests unreliable.

Many respondents provided multiple responses. The majority (80%) of all responses list the following factors as crucial in explaining African-American overrepresentation in the system: (1) family matters; (2) socio-economic matters; and (3) the juvenile's environment. These reasons are similar across all occupational categories; at least 70% of the responses list these three factors as being most critical. A higher proportion of responses from minorities, private attorneys, and TYC personnel listed "system being unfair" as a reason. The "other" category includes not only the individual factors outlined in Figure 8.3, but the juvenile's "lack of personal responsibility," as well.

Respondents were also asked to suggest three main corrective actions to remedy the overrepresentation of African-American youth. Forty-one percent of the responses concerned the need for more youth-oriented programs that address background risk factors influencing delinquency. Addressing family problems (28.1% of responses) and improving economic opportunities for African Americans (16.6%) were other most often mentioned solutions. The remaining responses, each of which accounted for 2–3% of the total, were combined into an "other" category, which constituted 14.2% of the responses (see Figure 8.4).

TABLE 8.5 Suggested Solutions for the Overrepresentation of African-American Youth, by Race/Ethnicity and Occupation of Respondents (%)

	Improve economic opportunities	Programs to fix risk factors	Fix family problems	Other	Weighted *N*
Race/ethnicity					
African American	11.8	39.4	28.1	20.8	94
Anglo	18.4	40.6	28.4	12.7	327
Hispanic	16.4	45.4	26.1	12.2	66
Occupation					
Judges	19.6	41.3	28.3	10.9	60
Prosecutors	12.4	34.3	39.1	14.3	36
Attorneys	21.3	40.4	21.3	17.0	122
Juvenile probation	15.4	43.7	23.2	17.6	209
Police officers	12.5	34.4	53.1	0	52
TYC staff	11.1	51.9	37.1	0	7

Table 8.5 presents suggested solutions to African-American overrepresentation across the racial/ethnic and occupational categories of respondents. Programs that address background risk factors and family problems were the two most frequently cited recommendations, the former being mentioned more often than the latter. Most respondents felt that the single best solution was to allocate more resources to programs that address background risk factors influencing delinquency.

The question regarding overrepresentation was also asked with respect to Hispanic youth. Overall, 63.3% of the respondents agreed with the statement that "Hispanics are represented at a significantly higher percentage in the juvenile justice system than they are in the general population in Texas." There are statistically significant differences across racial/ethnic categories: 79% of African-American, 70.6% of Hispanic, and 58% of Anglo respondents agreed that Hispanic youth are overrepresented (see Table 8.6). Judges, attorneys, probation officers, and TYC staff were more likely than either prosecutors or police officers to agree with the statement. Again, however, the analysis indicates that this difference is statistically significant. The majority of respondents from all occupational groups agreed with the statement on Hispanic overrepresentation.

Among the three main factors identified by respondents as being responsible for Hispanic overrepresentation were these: (1) family matters (30.6% of responses); (2) socio-economic matters (29%); and (3) matters related to the juvenile's environment (24.3%). Some respondents mentioned that the juvenile justice system has problems and/or is unfair to minorities (5.9%). Others suggested that a lack of responsibility on the

TABLE 8.6 Agreement/Disagreement with the Statement on Overrepresentation of Hispanic Youth, by Race/Ethnicity and Occupation of Respondents (%)

	Disagree	Neither agree/disagree	Agree	Weighted *N*
Race/ethnicity				
African American	16.1	4.4	79.4	67
Anglo	31.0	11.1	58.0	335
Hispanic	19.4	10.1	70.6	97
			χ^2 13.5 (4); $p < .01$	
Occupation				
Judges	27.7	9.6	62.8	61
Prosecutors	38.4	11.8	50.0	35
Attorneys	25.5	6.9	67.6	114
Juvenile probation	18.2	15.9	65.9	213
Police officers	37.8	9.8	52.4	67
TYC staff	30.0	6.7	63.3	8
			χ^2 20.7 (10); $p < .01$	

part of accused youth (3.3%) also contributed to the overrepresentation of Hispanic youth (see Figure 8.5). All of these factors corresponded to those listed earlier for the possible reasons associated with the overrepresentation of African-American youth in the juvenile justice system in Texas.

Table 8.7 presents the factors that are perceived to contribute to the overrepresentation of Hispanic youth across respondents' racial/ethnic and occupational strata. As in the case of African-American youth, the majority of responses focused on family and socio-economic matters and on the juvenile's environment. Minority respondents were more likely to include the unfairness of the system as a reason, but these responses had very low percentages (African American, 10.4%; Hispanic, 7.4%). Prosecutors (31.2%), police officers (36.8%), and TYC personnel (29.0%) were more likely than respondents from other occupational categories to list family matters. Judges, attorneys, and probation officers were more likely to identify socio-economic matters as crucial to the overrepresentation of Hispanics in the juvenile justice system.

As shown in Figure 8.6, the most frequently mentioned solutions to the overrepresentation of Hispanic youth include developing programs to address background factors that influence delinquency (42%), resolving family problems (29.6%), and improving economic opportunities (16.6%). Almost 12% of responses were in the "other" category. It is noteworthy that the first three solutions listed here are identical to those suggested as possible solutions to the overrepresentation of African-American youth.

FIGURE 8.5 Factors Most Frequently Associated with the Overrepresentation of Hispanic Youth in the Juvenile Justice System

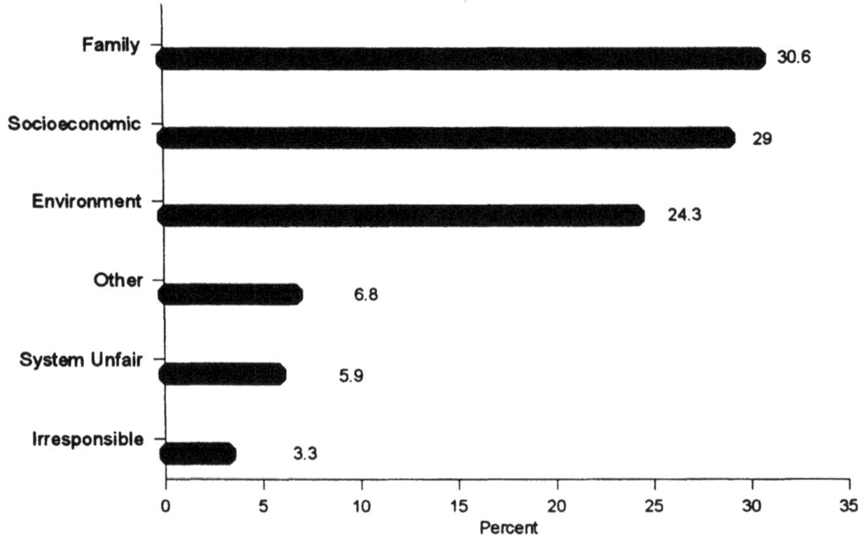

TABLE 8.7 Factors Related to the Overrepresentation of Hispanic Youth, by Race/Ethnicity and Occupation of Respondents (%)

	Family	Socio-economic	Juvenile's environment	Unfair system	Other	Weighted *N*
Race/ethnicity						
African American	27.3	31.2	15.6	10.4	15.5	73
Anglo	30.0	25.3	25.8	4.2	14.7	375
Hispanic	26.3	31.2	18.1	7.4	17.0	117
Occupation						
Judges	25.9	30.6	21.3	5.6	16.6	105
Prosecutors	31.2	23.0	23.7	3.4	19.7	107
Attorneys	25.4	28.8	20.3	6.8	19.7	54
Juvenile probation	26.5	30.2	24.0	5.2	14.1	183
Police officers	36.8	24.1	21.8	6.9	11.4	84
TYC staff	29.0	21.0	26.3	10.5	13.2	38

Table 8.8 presents suggested solutions to the overrepresentation of Hispanics across respondents' racial/ethnic and occupational categories. Cross-racial/ethnic differentials are minimal. Likewise, occupational positions do not appear to make a difference. A major proportion of the suggested solutions pertain to the need for additional programs that will address background risk

FIGURE 8.6 Suggested Solutions for the Overrepresentation of Hispanic Youth

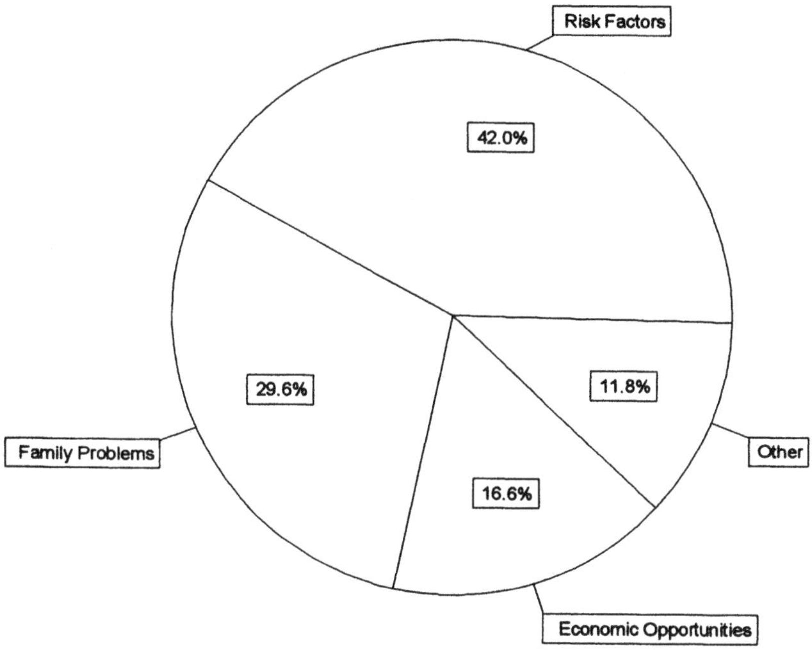

TABLE 8.8 Suggested Solutions for the Overrepresentation of Hispanic Youth, by Race/Ethnicity and Occupation of Respondents (%)

	Improve economic opportunities	Programs to fix risk factors	Fix family problems	Other	Weighted *N*
Race/ethnicity					
African American	17.0	47.2	23.7	12.1	76
Anglo	17.4	42.2	27.0	13.5	282
Hispanic	17.0	44.5	29.1	9.4	108
Occupation					
Judges	13.4	46.3	28.1	12.2	533
Prosecutors	12.5	42.5	36.3	8.8	27
Attorneys	18.9	46.0	21.6	13.5	96
Juvenile probation	18.4	41.8	25.3	14.5	232
Police officers	15.0	43.3	38.3	3.3	49
TYC staff	18.5	51.9	29.6	0	7

factors that promote juvenile delinquency (43.6%); resolving family problems is the next most frequently mentioned corrective (30.7%).

Some studies have suggested that juvenile justice practitioners face unique problems when communicating with the family of minority youth (Bishop and Frazier, 1996). These problems could lead to situations in which minority youth are detained at intake more often than other youth, as was determined in the analyses of data from County-1 and County-2. To address this matter, a series of communication-oriented questions were posed to respondents. Fifty-one percent of eligible respondents (i.e., those experienced in detention, adjudication, and disposition decisions) did not have problems communicating with the parents of, or adults responsible for, minority youth after the youth had been arrested and brought to the juvenile probation department. However, 43.2% (*N* = 227) of the sample did have communication problems; of those, 71% indicated that the parents' or other responsible adults' lack of access to a telephone and transportation impeded communication or contact. Interviewers also obtained 239 open-ended responses pertaining to communication barriers between families and juvenile authorities. Analyses of these open-ended responses identified the following as critical: (1) apathy of the parents (23.4% of responses); (2) language barriers (23.4%); (3) frequent mobility among families, which often meant that unreliable addresses and phone numbers were provided (23.8%); and (4) distrust of the legal system (8.3%). Five percent mentioned problems that minority working parents had in keeping appointments.

Do respondents across racial/ethnic and occupational strata report similar barriers to communication? Table 8.9 lists responses related to difficulties

TABLE 8.9 Difficulties in Contacting Minorities, by Race/Ethnicity and Occupation of Respondents (%)

	Language	Frequent mobility	Apathy	Working parents	Distrust legal system	Other	Weighted *N*
Race/ethnicity							
African American	39.0	22.3	22.3	11.9	16.5	0	25
Anglo	33.4	26.0	26.0	4.4	9.5	0	154
Hispanic	22.6	22.6	22.6	3.8	9.6	5.2	31
Occupation							
Judges	10.4	34.5	37.9	0	17.2	0	19
Prosecutors	14.7	38.2	29.4	11.8	5.9	0	11
Attorneys	30.0	25.0	20.0	5.0	10.0	10.0	52
Juvenile probation	43.5	19.4	21.0	4.8	11.3	0	91
Police officers	25.0	27.5	35.0	7.5	5.0	0	33
TYC staff	30.8	23.1	30.8	0	15.4	0	4

contacting minority families across respondents' racial/ethnic and occupational categories. African-American respondents, judges, and TYC staff were more likely to highlight "distrust" of the legal system as a serious obstacle.

Another critical issue concerns why minorities represent 80% of the youth confined in TYC facilities (see Jeffords, Lindsey, and McNitt, 1993). To address this, respondents in the sample were asked about the scarcity of placement slots for minority youth. Sixty-five percent of the 334 respondents experienced in disposition decisions felt that their ability to place minority youth in community-based treatment programs was affected by the scarcity of such placement resources. Hispanic respondents were significantly more likely to rate scarcity of placement slots as being important (see Table 8.10). Furthermore, a higher proportion of attorneys were more likely than practitioners in the other occupations to rate this as important. All eligible respondents were then asked to rate the importance of the problem of scarce placement resources. Overall, respondents ranked the lack of placement slots a 2.8 on a 3-point scale, where 1 means "not important" and 3 means "very important." No differences by the race/ethnicity or occupation of respondents are evident.

Of 209 practitioners who responded to the question on minority commitments to TYC, 63% indicated that they had to rely on commitments to TYC when placement slots elsewhere were unavailable. There were no differences in responses by the race/ethnicity of respondents. A larger proportion of attorneys (80%) were likely to list this as important (Table 8.11).

Finally, respondents were asked about the impact of private insurance on placement decisions. Seventy percent of the 343 eligible respondents indicated that the availability of private insurance from the juvenile's family affected decisions about where he/she was placed. A higher proportion of African Americans ($p < .01$) and probation officers were likely to rank this as a crucial matter (see Table 8.12). Respondents ranked the issue of private insurance a 2.54 on a 3-point scale, where 3 meant "very important." Prosecutors and judges considered this factor to be less significant.

It should be noted that judges have final authority over placement decisions and that individuals from other occupational backgrounds merely play advisory roles in these decisions. Bearing this fact in mind, it should be noted that 63% of the judges in the sample felt that insufficient resources was an important factor in determining placement decisions. They were evenly split on the issue of whether the shortage of placement slots results in minorities being placed in TYC facilities. Finally, 60% of the judges felt that the availability of private insurance was a factor in placement decisions (see Table 8.12). Judges' responses to these questions did not significantly differ from those of other respondents.

The results of this section show that, overall, most respondents believe that minorities are overrepresented in the juvenile justice system. Respondents

TABLE 8.10 Factors Influencing Placement Decisions by Respondents' Job Position and Race/Ethnicity

	Mean scores			
Job position	Importance of lack of resource for placement		Importance of private insurance for placement	
	N	Mean	N	Mean
Overall	18	2.84	28	2.57
Judge	42	2.74	43	2.26
Prosecutor	58	2.74	53	2.28
Probation	60	2.77	91	2.6
Attorney	25	2.88	21	2.62
Police	10	2.90	6	2.67
TYC	2	2.5	5	2.4

	Mean scores			
Race/ethnicity	Importance of lack of resource for placement		Importance of private insurance for placement	
	N	Mean	N	Mean
Overall	197	2.80	219	2.54
Anglo	142	2.81	161	2.55
Hispanic	37	2.75	30	2.51
African American	18	2.84	28	2.57

Importance of lack of resources for placement decisions (%)			
Job position	Yes	No	Total
Judge frequency	27.95	16.9	44.85
Overall %	8.37	5.06	13.44
Row %	63.32	37.68	N/A
Column %	12.87	14.49	N/A
Prosecutor frequency	19.72	11.22	30.94
Overall %	5.91	3.36	9.27
Row %	63.74	36.26	N/A
Column %	9.08	9.62	N/A

TABLE 8.10 Factors Influencing Placement Decisions by Respondents' Job Position and Race/Ethnicity—*Continued*

Job position	Yes	No	Total
Probation frequency	89.67	67.62	157.29
Overall %	26.87	20.26	47.13
Row %	57.01	42.99	N/A
Column %	41.30	57.97	N/A
Attorney frequency	70.2	18.2	88.4
Overall %	21.03	5.45	26.49
Row %	79.41	20.59	N/A
Column %	32.34	15.60	N/A
Police frequency	9.02	.82	9.84
Overall %	2.70	.25	2.95
Row %	91.67	8.33	N/A
Column %	4.15	.70	N/A
TYC frequency	.54	1.89	2.43
Overall %	.16	.57	.73
Row %	22.22	77.78	N/A
Column %	.25	1.62	N/A
Total	217.1	116.65	333.75
	65.05	34.95	100.00
Race/ethnicity	Yes	No	Total
Anglo frequency	138.57	88.15	2,260.72
Overall %	41.52	26.41	67.93
Row %	61.12	38.88	N/A
Column %	63.83	75.57	N/A
Hispanic frequency	48.2	12.06	60.26
Overall %	14.44	3.61	18.06
Row %	79.99	20.01	N/A
Column %	22.20	10.34	N/A
African-American frequency	30.33	16.44	46.77
Overall %	9.09	4.93	14.01
Row %	64.85	35.15	N/A
Column %	13.97	14.09	N/A
Total	217.1	116.65	333.75
	65.05	34.95	100.00

N/A = not applicable

TABLE 8.11 Resources Influenced Decision to Commit to TYC by Respondents' Job Position and Race/Ethnicity

Job position	Yes	No	Total
Judge frequency	13.65	13.65	27.3
Overall %	6.52	6.52	13.03
Row %	50.00	50.00	N/A
Column %	10.34	17.62	N/A
Prosecutor frequency	10.88	8.5	19.38
Overall %	5.19	4.06	9.25
Row %	56.14	43.86	N/A
Column %	8.24	10.97	N/A
Probation frequency	49.98	38.22	88.2
Overall %	23.86	18.25	42.11
Row %	56.67	43.33	N/A
Column %	37.87	49.34	N/A
Attorney frequency	52	13	65
Overall %	24.83	6.21	31.04
Row %	80.00	20.00	N/A
Column %	39.40	16.78	N/A
Police frequency	4.92	4.1	9.02
Overall %	2.35	1.96	4.31
Row %	54.55	45.45	N/A
Column %	3.73	5.29	N/A
TYC frequency	.54	0	.54
Overall %	.26	0	.26
Row %	100.00	0	N/A
Column %	.41	0	N/A
Total	131.97	77.47	209.44
	63.01	36.99	100.00

Race/ethnicity	Yes	No	Total
Anglo frequency	77.61	53.3	130.91
Overall %	37.06	25.45	62.5
Row %	59.29	40.71	N/A
Column %	58.81	68.80	N/A
Hispanic frequency	32.51	15.69	48.2
Overall %	15.52	7.49	23.01
Row %	67.45	32.55	N/A
Column %	24.63	20.25	N/A
African-American frequency	21.85	8.48	30.33
Overall %	10.43	4.05	14.48
Row %	72.04	27.96	N/A
Column %	16.56	10.95	N/A
Total	131.97	77.47	209.44
	63.01	36.99	100.00

TABLE 8.12 Role of Private Insurance in Placement Decisions by Respondents' Job Position and Race/Ethnicity

Job position	Yes	No	Total
Judge frequency	27.95	18.85	46.8
Overall %	8.14	5.49	13.63
Row %	59.72	40.28	N/A
Column %	11.55	18.63	N/A
Prosecutor frequency	18.02	14.28	32.3
Overall %	5.25	4.16	9.41
Row %	55.79	44.21	N/A
Column %	7.44	14.11	N/A
Probation frequency	135.24	26.46	161.7
Overall %	39.4	7.71	47.11
Row %	83.64	16.36	N/A
Column %	55.87	26.15	N/A
Attorney frequency	54.6	36.4	91
Overall %	15.91	10.6	26.51
Row %	60.00	40.00	N/A
Column %	22.55	35.98	N/A
Police frequency	4.92	4.1	9.02
Overall %	1.43	1.19	2.63
Row %	54.55	45.45	N/A
Column %	2.03	4.05	N/A
TYC frequency	1.35	1.08	2.43
Overall %	.39	.31	.71
Row %	55.56	44.44	N/A
Column %	.56	1.07	N/A
Total	242.08	101.17	343.25
	70.53	29.47	100.00

Race/ethnicity	Yes	No	Total
Anglo frequency	158.87	78	236.87
Overall %	46.28	22.72	69.01
Row %	67.07	32.93	N/A
Column %	65.63	77.10	N/A
Hispanic frequency	40.85	17.29	58.14
Overall %	11.90	5.04	16.94
Row %	70.26	29.74	N/A
Column %	16.87	17.09	N/A
African-American frequency	43.26	5.88	48.24
Overall %	12.34	1.71	14.05
Row %	87.81	12.19	N/A
Column %	17.50	5.81	N/A
Total	242.08	101.17	343.25
	70.53	29.47	100.00

suggested the following factors as reasons for overrepresentation: (1) the breakup of the family; (2) socio-economic problems; and (3) the juvenile's environment. Moreover, respondents felt that addressing family matters and background factors that contribute to delinquency could ameliorate minority overrepresentation. Respondents also identified what they perceived as communication problems with minority females. Finally, respondents also provided information that can help elucidate why minorities are overrepresented in TYC facilities—lack of community-based resources.

Views on the Juvenile Justice System in Texas

Respondents were also asked to provide their impressions about the problems with and strengths of the juvenile justice system in the state, as well as possible solutions to any perceived problems. This section examines the open-ended responses to these questions. A total of 1,058 responses were coded and entered; each of the 526 respondents averaged two responses per question.

According to the respondents, the three main problems of the state system are as follows: (1) lack of resources—26%; (2) lack of work-related autonomy—24%; and (3) lack of programs that address background risk factors that are correlated with delinquency—21.4%. Additionally, about 16% of the respondents mentioned problems in the processing of juveniles in the system (delays, paperwork, lack of adequate programs, placement difficulties), and another 9% mentioned personnel-related matters (workload, remuneration) (see Figure 8.7).

Table 8.13 identifies various problems in the system across respondents' racial/ethnic and occupational strata. Most respondents, regardless of race/ethnicity, highlighted similar issues. When examined by occupation, a higher proportion of attorneys and probation officers selected personnel problems, and a higher proportion of TYC staff listed the need to address risk factors for juvenile delinquency. For possible solutions to these problems, respondents provided 893 answers. The three most frequently mentioned solutions to these problems were the following (see Figure 8.8): (1) improvements in the system for processing juveniles—29% of responses; (2) increasing funding/resources, which also included workload, staffing, and remuneration problems—35%; and (3) programmatic solutions to address the background or risk factors for juvenile delinquency—22.1%.

Table 8.14 lists suggested solutions according to respondents' racial/ethnic and occupational strata. Roughly 25 to 35% of all respondents said that the three solutions outlined earlier were needed. Hispanic and Anglo respondents were more likely than African Americans to list the need for additional funding and resources. African Americans were more likely to mention the need for more programs to address background factors for juvenile delinquency. Roughly one-third of the respondents mentioned the

FIGURE 8.7 Primary Problems Targeted by Respondents

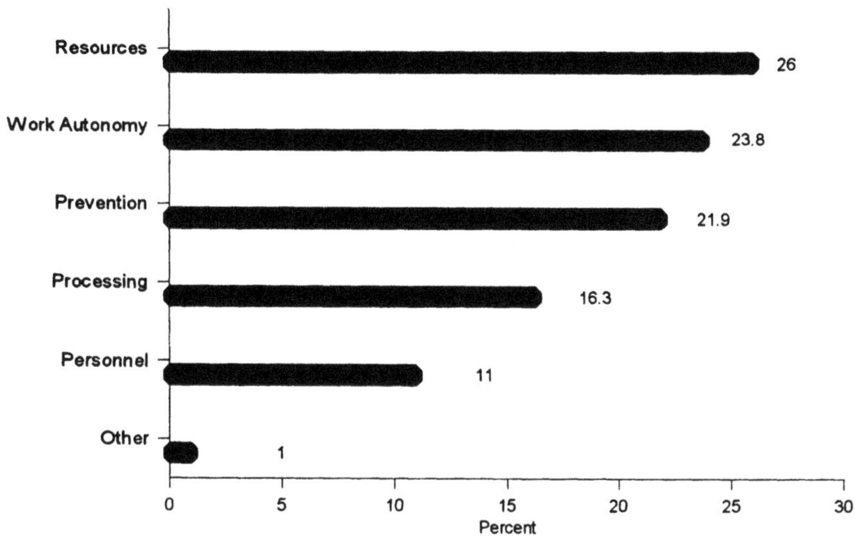

TABLE 8.13 Perceptions of Various Problems in the Juvenile Justice System, by Race/Ethnicity and Occupation of Respondents (%)

	Personnel issues	Lack of resources	Work-related autonomy	Address background factors	Problems juvenile process	Weighted *N*
Race/ethnicity						
African American	11.8	24.4	24.9	24.2	14.6	122
Anglo	10.5	26.2	24.2	21.6	17.3	703
Hispanic	12.2	28.1	21.8	21.9	14.5	198
Occupation						
Judges	9.8	32.6	24.5	20.7	12.5	119
Prosecutors	5.0	29.6	26.6	21.5	17.0	76
Attorneys	14.7	24.2	2.42	20.0	16.8	149
Juvenile probation	12.1	29.1	19.9	23.8	14.2	415
Police officers	6.6	17.0	31.9	20.3	16.8	144
TYC staff	5.1	11.9	28.8	32.2	20.3	16

need for changes in the processing of juveniles in the system. Police and prosecutors were more likely than practitioners in the other occupations to make this suggestion.

The question regarding the three main strengths of the Texas juvenile justice system elicited 802 responses. Thirty-six percent of the respondents

FIGURE 8.8 Primary Areas of Improvement Targeted by Respondents

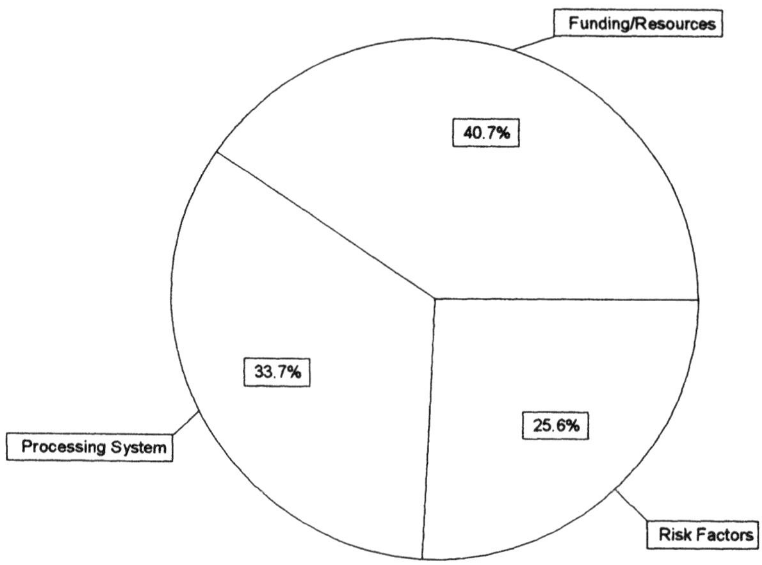

TABLE 8.14 Suggested Solutions to Problems in the Juvenile Justice System, by Race/Ethnicity and Occupation of Respondents (%)

	Programs addressing background factors	Funding/ resources	Changes in juvenile processing	Weighted *N*
Race/ethnicity				
African American	33.8	32.6	33.6	94
Anglo	28.9	35.1	36.0	536
Hispanic	26.0	36.4	32.6	151
Occupation				
Judges	25.8	41.7	32.6	86
Prosecutors	14.1	35.8	45.1	59
Attorneys	35.1	32.5	32.5	200
Juvenile probation	30.8	38.4	30.8	329
Police officers	18.4	22.8	58.8	94
TYC staff	26.5	30.6	42.9	13

mentioned the system's facilities, 24% mentioned new laws, 24% mentioned the services the system provides for "kids" when they get into trouble, and 5% replied "none." The remaining 11% comprised miscellaneous responses, which were combined into an "other" category.

Views on Delinquency

A juvenile's propensity to commit delinquent acts may have important implications for how he/she is treated within the juvenile justice system. Consequently, a clear understanding of the antecedents of crime and delinquency is a prerequisite for achieving long-term solutions to the problem of the disproportional representation of minorities in the juvenile justice system. Previously, respondents underscored the need to address background factors that are correlated with delinquency. Questions in this section of the survey provided respondents with an opportunity to identify what they perceived to be the main influences on delinquency and so help identify the background risk factors that promote delinquency.

Respondents were given a list of 25 possible causes of or explanations for delinquent behavior and were asked to rate their importance on a scale of 0–5, with 0 representing "not important at all" and 5 representing "very important." The responses were collapsed and re-coded, such that 0–1 were grouped in the "not important" category; 2–3 were put in the "somewhat important" category; and 4–5 were put in the "very important" category. Table 8.15 summarizes the results for this set of 25 questions; the factors that the majority of the sample ranked as "important" are listed first. Table 8.15 shows that the majority of all respondents mentioned the lack of parental supervision (97.3%) and the lack of discipline by parents (91.4%) as important correlates of delinquency. On a scale of 1–3, where 1 meant "not important" and 3 measured "very important," the mean score for a lack of parental supervision was 2.97; the mean score for a lack of discipline by parents was 2.91. Other factors, such as the influence of negative peer groups (82.8%) and abuse of alcohol or drugs by youth (79.1%), were also rated as "important" by a majority of the respondents. These were ranked 2.82 and 2.79, respectively. There were no major differences by race/ethnicity or occupation of the respondents.

At least 60% of the respondents rated the following factors as "very important" correlates of delinquency: (1) inner city kids viewing violence as a way to resolve differences (66.2%); (2) making personal choices to commit delinquent acts (65.5%); (3) living in high-crime neighborhoods (64.2%); (4) not knowing positive ways to interact with others (64.1%); (5) having psychological or emotional problems (62.5%); (6) performing negatively in school (61.4%); and (7) having siblings who are delinquent

TABLE 8.15 Responses to the List of Factors Mentioned, from Most to Least Important (%)

Factors mentioned	Not important (1)	Somewhat important (2)	Very important (3)
Lack of parental supervision	.5	2.2	97.3
Lack of discipline by parents	1.0	7.8	91.4
Influence of negative peer group	.8	16.4	82.8
Abuse of alcohol or drugs by the youth	.6	20.3	79.1
Inner city kids see violence as a way to resolve differences	4.2	29.3	66.2
Making personal choices to commit delinquent acts	5.7	28.9	65.5
Living in a neighborhood where a lot of criminal activity takes place	2.1	33.5	64.2
Not knowing positive ways to interact with other youth	2.5	33.3	64.1
Having psychological or emotional problems	3.6	33.9	62.5
Negative performance in school	4.2	34.3	61.4
Having siblings who are delinquents	3.9	34.9	60.9
Inability to control impulses	5.2	34.7	59.9
Being a victim of child abuse	4.1	89.6	58.6
Failure in socialization of youth	2.2	41.7	56.1
Living with mother only	10.6	41.1	48.2
Violent and destructive media images	5.6	46.8	47.4
Media advertising showing need for material possessions	9.6	49.4	40.9
Having little opportunity for work	10.0	41.1	40.8
Having learning disabilities	11.8	82.1	34.3
The economic structure	13.2	54.1	32.4
The socio-economic inequality in this county	15.5	77.2	31.8
Being poor	16.5	51.0	31.5
Inadequate schools	15.6	53.8	30.6
Living with relatives other than parents	14.1	56.4	29.3
Having a natural tendency for delinquent behavior	37.7	52.8	19.4

(60.9%). The mean importance score for these variables were as follows: (1) using violence as a way to resolve differences (2.62); (2) making personal choices (2.59); (3) living in high-crime neighborhoods (2.62); (4) not knowing positive ways to interact (2.62); (5) having psychological or emotional problems (2.59); (6) performing negatively in school (2.57); and (7) having delinquent siblings (2.57).

Other factors that the majority of respondents ranked as "important" were (1) the inability to control impulses (59.9%); (2) being a victim of child abuse (58.6%); and (3) failure in socialization of youth (56.1%). The mean importance scores for these factors were 2.55, 2.55, and 2.54, respectively. Fourteen of the twenty-five items listed in Table 8.15 were rated as "very important" by a majority of the respondents. The scores for the 14 factors ranged from a low of 2.54 to a high of 2.97.

As shown in Table 8.15, the remaining factors were not rated "very important" by a majority of respondents. These factors and their mean scores of significance were as follows: (1) living with the mother only (2.38); (2) exposure to media violence (2.4); (3) exposure to media advertising (2.38); (4) having little opportunity to work (2.31); (5) having learning disabilities (2.22); (6) the economic structure (2.19); (7) being poor (2.15); (8) inadequate schools (2.15); and (9) living with relatives other than parents (2.15). Although less than one-half of the respondents felt that these factors were important, their rankings were all above 2, indicating that those who thought these factors were important ranked them as "somewhat important." Having a natural tendency toward delinquent behavior was seen as the least important factor in delinquency, with 38% of the respondents rating it as "not important." The mean score for this factor was 1.82.

Ratings of Factors by Respondents' Profile

An interesting question is whether responses to factors influencing delinquency vary according to the race/ethnicity or occupation of the respondent. Since many of the cells have small numbers, the use of inferential statistics may be inappropriate for many of these data. Among the top four factors behind delinquency, listed in Table 8.15, no noticeable differences by occupation or race/ethnicity are evident. As for the other factors, a smaller proportion of prosecutors than practitioners in the other occupations was inclined to think that "inner city kids see violence as a way to resolve differences." Similarly, smaller proportions of police and attorneys supported the view that "making personal choices to commit delinquent acts" was an important factor influencing delinquency. A larger share of Anglo respondents were likely to rate this as an "important" factor

In general, smaller proportions of judges, prosecutors, and police officers felt that "not knowing positive ways to interact" (or having poor social skills) and "living in bad neighborhoods" were important predictors of delinquency. A higher proportion of respondents in both minority groups believed that having poor social skills is correlated with delinquency. African Americans were more likely to pinpoint high-crime neighborhoods as a factor in delinquency. Except for prosecutors and attorneys, the majority of respondents from most occupational groups rated negative performance in school or poor grades as "very important." Over two-thirds of minority respondents felt this way, in contrast to 58% of Anglo respondents.

Proportionally larger numbers of judges and probation officers indicated that having psychological and emotional problems influenced delinquency. Seventy-one percent of Hispanic respondents indicated that this was an important factor, a larger proportion than for the other two groups. Prosecutors and attorneys were less likely to support the view that negative school performance or bad grades contribute to delinquency. In contrast, a larger share of minority respondents felt that negative performance in school contributed to delinquency. Attorneys and TYC staff were more likely to place importance on the role of delinquent siblings. Hispanics tended to support this view, as well. Police and prosecutors indicated that "an inability to control impulses," or poor self-control, was less likely to influence delinquency. No differences by race/ethnicity are evident.

Judges, probation officers, and attorneys were more likely to believe that child abuse influences delinquency. Proportionally, more Anglo and Hispanic respondents supported this perspective. Except for prosecutors, a majority of respondents from all occupational groups believed that failure in socialization contributes to delinquency. A larger proportion of Hispanic and African-American respondents also supported this view. Larger proportions of police, probation officers, attorneys, and, to a lesser extent, judges believed that living with a single mother was a factor influencing delinquency. A larger number of Hispanic and African-American respondents also supported this view.

A majority of judges rated media portrayals of violence as "very important." Hispanics and African-American respondents also supported this item in larger proportions. Concerning the role of media advertising, a majority of probation officers felt that it was an important factor influencing delinquency, the only group that felt this way.

Are there differences according to occupation or race/ethnicity in responses regarding the influence of economic factors on delinquency, such as opportunities to work, economic structure, socio-economic inequality, or being poor? Less than 40% of respondents from all occupational groups rated these factors as "very important." However, minority respondents, especially African Americans, were more likely to rate economic factors as "very important." A higher proportion of minority respondents were also likely to list socio-economic inequality and the economic structure as factors influencing delinquency. Being poor, attending inadequate schools, living with relatives, and having a natural tendency toward delinquent behavior were ranked as "moderately important" or "somewhat important" by a majority of respondents in the survey.

Finally, researchers compared the rankings of the scores assigned to each of the 25 factors, by race/ethnicity and occupation. Using these factors as dependent variables, a series of ANOVA models was generated. If a main effect for the race/ethnicity or occupation of the respondent was indicated, pair-wise comparisons between means were done using Scheffle's method. The ANOVA analysis identified five factors that showed a main effect either for the race/ethnicity or occupation of the respondent. This means that, in rankings of five items, significant differences exist according either to the race/ethnicity or occupation of the respondent. Given the fairly large number of respondents who rated these factors, the findings presented here should be more robust than those of the earlier ANOVA analyses.

A statistically significant difference between all minority and Anglo respondents exists for the two factors pertaining to economic influences on delinquency, namely, the role of the economic structure and socio-economic inequality. There was also a race/ethnicity effect with respect to the role of inadequate schools in influencing delinquency. For economic structure, the critical difference in mean values was between Anglo respondents and both minority groups.

The results from the ANOVA analysis showed that for two factors there were two main effects for occupational strata: natural delinquent tendencies and psychological factors as correlates of delinquency. In the case of natural delinquent tendencies, the rankings that TYC staff assigned to this factor were significantly higher than the rankings given to it by attorneys.

Open-ended responses were requested on factors that respondents felt were important influences on delinquency. Two hundred and forty-eight open-ended responses were obtained (see Tables 8.16 and 8.17). Of these, 103 (41.7%) mentioned family background; 23.9% mentioned matters related to the juvenile's environment, such as high-crime neighborhoods, poor role models, and the presence of gangs; and 19% mentioned the juvenile's personal values. Nine percent listed socio-economic and educational factors as contributing to delinquency. The "other" category comprises views in which respondents felt that welfare dependency and the fact that youth face no consequences for their actions promoted delinquency.

TABLE 8.16 Other Factors Related to Delinquency, by Occupation of Respondents (%)

Factor	Judge	Prosecutor	Probation officer	Attorney	Police officer	TYC staff
Family	27.9	35.9	41.1	58.3	25.0	36.4
Socio-economic	4.7	4.7	5.7	4.2	0	0
Education	7.0	6.3	5.7	4.2	0	2.2
Youth's environment	27.2	26.6	20.0	20.8	36.1	2.3
Personal values	27.9	23.4	21.4	8.3	19.4	9.1
Other	4.6	3.1	5.7	4.2	9.5	0
Weighted totals	28	22	103	63	29	3

TABLE 8.17 Other Factors Related to Delinquency, by Race/Ethnicity of Respondents (%)

Factor	African American	Anglo	Hispanic
Family	46.2	43.5	32.1
Socio-economic	4.8	3.0	9.1
Education	9.6	4.1	4.5
Youth's environment	19.7	21.0	37.2
Personal values	12.3	21.3	13.7
Other	7.5	7.3	3.5
Weighted totals	31	170	47

The majority of responses from all occupations listed family matters, the youth's environment, and personal values as additional factors. Minority respondents, although not disagreeing with these factors, also listed education and socio-economic factors as "important." Anglo respondents were more likely than minorities to mention "personal values" as a factor. The factors that respondents identified as "important" in influencing delinquency fit with a body of research that views these as "risk factors" for delinquency and other forms of deviant behaviors among youth (Center for Substance Abuse Prevention, 1993). This body of research has divided risk factors into the following categories:

1. *Individual* factors are personal attributes associated with risk for delinquent behavior. A number of factors highlighted in this survey fit into individual-level risk factors. Making personal choices to commit delinquent acts, being unable to control impulses, and having psychological and emotional problems are examples of individual risk factors.
2. *Family* risk factors are important because families provide the most important and enduring context for individual development. Lack of parental supervision, lack of discipline by parents, having siblings who are delinquent, being a victim of child abuse or neglect, and failure in socialization of youth are examples of family risk factors.
3. *School* risk factors have a direct and an indirect impact on delinquent behavior. Factors that respondents highlighted, such as poor academic performance, heightened discipline problems, and disengagement from school life, can be considered school risk factors. Survey respondents mentioned negative school performances and poor social skills, both of which can be seen as examples of school-related risk factors.
4. *Peer* risk factors are also linked to delinquent behaviors. Respondents list the influence of negative peer groups and abuse of alcohol or drugs by youth (which usually occur in peer groups), and these should be seen as aspects of peer risk factors.

Case Scenario Evaluation

After some deliberation, it was decided to test for the presence of possible prejudice in decision making through the survey process. In addition to what has been examined in other studies, it was decided that this research would examine whether a third set of factors associated with decision makers' work environment plays a critical role in influencing outcomes. To a certain extent, many legal institutions operate without clear guidelines for decision makers. Courts and juvenile departments enforce the law, and to a certain extent, the various actors represent an occupational subgroup. Law is made up of rules, but these rules do not dictate with any precision how various practitioners must dispose of cases. The process essentially breeds a great deal of discretion. Individual decision makers also must work within a system where judges, prosecutors, defense attorneys, probation officers, and law enforcement personnel act as functionally interdependent actors. What goes on within the juvenile process has been described as a craft, which means a combination of work and politics (Fleming, Nardulli, and Eisenstein, 1992). Individual decision makers have career aspirations and their upward mobility within departments in influenced by the degree to which departmental/organizational goals are fulfilled. Organizational goals and expectations are often expressed in terms of numbers of cases processed and disposed within a certain time interval. As workloads increase, pressure to keep the cases flowing may also increase and decision makers may lack or perceive a lack of sufficient time to review cases objectively and thoroughly.

Juvenile probation departments themselves face political pressures from the outside such as their supervisory boards and public interest groups. Electoral politics also influence organizational dynamics. These external pressures may translate into new goals and emphases for staff to pursue. Within this context, individual decision makers often face external pressures and such pressures could translate into decisions based less upon objective criteria and more in terms of prejudicial attitudes about minorities. These prejudicial attitudes and racial stereotypes may play a critical role in influencing whether minority delinquents are arrested, detained, petitioned to court, adjudicated delinquent, and subsequently sentenced to severe dispositions more often than majority youth. There is experimental research which supports the argument that individuals under pressure are more likely to rely on stereotypes as the basis for decisions (Eaton and Kruglanski, 1991; Kruglanski and Freund, 1983).

Several well-controlled studies provide further evidence that perpetrators are treated differently depending on their racial or ethnic group membership. Furthermore, these studies suggest that differential treatment might be mediated by stereotypical assumptions about characteristics and behaviors of minorities and even by differential causal attribution. Thus, the same behavior is perceived as more violent (Duncan, 1976), and more mean and threatening (Sager and Schofield, 1980) when it is performed by African Americans than by Caucasians. Studies comparing social perceptions of Hispanics and Caucasians corroborated that minorities and majorities are perceived differently even when there are no differences in their behavior (Bodenhausen and Wyer, 1985; Bodenhausen and Lichenstein, 1987). For example, the same behavior was perceived as significantly more aggressive when performed by a person whose name suggested Hispanic origin (i.e., Carlos Ramirez) than when performed by an individual whose name suggested a white person, or even when not particularly associated with any race or ethnic group. Moreover, these stereotypical judgments were especially strong in situations where observers had to make complex and consequential decisions (e.g., decisions about the guilt or innocence of defendants in criminal trials, and the punishment that was appropriate for their offenses) than when observers had to make relatively simple and inconsequential judgments (e.g., judgments about the personality traits of an individual) (Bodenhausen and Lichenstein, 1987). Considering that decisions made at every stage of the processing of minority delinquents are complex and undoubtedly consequential, it is reasonable to hypothesize that decisions may be influenced by stereotypical expectations, if indeed, these expectations actually exist.

Differential social perception does not appear to be the only factor contributing to unequal treatment of minority youth. In addition, there is evidence to suggest that inferences about the causes of crime and projections about future conduct also differ depending upon race or ethnic origin. Causes of the same criminal behavior are perceived differently depending on whether a perpetrator belongs to a majority group or a minority group for which criminal propensities are assumed. Criminal behaviors committed by minorities tend to be attributed to stable, relatively fixed, and permanent aspects of the individual, his culture, or his environmental context whereas the crime of whites tends to be causally attributed to temporary and transitional factors that are episodic at best (Duncan, 1976; Bodenhausen and Wyer, 1985). Given these differences in attributing the causes of crime, it is hardly surprising that expectations for future conduct may differ as well. When compared to majority offenders, minorities are expected to be more likely to menace society by committing more future crimes and more serious crimes as well. These stereotypical attributions and expectations sometimes even persist in spite of the presence of evidence to the contrary (Bodenhausen and Wyer, 1985; Bodenhausen and Lichenstein, 1987).

Thus, there is ample theoretical support for the notion that latent racial stereotypes may influence the handling of minority youth. Yet, the systematic measurement of these effects has remained elusive. It cannot be realistically expected that decision makers will readily and openly admit to racial prejudice or bias and the subsequent actual discrimination. Consequently, measuring the role of subjective factors poses methodological difficulties.

The social psychological literature indicates that people are either unaware of prejudicial attitudes or are unwilling to openly admit that their decisions, judgments, and behavior are under the strong influence of racial and ethnic stereotypes (Fisk and Taylor, 1991). This has important methodological implications. Measurement techniques in which respondents are asked directly to express their racial and ethnic attitudes produce results that are significantly different from those obtained by unobtrusive techniques. To obtain valid estimates of stereotypical expectations and attributions, unobtrusive and quasi-experimental techniques are highly desirable. One particular strategy that has been discussed in the literature is the error-choice method (Webb, Campbell, Schwartz, and Sechrest, 1966). In this method, respondents are presented with a series of multiple-choice items purporting to assess their factual knowledge about the chosen domain. Many of these items concern facts and have correct answers among the response alternatives. Several of the items, however, have only incorrect or ambiguous response alternatives, and they are devised so that respondents' choices among them are indicative of stereotypical opinions. The error-choice method has been successfully implemented to measure attitudes toward a number of socially sensitive issues (Hammond, 1948). Quasi-experimental techniques are procedures similar to those presented.

In the present study, respondents were read a case scenario, which described hypothetical delinquent acts committed by a given juvenile. The scenario had a randomly chosen racial/ethnic identifier for the juvenile (African-American, Hispanic, Anglo, or no-ethnic-identifier-mentioned) and a name for the juvenile. The juvenile's criminal history was randomly selected between a first and a third offense. This random assignment of racial/ethnic identifiers and criminal histories was computer controlled. The format of the scenario was as follows:

> A sixteen-year old [Anglo/African American/Hispanic/Youth] named [Christopher Koenning/Tyrone Franklin/Juan Fernandez/The Youth] was arrested and charged with possession of less than one gram of cocaine. He was arrested in the company of a gang member. This is the [first time/third time] that [Christopher Koenning/Tyrone Franklin/Juan Fernandez/The Youth] has been arrested. (If third time is used in the scenario, then the previous two times were for possession of a handgun.)

Seven outcomes or conclusions were assessed in this procedure. The respondents were asked to rate their perception of the seriousness of the offense described in the case scenario. Later, they were asked to suggest actions that the youth would be subjected to at the pre- and post-adjudication stages. Responses varied on a scale of 0–5, with 0 representing "not at all likely" and 5 representing "extremely likely." These responses were re-coded such that 4 and 5 were rated "extremely [serious, dangerous, likely]"; 2 and 3 as "somewhat [serious, dangerous, likely]"; and 0 and 1 as "not at all [serious, dangerous, likely]." Respondents were also asked to rate the likelihood that the juvenile offenders would commit similar or other offenses in the future.

Tables 8.18, 8.19, and 8.20 present respondents' opinions of the seriousness of the offense, the likelihood of a juvenile committing a similar and other offenses in the future, and the racial/ethnic and occupational strata of respondents. The majority of response rankings were distributed between the "extremely serious" and the "extremely likely" categories.

A series of multiple regression equations were generated, each designed to measure the effects of a series of independent variables on a selected dependent variable. The goal was to determine if the juvenile's race/ethnicity and criminal history and the race/ethnicity of the respondent had a bearing on the perception of the offense and the actions recommended. The dependent variables were based on a scale of 0–5. The independent variables (dummy variables) included in the multiple regression equations were these:

1. *Race/ethnicity of the juvenile:* African American, Hispanic, no race specified. Anglo was the reference category.
2. *Race/ethnicity of the respondent:* Hispanic, African American. The reference group was Anglo.
3. *The respondent's educational level:* Bachelor's degree, professional degree. The reference group was respondents with no degree.
4. *Prior history of the juvenile:* Third offense versus first offense. The first offense was the reference category.

TABLE 8.18 Ratings of the Seriousness of the Offense, by Race/Ethnicity and Occupation of Respondents (%)

	Not at all serious	Somewhat serious	Extremely serious	Weighted total
Race/ethnicity				
African American	0	26.3	73.8	68
Anglo	2.6	33.5	63.9	334
Hispanic	2.1	20.2	77.6	101
Occupation				
Judges	4.4	23.9	71.7	60
Prosecutors	5.3	34.5	60.2	38
Attorneys	2.1	36.2	61.7	12
Juvenile probation	1.3	29.6	69.1	219
Police officers	1.2	22.0	76.8	67
TYC staff	0	34.5	65.5	8

Table 8.21 presents the results of the least-squares regression models. This, and the other regression tables presented in this chapter, list the unstandardized coefficients (b), the standardized betas, and the standard error (s.e.), which allows readers to determine the importance and the significance of the relationships. The standardized coefficients (beta) provide the relative weighting of factors explaining respondents' perceptions of the nature of the offense, or of the actions taken after the juvenile is referred to juvenile authorities. The higher the beta for a predictor variable, the more

TABLE 8.19 Ratings of the Likelihood of Committing Similar Offenses, by Race/Ethnicity and Occupation of Respondents (%)

	Not at all serious	Somewhat serious	Extremely serious	Weighted total
Race/ethnicity				
African American	2.4	7.4	90.2	62
Anglo	.3	15.4	84.3	332
Hispanic	0	6.8	93.2	101
Occupation				
Judges	1.1	4.6	94.3	57
Prosecutors	.9	14.7	84.4	37
Attorneys	0	20.7	79.5	114
Juvenile probation	.7	11.8	87.5	212
Police officers	0	8.5	91.5	67
TYC staff	0	7.1	92.9	8

TABLE 8.20 Ratings of the Likelihood of Committing Other Offenses, by Race/Ethnicity and Occupation of Respondents (%)

	Not at all serious	Somewhat serious	Extremely serious	Weighted total
Race/ethnicity				
African American	2.3	19.8	78.0	65
Anglo	1.4	17.5	81.1	333
Hispanic	.7	12.5	86.9	99
Occupation				
Judges	2.2	6.0	92.2	59
Prosecutors	1.9	16.8	81.3	36
Attorneys	2.3	22.7	75.0	114
Juvenile probation	.7	20.0	79.3	213
Police officers	1.2	7.3	91.5	67
TYC staff	0	7.1	92.9	8

TABLE 8.21 Multiple Regression Models of Case Scenario Juvenile Outcomes

	Seriousness of offense		Dangerousness of offense		Likely to commit similar offense		Likely to commit other offenses		Is a threat to society	
	Unstd. coef. (s.e)	Beta	Unstd. coef. (s.e)	Beta	Unstd. coef. (s.e.)	Beta	Unstd. coef. (s.e.)	Beta	Unstd. coef. (s.e.)	Beta
Juvenile's race/ethnicity										
African American	–.22	–.08	–.05	–.02	–.03	–.02	.71	.10	.02	.001
	(.12)		(.16)		(.11)		(.12)		(.15)	
Hispanic	–.31*	–.12	–.08	–.03	–.32*	–.16	–.09	–.04	.001	.003
	(.15)		(.16)		(.12)		(.14)		(.16)	
Not specified	–.22	–.09	–.13	–.05	.15	.08	.30*	.15	.17	.07
	(.12)		(.14)		(.09)		(.11)		(.13)	
Respondent's race/ethnicity										
African American	.13	.04	.08	.02	.02	.001	–.15	–.06	–.12	–.04
	(.14)		(.14)		(.13)		(.13)		(.14)	
Hispanic	.24*	.09	.24	.08	.07	.03	–.02	–.01	.07	.03
	(.11)		(.14)		(.08)		(.09)		(.12)	
Respondent's education										
B.S. degree	–.42**	–.20	–.38*	–.16	–.16	–.10	–.22	–.12	–.18	–.08
	(.14)		(.14)				(.12)		(.15)	
Professional degree	–.56**	–.27	–.86*	–.37	–.17	–.11	–.29*	–.16	–.35*	–.16
	(.15)		(.15)		(.12)		(.13)		(.17)	
Juvenile's criminal history										
First offense	–.77***	.37	–.72***	.31	–.67**	.41	–.77**	.42	–1.12***	.49
	(.10)		(.11)		(.08)		(.09)		(.11)	
Intercept	4.8		4.5		4.9		4.8		4.6	
	(.16)		(.13)		(.14)		(.15)		(.18)	
Multiple R^2	17.4%		17.1%		19.9%		20.4%		24.6%	
Wald F value	1,023***		704		2,626***		1,915***		1,071***	

$^{*}p < .05$ $^{**}p < .01$ $^{***}p < .001$

important that variable is in influencing the dependent variable. The maximum predicted effect (MPE), discussed in Chapter 5, can also be used as another indicator of the relative strength of each factor. Generally, a positive coefficient indicates that the factor is associated with a perception of the offense as being more serious, or that a more severe action was recommended after the juvenile's referral to probation. Interpretations are always made in relation to a reference category, which, in the case scenario, is Anglo for the juvenile's race/ethnicity.

In the equation modeling the *seriousness of the offense,* the significant effects are the following (in order of importance): (1) the criminal history of the juvenile; (2) whether the respondent had a professional or a bachelor's degree; (3) whether the juvenile in the case scenario was Hispanic; and (4) whether the respondent was Hispanic. These were the most important and statistically significant variables in explaining the perceived seriousness of the offense. The fact that the juvenile committed a third offense, as opposed to a first offense, was considered the most important factor. The higher the respondent's educational level, the lower his/her rating of the seriousness of the offense. Generally, respondents with bachelor's or professional (or graduate) degrees rated the offenses described in the case scenario as less serious. In terms of race/ethnicity effect, if the juvenile was described as Hispanic, respondents considered the offense to be less serious than if an Anglo juvenile had committed the same offense. Hispanic respondents rated the offense as more serious than did their Anglo peers.

In the equation modeling the *perceived dangerousness of the offense,* the two most important variables were the criminal history of the juvenile and the educational level of the respondent (bachelor's or professional degree). Again, the more extensive the juvenile's criminal history, the higher the respondent's rating of the perceived dangerousness of the offense. The higher the respondent's educational level, the less dangerous he/she perceived the offense to be. Neither the race/ethnicity of the juvenile nor that of the respondent affected the perception of the dangerousness of the offense.

In the equation modeling the likelihood of the juvenile *committing a similar offense* in the future, the significant and most important variables were the juvenile's criminal history and his/her Hispanic ethnicity. Youth with more extensive criminal histories were judged to be more likely to commit similar offenses in the future. When the case scenario described the juvenile as Hispanic, respondents felt that he/she would be less likely than an Anglo juvenile to commit similar offenses in the future.

In the equation modeling the likelihood of the juvenile *committing other offenses* in the future, the most important variables were the juvenile's criminal history, whether the respondent had a professional degree, and whether the juvenile's race/ethnicity was specified in the case scenario. The more extensive the juvenile's criminal history, the greater the perceived likelihood of that individual committing other offenses in the future. Respondents with professional degrees rated the likelihood of the juvenile committing future offenses lower than did their counterparts who did not have college degrees. Not specifying the juvenile's race/ethnicity in the case scenario was associated with a greater likelihood of future criminal activity. Finally, if the juvenile's race/ethnicity was *not* provided, respondents perceived him/her as more likely than an Anglo juvenile to commit future offenses.

The *perceived threat of the juvenile offender* to society was the dependent variable for the fifth model. The important predictors were the juvenile's criminal history and whether the respondents had professional or graduate degrees. A more extensive criminal history was associated with a greater perceived threat to society. Respondents with graduate degrees viewed the offense as less threatening to society, compared to their peers without college degrees.

In all five models, criminal history was the most important factor influencing perceptions. In Model 1, a first-time offender is ranked .77 points lower than a third-time offender on the seriousness of the offense, all other factors being constant. These differences are statistically significant. The variance explained by the independent or predictor variables, represented by the Multiple R^2, ranged from about 17.4% to 24.6%. Generally, having a more serious criminal history was associated with a maximum predicted estimate of between 16% and 25% in the dependent variables being examined.

The two remaining multiple regression analyses involved recommendations for actions to be taken in the pre-adjudication and disposition stages. Respondents were asked to judge what would happen after the juvenile had been turned over to the juvenile probation authorities. At the pre-adjudication stage, the actions selected by the respondents were ranked (a list was provided and open-ended responses were encouraged). The 516 responses were re-coded from the least severe (charges dropped, juveniles sent home—35.6% of responses) to the most severe (detention in a facility—46.9% of responses). Diversion to alternative programs (13.3% of responses) and in-home detention (4% of responses) were ranked between these two extremes.

In the regression analyses of the severity of pre-adjudication actions, the factors associated with the recommended actions were these: (1) the juvenile's criminal history; (2) the respondent's educational level; and (3) whether the respondent was Hispanic, rather than Anglo. The more extensive the criminal history, the more likely severe pre-adjudication actions were recommended. Respondents with bachelor's degrees recommended less severe actions than those without college degrees. Hispanic respondents chose less severe pre-adjudication actions than did Anglo respondents.

Five hundred and sixteen post-adjudication outcomes were provided by respondents. These were based on a provided list and open-ended

TABLE 8.22 Results of Multiple Regression on the Severity of Respondents' Pre- and Post-Adjudication Actions

	Severity of actions (pre-adjudication)		Severity of punishment (post-adjudication)	
	Unstand. coef. (s.e.)	Beta	Unstand. coef. (s.e.)	Beta
Juvenile's race/ethnicity				
African American	.07 (.19)	.02	–.08 (.12)	–.04
Hispanic	.11 (.19)	.03	–.08 (.11)	–.04
Not specified	.06 (.18)	.02	–.10 (.11)	–.05
Respondent's race/ethnicity				
African American	–.30 (.20)	–.07	–.05 (.13)	–.02
Hispanic	–.36* (.17)	–.11	–.01 (.10)	–.01
Respondent's education				
B.S. degree	.39* (.17)	.14	–.04 (.10)	–.02
Professional degree	.09 (.18)	.03	–.08 (.10)	–.05
Juvenile's criminal history				
First offense	–1.01*** (.13)	.36	–.71*** (.07)	.41
Intercept	2.92 (.21)		1.97 (.13)	
Adjusted R^2	14.3%		18.3%	
Wald F value	211***		261***	

$^*p < .05$ $^{***}p < .001$

responses. The responses were re-coded from the least severe (probation at home—71.6% of responses) to the most severe (placement in a secure facility or certification as an adult—20.5% of the responses). Outside-home probation was the intermediate category (8% of responses). In the analyses of post-adjudication outcomes, the juvenile offender's criminal history was the only statistically significant variable in explaining the severity of post-adjudication recommendations. The most extensive criminal histories were associated with more severe dispositions (see Table 8.22).

Clearly, the juvenile offender's criminal history was the strongest predictor of respondents' perceptions of the seriousness of the juvenile's offense, of the likelihood of future criminal activities, and of actions taken at the pre- and post-adjudication stages. Someone with a first offense is ranked a significant 1.01 points lower than a juvenile with two prior offenses, in terms of the severity of pre-adjudication actions recommended by respondents (see Table 8.22). The respondent's educational level was another consistent predictor of perceptions, with one education variable being significant in five of the seven models considered. The race/ethnicity of the juvenile, especially being Hispanic, and the respondent's race/ethnicity were significant in three models, but no clear pattern is discernible. It is unclear why offenses committed by Hispanic youth were ranked as less serious or why the likelihood of their committing other similar offenses was ranked lower than that of Anglo youth. However, it is noteworthy that a juvenile's race/ethnicity is not correlated with the recommended actions at pre- and post-adjudication stages. Finally, the race/ethnicity of the respondent was significant in determining perceptions and actions in two models. Hispanic ethnicity was associated with a less serious perception of the offense, and Hispanics were less likely to recommend severe actions at the pre-adjudication stage.

CONCLUSION

The analyses of the survey data reported earlier provide valuable information on how a group of experienced practitioners view juvenile justice processing in the state of Texas. Various topics were raised, including the question of minority overrepresentation in the juvenile justice system. The majority of respondents agreed with the statement that minorities are overrepresented in the juvenile justice system. Respondents also provided perceived reasons for this problem and suggested possible solutions. Some practitioners identified difficulties in contacting or communicating with the parents of minority youth. Respondents with experience in disposition decisions highlighted some of the problems decision makers encounter in placing minority youth after the disposition stage. Based on the responses to questions about the scarcity of placement slots and the role of private insurance, researchers can now have a better understanding of why many minority youth are placed in TYC facilities (Jeffords, Lindsey, and McNitt, 1993).

These practitioners evaluated a case scenario presented to them and selected criminal history as the strongest factor influencing perceptions of the offense committed in the case scenario. The case history of the juvenile and the educational level of the respondent also determined recommendations for pre- and post-adjudication actions. The race/ethnicity of the juvenile and of the respondent were significant on two counts. However, neither the race/ethnicity of the respondent nor of the juvenile was a major predictor of most judgments made by critical decision makers.

Respondents identified problems with the system and suggested solutions to these problems. Allocating more resources to the system, improving the efficiency of juvenile processing, and improving programs that address background risk factors to delinquency are the most commonly cited solutions to the problems that they outlined. Respondents also highlighted the strengths of the system, and what they consider to be the main factors that contribute to delinquency among juveniles.

A number of the suggested solutions underscored the need to develop programs that would address the background risk factors that contribute to delinquency. Respondents were asked to rate 25 different factors influencing delinquency, as well as to provide open-ended responses to possible influences on delinquent behavior. These analyses give researchers and policymakers an indication of the type of risk factors that should be targeted by new programs.

NOTE

1. When the telephone survey was terminated, there were 212 call-backs or potential interviews being pursued, 34 wrong numbers, and 101 unqualified respondents. Judges, prosecutors, and attorneys who no longer dealt with juvenile cases or, in some cases, whose names were listed by mistake in directories and membership lists constituted the majority of these 101 individuals.

9

Summary and Implications

SUMMARY

The research reported in this work was an effort to investigate possible disproportionate minority confinement (DMC) in the Texas juvenile justice system. The focus of the study was whether members of certain racial or ethnic groups (e.g., African Americans and Hispanics) were processed selectively and differently across the various stages of the juvenile justice system compared to majority youth. In particular, the research problem involved whether African-American and Hispanic youth, compared to their Anglo peers, were processed more harshly at the following decision-making stages: (1) detention during the pre-adjudication stage; (2) referral to the DA for prosecution; (3) referral to court for subsequent adjudication; and (4) sentencing to secure confinement, because of their minority status as opposed to legally relevant criteria which would explain and justify the differential treatment.

It was noted at the outset of this volume that the disproportionate minority confinement issue is reminiscent of the criminological debate which began in the 1960s concerning the "dark figure of crime" and the nature of the "real" relationship surrounding race and involvement in delinquency, in contradistinction to the "image" of crime prevalent in official crime data. On one hand, the disproportionate minority processing debate was shown to involve a "differential selection" thesis which maintains that minority youth are arrested, detained, adjudicated, and incarcerated because of their minority status and regardless of the nature, extent, and quality of their delinquent acts and prior criminal history. Alternatively, the disproportionate minority processing issue also concerns a "differential involvement" thesis which argues that minority youth are differentially handled by the system, not because of their race or ethnic status, but rather, because of a variety of legal factors such as a more serious current offense (e.g., delinquency involving personal violence or drug violations which the system may be trying to crack down on), a more extensive prior record of delinquency, accelerating recidivism, or even a history of previous lenient dispositions which have failed. Thus, unlike the differential selection thesis which posits racial bias or the stereotyping of minorities as more dangerous, the differential involvement approach posits legitimate and legally permissible factors which result in the handling of certain cases more selectively (e.g., harshly) than others.

It was demonstrated that much of the prior research into minority overrepresentation has been promulgated and shaped by federal mandates, and undoubtedly influenced by the attendant socio-political interests which often accompany such mandates. The discussion attempted to show that these federal mandates and constraints are manifestly political rather than scientific, represent ideological rather than substantive concerns, and thereby, the federal mandates have tainted the process of objective scientific inquiry. The quality of research undertaken concerning the disproportionate minority confinement issue has been diminished, and consequently, has produced a set of available findings that are highly inconclusive. It was also shown that, despite the inconclusiveness of the research data, numerous federal government publications, and a cadre of researchers who play a significant role in assisting OJJDP in its disproportionate minority confinement agenda, portray the research to the contrary, and often convey the mistaken and or distorted notion that "substantial" or "widespread" evidence exists that minority youth are being discriminated against through racist policies in the juvenile justice system across the country. The review maintained that this mischaracterization of the research literature, and the indictment of countless cores of juvenile justice practitioners, only serves to further complicate and politicize the issue and deflect attention away from the real issue. The issue which cries out for attention and solutions is the reasons for differential involvement on the part of minority youth.

A study design was developed which attempted to overcome some of the deficiencies in many prior studies. The design called for the selection of three Texas counties for which extensive case-level data collection would occur. The three counties selected represented a useful basis for comparative analyses. Two of the large urban counties in Texas were chosen; one is among the very largest, not only in the state, but also, in the nation, and a small rural county was also included. The research collected and analyzed two kinds of juvenile justice system data in the three counties.

The first set of data collected and analyzed were aggregate statistics pertaining to arrests of juveniles as recorded by the Texas Department of Public Safety for the period 1990–1994. These arrest statistics were supplemented by a second set of aggregate data from the Texas Juvenile Probation Commission concerning the delinquency cases that were referred to probation departments for further processing. These aggregate counts of arrests and referrals were then merged with population data so that incidence rates across gender, and race/ethnicity categories could be computed and analyzed. Moreover, because these aggregate data cover the period 1990–1994, they comprise a useful baseline period with which to assess the differential involvement of juveniles in various categories of crime. Texas has been experiencing population growth over the past several years, and as of 1994, Texas became the second most populous state after California. It is thus crucially necessary to document the extent to which population growth and the trends in juvenile crime are related.

In addition to aggregate data, the study conducted data collection and analysis on a random sample of offenders in each county using county automated case-management systems. This procedure facilitated the tracking of individual cases through the various processing points of the juvenile justice system. Through the application of multivariate statistical models, the research was able to investigate and determine if particular categories of youth were being processed differently as their cases moved from stage to stage of the juvenile justice system. The use of client tracking data provided two major advantages to the study. First, the assessment could directly calculate differences in the handling of youth with reference to stage-specific transition probabilities as opposed to the imprecise inferences that must be drawn from summary data. Second, client tracking permitted the establishment of relationships between case characteristics (e.g., prior record, instant offense severity) and processing decisions, and thereby permitted the determination of whether there are any race or ethnicity biases in these relationships.

A supplementary, but highly important, prong of the research project was the use of survey methodology to conduct a statewide study of the attitudes and opinions of juvenile justice practitioners. The surveys address a range of significant issues concerning the processing of delinquency cases, factors related to the genesis of delinquency, general concerns about delinquency, and the resources available in the juvenile system to respond to the problem of delinquent behavior. The use of the survey methodology was crucially necessary to tap into the underlying factors, and perhaps the value system, that various juvenile justice decision makers may be using in rendering processing decisions as a juvenile moves through the system. Further, the use of a statewide telephone survey to supplement the case-level data collection in the three study counties provided very useful comparative data that enhanced the determination of whether minority overrepresentation occurs and the identification of factors correlated with such overrepresentation.

In summary, the present study was conceived and conducted to first document the nature and extent of comparative minority involvement in the juvenile justice system in Texas, and then analyze juvenile justice decision making throughout four stages of juvenile justice processing. The study employed a multi-focused data-collection strategy which permitted the integration of various kinds of data. The findings are based on a range of appropriate statistical analyses, including the use of highly sophisticated multivariate prediction models. The research was a highly collaborative and cooperative effort among the researchers, state agencies, and county level criminal justice officials. This collaboration facilitated the conduct of the research and enhances the validity of the findings. Most important, the results reported stem from a rigorous statistical assessment of delinquency case processing through the stages of the juvenile justice system, and the research thus provides a meaningful basis for policy and program development in the future.

SUMMARY OF FINDINGS

Aggregate Measures of Delinquency

The analysis examined arrest rate data from the Department of Public Safety, and these data indicated that minority youth had been arrested for (and by implication are associated with) a higher number and greater severity of criminal activities than are Anglo youth. Based on statewide data, the inter-racial/ethnic differences between Anglo and African-American youth were particularly pronounced for violent, drug, and weapon arrests. Statewide, between 1990 and 1994, African-American youth were 5.4 times more likely than Anglo youth to be arrested for drug offenses and were 7.3 times more likely than Anglos to be arrested for violent offenses. The African-American/Anglo differences within the targeted counties were even larger, whereas the differences between Anglos and Hispanics were generally smaller. For example, based on average rates over the five-year period statewide, Hispanic youth were 2.6 times more likely than Anglo youth to be associated with violent offenses. In County-1 and, to a certain extent, in County-2 violent index arrest rates of African-American males climbed steadily during the period under study, whereas index arrest rates of Anglo and Hispanic males declined. Drug arrests for all males in County-1 and County-2 increased between 1990 and 1995. Weapon arrests of African-American and Anglo youth declined in both urban counties during the same time period.

Arrests of female youth occur at much lower rates than those of male youth. Among offenses, index and property crimes have the highest incidence among females. Minority female youth have higher arrest rates than do Anglo female youth, but the inter-racial/ethnic differences are generally smaller than those for males. Finally, arrest rates for offenses among females involving drug possession and violence increased among all three ethnic groups in County-1 and County-2. Similar to the trend observed for males, weapon arrests for females declined in the two urban counties.

The analysis also examined referral data from the Texas Juvenile Probation Commission, and these data showed the same basic findings as were found for arrests. That is, African-American youth were referred at higher rates than their Anglo and Hispanic peers. This particular trend is especially apparent with respect to violence, drugs, and weapon offenses for which the African-American-to-Anglo referral ratios were substantial. Like the arrest data, the Texas Juvenile Probation Commission data showed that the number of drug and violent offense referrals has risen over the five-year period (1990–1994), particularly for minority youth.

It was found that referrals for females occur at lower rates than those for males. Yet, it was also found that minority females have higher referrals than Anglo females, but the inter-racial/ethnic differences are generally smaller than those for males. Finally, females generally commit more index offenses involving property as compared to violence, and fewer drug or weapon crimes. However, although the incidence rates were low compared to males, statewide referrals for drug and violent offenses among all three ethnic groups increased during the 1990–1994 time period.

Disproportionate Representation Indices (DRI) for the aggregate data were also studied. In every instance, the DRI results indicated that Anglos had a DRI of less than 1.0 for both males and females. Anglos of either gender were underrepresented for all five offense types, for all three targeted counties, and for statewide data. The opposite was true for African Americans. African-American youth had the highest DRIs, and all were greater than 1.0, for all offense types and for all locations. Both male and female African-American youth were disproportionately arrested for all offenses, particularly those involving violence and drug and weapons charges. Hispanics fell between the Anglos at the low end and African Americans at the high end. However, there were cases where Hispanics were underrepresented. For example, in County-3, Hispanic males were underrepresented for all offense types, with the exception of index property crimes for which they were at parity. Similarly, Hispanic females in County-3 were underrepresented for violent and property crimes and only slightly overrepresented for total index crime (DRI = 1.14).

With very few exceptions (as noted previously), the aggregate data indicate that minority youth are overrepresented with respect to both juvenile arrests and referrals. There are, of course, alternative ways in which these results may be interpreted. First, minority youth may be overrepresented at the front end of the juvenile justice system because law enforcement differentially handles such youth. Differential police handling can involve the following: (1) more diligent patrols of minority areas; (2) singling out of minority youth for more intense scrutiny (i.e., you find what you look for); (3) discretionary arrest practices such that minority youth are arrested for their offenses (particularly the more serious), while Anglo youth are allowed to escape with just a warning. In essence, this differential police handling is the foundation of the "differential selection" thesis—minority youth show up more often in police statistics because the police are more prone to patrol areas where they will find minority youth committing crimes for which they will be arrested. Alternatively, minority youth are overrepresented with respect to juvenile arrests and referrals because they are involved in more crimes, more serous crimes, and/or crimes which have higher clearance rates (like violent crimes), thus increasing the chances of detection and arrest.

The debate cannot be resolved here, owing to the absence of data concerning the law enforcement stage and the associated police behavior when dealing with minority youth. However, in the absence of compelling competent evidence that law enforcement officers in Texas, or elsewhere for that matter, are biased and discriminatory, and routinely employ racial stereotypes, it strains credibility to assert that minority overrepresentation in arrest or referrals is more likely to be a function of differential "selection" compared to differential "involvement." In fact, the latter would be an equally, if not more compelling argument. Simply, it can justifiably be hypothesized that law enforcement officers might be expected to arrest as many suspected delinquents as possible (whether they be Anglo or minority group members) given probable cause, and allow juvenile justice authorities to sort out the subsequent decision making. If minority youth show up in the arrest statistics more often, then it is likely that their behavior, and the seriousness thereof, places them at much higher risk of detection and arrest, and then, subsequent to such arrest, detention, referral for prosecution, and so on. Interestingly, Smith et al. (1984) have provided results from very sophisticated analyses concerning race and arrest decisions which indicate that it may be the victim's race/ethnicity rather than that of the offender that is a more significant determinant of police arrest practices.

In any case, more research is needed which focuses on police practices and the extent to which such practices represent either conscious or subconscious attitudes and racial stereotypes which result in the purposive or unintentional differential scrutiny and/or arrest of minority youth. It is necessary to examine law enforcement practices, because after all, they are the major mechanism by which youth are referred to the juvenile justice system. While the decision-making process within the court process, beginning with the intake stage, may be free from differential handling of minorities, racist practices may operate before the youth are referred and the system data would not reflect such practices. Meanwhile, the prevailing evidence, from a variety of sources (including aggregate statistics, and individual-level research studies), would seem to suggest that minority youth are indeed differentially involved in delinquent activities, especially the more serious criminal acts which place them at risk for greater arrest probabilities. Future research should endeavor to resolve this point.

Case-Level Data

Individual case-level data were collected and analyzed for three Texas counties pertaining to four distinct decision points in the juvenile justice system: detention; referral of juvenile to the DA's office; court referral; and court disposition (with an emphasis on commitment to a secure facility). In theory, there were a total of 39 distinct possibilities for the differential handling of minority youth (4 system stages × 3 counties × 3 offender groups: all cases, males, and females, plus status offenders in the three counties). We only found eight occurrences for which differential handling of minorities occurred. More important, not all such occurrences were unfavorable, as three occurrences represented differential handling which favored the minority youth compared to Anglos. Thus, the present study found only five instances out of a possible 36 for which minority youth received unfavorable system processing. Of course, these findings cannot be generalized to other jurisdictions across the country. Yet, they are important because they indicate that when careful attention is placed on measuring the full range of variables necessary to explain case processing decisions, and when appropriate statistical analyses are performed, there is considerably less, and generally, quite explainable, differential handling of minority delinquents.

County-1. County-1 is one of the largest counties in Texas, with a population in excess of several million people. Generally, the results indicate that processing decisions in County-1 were based on three legally permissible offense measures: (1) severity of the current alleged offense; (2) number of prior delinquent acts; and (3) severity of prior delinquent acts. However, County-1 exhibited five of the eight differential minority handling occurrences and four of the five that represented unfavorable situations for minority youth. First, Hispanics overall and, second, Hispanic males were significantly more likely than Anglo males to be detained. Third, Hispanic and African-American males were both significantly more likely to be referred to court, compared to similarly situated Anglo males. Fourth, however, Hispanic females were significantly less likely than Anglo females to be referred to the DA's office for possible prosecution.

It was suspected that gang membership/activity might be a likely candidate for the unfavorable effects for Hispanics, overall and for males, and the one for African Americans. That is, County-1 had a significant delinquent gang problem in which Hispanic and African-American youth gangs were very active. The analyses were unable to control for gang membership in the County-1 analyses, due to the lack of reliable gang information in the database. Yet, it is still likely that if gang membership had been available as a control variable in the models, it likely would have influenced the differential effects found for Hispanic or African-American youth.

Beyond these four instances, the data indicate that at the crucial final disposition stage (i.e., the secure confinement decision), there is no evidence indicating that minority youth in County-1 receive differential (i.e., much harsher) handling from authorities than their Anglo counterparts.

County-2. County-2 had 12 possible occurrences for possible differential handling of minorities, as there were no females who received a final disposition of incarceration. Like County-1, the results for County-2 indicate that, with two exceptions (out of 12), juvenile justice authorities utilize legally permissible factors in making decisions on how to handle cases. This was the finding for "all cases" for all four decision points. County-2 did have two differential occurrences—one unfavorable and one favorable. African-American males were significantly more likely to be detained than their Anglo counterparts. However, both Hispanic and African-American females were significantly less likely to be detained compared to Anglo girls.

The results for County-2 indicate that, almost always, legally permissible and substantively meaningful factors represent the operative criteria upon which juvenile justice officials make their decisions. Consistently, severity of current offense, severity of prior offenses, and number of prior delinquent acts emerged as significant correlates of decision making for all cases and for males and females separately.

County-3. The single most important finding concerns the fact that neither race nor ethnicity was a significant factor for the two decision points in County-3 (detention and case referral to the court). Once statistical controls were introduced, no race/ethnicity effect for court probation persisted (a substitute dependent variable). Females were less likely to be prosecuted, but since only a few females were involved, the impact of gender preferences in favor of girls is not a substantial problem.

Survey of Practitioners

Minorities in the juvenile justice system. Overall, 59.6% of all respondents agreed that African-American youth are overrepresented in the Texas juvenile justice system. Across the six occupational strata, prosecutors were most likely to agree that African-American youth are overrepresented (62.8%), whereas the least likely to think so were police officers (54.9%). The results were similar with respect to Hispanic youth as a majority of respondents, 63.3%, believed that "Hispanics are represented at a significantly higher percentage in the juvenile justice system than they are in the general population in Texas." There were significant differences across racial/ethnic categories: 79% of African-American, 70.6% of Hispanic, and 58% of Anglo respondents agreed that Hispanic youth are overrepresented. Judges, attorneys, probation officers, and TYC staff were more likely than either prosecutors or police officers to agree with Hispanic overrepresentation. However, a majority of respondents across all occupational groups agreed with the statement on Hispanic overrepresentation.

Juvenile justice practitioners identified identical reasons for the perceived overrepresentation of African-American and Hispanic youth in the Texas juvenile justice system. With respect to African Americans, the most frequently stated response was "family background." Just under one-third (30.7%) of the responses listed the weakening of the family unit, single-parent households, absence of a father, lack of parental role models, or dysfunctional families. Socio-economic issues ranked a close second, as 29.6% of the respondents listed lack of employment opportunities, lack of educational attainment, and welfare dependence as factors critical to this issue. Factors related to the juvenile's environment ranked third: 21% of the responses listed high-crime neighborhoods and gang activities as crucial to the overrepresentation of African-American youth. A small percentage of respondents mentioned that the juvenile justice system has problems and/or is unfair to minorities (6.4%). Similarly, another small component, 4.8%, suggested a lack of responsibility on the part of accused youth. The three main factors identified by respondents as being responsible for Hispanic overrepresentation were the same: (1) family matters (30.6% of responses); (2) socio-economic matters (29%); and (3) matters related to the juvenile's environment (13.9%). Similar to the case for African Americans, only a few respondents mentioned that the juvenile justice system has problems and/or is unfair to minorities (5.9%). Others suggested that a lack of responsibility on the part of accused youth (3.3%) also contributed to the overrepresentation of Hispanic youth.

Respondents were also asked to suggest three main corrective actions to remedy the overrepresentation of African-American youth. Forty-one percent of the responses concerned the need for more youth-oriented programs that address background risk factors influencing delinquency. Addressing family problems (28.1% of responses) and improving economic opportunities for African Americans (16.6%) were other most often mentioned solutions. Regardless of occupational categories, respondents indicated a need for programs that address background risk factors and family problems as the two most frequently cited recommendations (the former being mentioned more often than the latter). Most respondents felt that the single best solution was to allocate more resources to programs that address background risk factors influencing delinquency. The most frequently mentioned solutions to the overrepresentation of Hispanic youth included developing programs to address background factors that influence delinquency (43.6% of responses), resolving family problems (30.7%), and improving economic opportunities for Hispanics (17.2%). It is noteworthy that the first three solutions listed here are identical to those suggested as possible solutions to the overrepresentation of African-American youth.

Views on the juvenile justice system in Texas. Additionally, about 16% of the respondents mentioned problems in the processing of juveniles in the system (delays, paperwork, lack of adequate programs, placement difficulties), and another 9% mentioned personnel-related matters (workload, remuneration). The possible solutions to these problems included some 893 answers. The three most frequently mentioned solutions to these problems were the following: (1) improvements in the system for processing juveniles—26% of responses; (2) increasing funding/resources, which also included workload, staffing, and remuneration problems—35%; and (3) programmatic solutions to address the background or risk factors for juvenile delinquency—22.1%. Roughly 25% to 35% of all respondents said that the three solutions outlined were needed. Hispanic and Anglo respondents were more likely than African Americans to list the need for additional funding and resources. African Americans were more likely to mention the need for more programs to address background factors for juvenile delinquency. Roughly one-third of the respondents mentioned the need for changes in the processing of juveniles in the system. Police and prosecutors were more likely than practitioners in the other occupations to make this suggestion.

Views on delinquency. The perception of an offender's propensity to commit delinquent acts may have important implications for how he/she is treated within the juvenile justice system. Consequently, a clear understanding of the antecedents of crime and delinquency is a prerequisite for achieving long-term solutions to the problem of the disproportional representation of minorities in the juvenile justice system. Previously, respondents underscored the need to address background factors that are correlated with delinquency. The majority of all respondents mentioned the lack of parental supervision (97.2%) and the lack of discipline by parents (92.2%) as important correlates of delinquency. Other factors, such as the influence of negative peer groups (82.5%) and abuse of alcohol or drugs by youth (79.2%), were also rated as "important" by a majority of the respondents. There were no major differences by race/ethnicity or occupation of the respondents.

At least 60% of the respondents rated the following factors as "very important" correlates of delinquency: (1) inner city kids viewing violence as a way to resolve differences (66.2%); (2) making personal choices to commit delinquent acts (65.2%); (3) living in high-crime neighborhoods (64.2%); (4) not knowing positive ways to interact with others (64.1%); (5) having psychological or emotional problems (62.5%); (6) performing negatively in school (61.4%); and (7) having siblings who are delinquent (60.9%). Other factors that the majority of respondents ranked as "important" were: (1) the inability to control impulses (59.9%); (2) being a victim of child abuse (58.6%); and (3) failure in socialization of youth (56.1%).

An interesting issue was whether responses surrounding the factors influencing delinquency varied according to the race/ethnicity or occupation of the respondent. Among the top four factors behind delinquency, no noticeable differences by occupation or race/ethnicity were evident. As for the other factors, a smaller proportion of prosecutors than practitioners in the other occupations was inclined to think that "inner city kids see violence as a way to resolve differences." Similarly, smaller proportions of police and attorneys supported the view that "making personal choices to commit delinquent acts" was an important factor influencing delinquency. A larger share of Anglo respondents were likely to rate this as an "important" factor.

In general, smaller proportions of judges, prosecutors, and police officers felt that "not knowing positive ways to interact" (or having poor social skills) and "living in bad neighborhoods" were important predictors of delinquency. A higher proportion of respondents in both minority groups believed that having poor social skills is correlated with delinquency. African Americans were more likely to pinpoint high-crime neighborhoods as a factor in delinquency. Except for prosecutors and attorneys, the majority of respondents from most occupational groups rated negative performance in school or poor grades as "very important." Over two-thirds of minority respondents felt this way, in contrast to 58% of Anglo respondents.

Proportionally larger numbers of judges and probation officers indicated that having psychological and emotional problems influenced delinquency. Seventy-one percent of Hispanic respondents indicated that this was an important factor, a larger proportion than for the other two groups. Prosecutors and attorneys were less likely to support the view that negative school performance or bad grades contribute to delinquency. In contrast, a larger share of minority respondents felt that negative performance in school contributed to delinquency. Attorneys and TYC staff were more likely to place importance on the role of delinquent siblings. Hispanics tended to support this view, as well. Police and prosecutors indicated that "an inability to control impulses," or poor self-control, was less likely to influence delinquency. No differences by race/ethnicity are evident.

Judges, probation officers, and attorneys were more likely to believe that child abuse influences delinquency. Proportionally, more Anglo and Hispanic respondents supported this perspective. Except for prosecutors, a majority of respondents from all occupational groups believed that failure in socialization contributes to delinquency. A larger proportion of Hispanic and African-American respondents also supported this view. Larger proportions of police, probation officers, attorneys, and, to a lesser extent, judges believed that living with a single mother was a factor influencing delinquency. A larger number of Hispanic and African-American respondents also supported this view.

A majority of judges rated media portrayals of violence as "very important." Hispanics and African-American respondents also supported this item in larger proportions. Concerning the role of media advertising, a majority of probation officers felt that it was an important factor influencing delinquency, the only group that felt this way.

Case scenario evaluation. In order to test for subtle forms of racial stereotyping, respondents were presented with case scenarios with which we tested statistical models surrounding the following topics: (1) perceived seriousness of the offense; (2) perceived dangerousness of the offense; (3) likelihood that the offender will commit offenses in future; and (4) overall perceived threat of the offender. In all analyses, criminal history was the most important factor influencing perceptions. Generally, having a more serious criminal history was associated with a maximum predicted estimate of between 16% and 25% in the dependent variables being examined.

The survey also provided for an analysis of the recommendations for the actions to be taken in both the pre-adjudication and disposition stages. Respondents were asked to judge what would happen after the juvenile had been turned over to the juvenile probation authorities. At the pre-adjudication stage, the actions selected by the respondents were ranked (a list was provided and open-ended responses were encouraged). The 516 responses were re-coded from the least severe (charges dropped, juveniles sent home—35.6% of responses) to the most severe (detention in a facility—46.9% of responses). Diversion to alternative programs (13.3% of responses) and in-home detention (4% of responses) were ranked between these two extremes.

The results clearly indicated that the factors associated with the recommended actions were the following: (1) the juvenile's criminal history; (2) the respondent's educational level; and (3) whether the respondent was Hispanic, rather than Anglo. The more extensive the criminal history, the more likely severe pre-adjudication actions were recommended. Respondents with bachelor's degrees recommended less severe actions than those without college degrees. Hispanic respondents chose less severe pre-adjudication actions than did Anglo respondents.

Five hundred and sixteen post-adjudication outcomes were provided by respondents. These were based on a provided list and open-ended responses. The responses were re-coded from the least severe (probation at home—71.6% of responses) to the most severe (placement in a secure facility or certification as an adult—20.5% of the responses). Outside-home probation was the intermediate category (8% of responses). In the analyses of post-adjudication outcomes, the juvenile offender's criminal history was the only statistically significant variable in explaining the severity of post-adjudication recommendations. The most extensive criminal histories were associated with more severe dispositions.

Clearly, the findings indicated that the juvenile offender's criminal history, not his/her race or ethnic background, was the strongest predictor of respondents' perceptions of the seriousness of the juvenile's offense, the likelihood of future criminal activities, and actions likely to be taken at the both the pre- and post-adjudication stages. Someone with a first offense is ranked a significant 1.01 points lower than a juvenile with two prior offenses, in terms of the severity of pre-adjudication actions recommended by respondents. The respondent's educational level was another consistent predictor of perceptions, with one education variable being significant in five of the seven models considered. The race/ethnicity of the juvenile, especially being Hispanic, and the respondent's race/ethnicity were significant in three models, but no clear pattern is discernible. It is unclear why offenses committed by Hispanic youth were ranked as less serious or why the likelihood of their committing other similar offenses was ranked lower than that of Anglo youth. However, it is noteworthy that a juvenile's race/ethnicity is not correlated with the recommended actions at pre- and post-adjudication stages. Finally, the race/ethnicity of the respondent was significant in determining perceptions and actions in two models. Hispanic ethnicity was associated with a less serious perception of the offense, and Hispanics were less likely to recommend severe actions at the pre-adjudication stage.

IMPLICATIONS

Race and Delinquency Involvement

The most important implication of this research and its associated commentary on disproportionate minority confinement concerns research and theory development into the connection between race/ethnicity and involvement in delinquency. The results indicate that criminology can ill afford to continue a research agenda that so adamantly refuses to acknowledge the existence of racial and ethnic differentials in the prevalence, incidence, and severity of delinquency, that it is unable to explain the causes of such differences. The findings show an absence of strong and consistent race and ethnic differentials in juvenile processing in Texas. In fact, the findings indicate that even when such differentials occur, they do not affect the most important stage of juvenile justice decision making—the final disposition stage. Thus, the disproportionate minority confinement issue with its presumptive stance of racial and ethnic discrimination must be unmasked and exposed as an ill-advised political diversion that has for too long deflected proper attention away from the fundamental issue. The fundamental issue is the extent to which race, and to a lesser extent ethnicity, are significantly associated with a more pronounced involvement in delinquency generally, and serious acts of delinquent behavior in particular. Yet, the literature continues to sidestep the issue, and offers instead, observations which obfuscate the key issue and continually propose the wrong research agenda. For example, Pope and Feyerherm have suggested the following:

> Thus, differential involvement in youth crime may, in part, account for the increasing number of minorities coming into contact with the juvenile justice system. However, differential involvement in crime is a different issue from what happens to youthful offenders once they enter the juvenile justice system. (1993: 1)

This research provides strong evidence with which to disagree with the view of Pope and Feyerherm. The differential involvement of minorities in youth crime is not a different (and separate) issue, in fact, it is the real essence of the disproportionate minority confinement problem. In effect, if a greater prevalence of minority youth commit delinquent offenses, then there will be more such youth available for processing at each point of the juvenile justice process compared to Anglo youth. Moreover, if minority youth do in fact commit more serious delinquent acts, have longer and more serious prior records, and perhaps, even have more recent court contacts than Anglo offenders, then they face a much greater risk of receiving "unfavorable," but legally permissible, decisions at each and every stage of the process. This risk of what the DMC advocates call harsh treatment will be higher for minority youth, not because they are members of a racial or ethnic minority, but rather, because the nature and severity of their delinquency careers warrant decisions such as detention, referral for prosecution, and even confinement upon adjudication. The consequence is that minority youth will be disproportionately represented at each and every stage of the juvenile justice process owing to legitimate legal criteria.

It is incorrect, as Pope and Feyerherm have done, to separate the issue of differential involvement from the issue of differential processing. It is this artificial and unjustified separation which allows the perpetuation of the OJJDP agenda and associated mandates. As has been noted previously, this agenda asserts that any evidence whatsoever of disproportionate minority confinement is immediately suspect and requires further assessment in order to avoid funding problems under the formula grant program. It would appear, therefore, that valuable resources are being wasted on juvenile justice processing issues rather than devoting the vast majority of such resources to the problem of delinquency proneness and the associated risk factors which place minority youth in a complex of social and environmental factors pushing them toward delinquent conduct.

Thus, the problem of disproportionate involvement of minorities in delinquency is almost surely one of societal inequities rather than practitioner racism, and equally surely, the juvenile justice system cannot be expected to overcome the societal disadvantages that place minority youth at much greater risk of starting a delinquency career, continuing it through their youth, and ultimately, making the transition to a life of adult crime as we have reported elsewhere (Tracy and Kempf-Leonard, 1996). Elliott has perhaps captured the real essence of the issue:

> Yet, once involved in a lifestyle that includes serious forms of violence, theft, and substance use, persons from disadvantaged families and neighborhoods find it difficult to escape. They have fewer opportunities for conventional adult roles, and they are more deeply embedded in and dependent upon the gangs and the illicit economy that flourish in their neighborhoods. (1994: 19)

A strong implication of this study is that future research should be less concerned with whether the extensive race and ethnic differences in criminality are real or represent nothing more than an artifact of society's response to delinquency. Future research must devote more attention, and more focused attention, to delinquency where it is located most often, and on the conditions which foster the differences that have been observed time and time again. It has been shown that the prevalence and incidence of juvenile crime differs by subgroups such as race, ethnicity, social class, and gender (Tracy and Kempf-Leonard, 1996). Particularly when measured by official records, minority groups of color are overrepresented and females are underrepresented among serious offenses, and females are overrepresented among status offenses and child welfare cases. Thus far neither the argument that these distributions reflect true behavioral differences nor the argument that police and other officials are selectively targeting subgroups has been found to be solely correct.

Thus, I strongly endorse the position offered by Sampson and Wilson (1995) that criminology must develop a macro-social or community-level focus in order to investigate and disentangle the structural and cultural correlates of crime. Two recent publications (Hawkins, Laub, and Lauritsen, 1998; Hawkins, Laub, Lauritsen, and Cothem, 2000) endorse and extend the suggestions of Sampson and Wilson (1995), and offer valuable insights as to what a community-level research agenda might look like and how it might elucidate previously elusive aspects of crime. Specifically they suggest that:

> Multilevel research designs and theories that reflect a variety of analytic methods can further the study of serious and violent juvenile crime, especially when attempting to identify and account for ethnic and racial differences. The insights gained from such research have policy-related implications. Public policy aimed at reducing serious and violent juvenile offending should adopt the goal of transforming urban communities, especially in light of past trends in the concentration of urban poverty. (Hawkins et al., 2000: 4)

The suggestions of these researchers are important. It must be stressed, therefore, that the only useful research agenda is one which acknowledges race differences, and then proposes a worthwhile strategy to understand and explain the many and complex effects. Moreover, the need to examine multi-level effects of economic well-being is underscored by a recent study that found crime was not attributable to social disorder, but rather the source of each crime was economic disadvantage, including concentrated poverty, and combinations of residential and commercial land use (Sampson and Raudenbush, 1999). A multi-level orientation clearly is critical if research will ever be able to identify, understand, and hopefully make progress in remedying the conditions that give rise to differential crime in the first place.

Researchers can make productive use of the information available from the 2000 U.S. Census as it will provide measures of the prevalence of economic prosperity, including median income, families living below the poverty line, welfare recipients, residential stability, owner-occupied houses, and female-headed households. The cleavages may actually have increased between the "haves" and "have nots" in the recent past so it will be important to assess the extent to which the spatially concentrated areas of poverty observed previously now have diminished or become more diffused. Such improvement would have significant effect on the crime attributed to relative deprivation, particularly the abject poverty of the underclass that Currie (1993) called "endemic." New suggestions for understanding the spatial distributions of race and social disadvantage make clear the need also to examine concentration, exposure, city-level centralization, clustering, evenness, and a combination "hyper-segregation" index of these five dimensions (Massey and Denton, 1988, 1989).

Of course, it is one thing to search for the societal correlates of delinquency and crime; it is quite another thing to convince government authorities and marshal support for the principle that the most effective crime fighting strategy is one which addresses the underlying social conditions and factors that facilitate or predispose some people to commit crimes. Ira Schwartz, who has devoted his professional life to the juvenile justice system, has noted that, "it is sheer folly to think that we will be able to tackle the juvenile crime problem effectively without addressing some of the country's broader domestic issues" (1987: 177). Schwartz's view makes a great deal of sense. It is abundantly clear that basic societal problems, and the most crucial one to be addressed in the near future, are the amelioration of those circumstances which lead to poverty and differential social and economic opportunity and to poor school achievement, which in turn are all strongly related to early involvement of juveniles with the police and juvenile courts. Prevention and intervention strategies that uncover and eliminate the social, psychological, physiological, and other, as yet to be determined, influences which produce these unacceptable social and moral faults in the development of our youth must be discovered and implemented. This posture must take the form of a national policy which is given the highest possible priority and which enjoys the allocation of substantial and sustained resources.

While it might be expected that local communities have an abundance of private social service organizations and grassroots movements that provide youth-oriented programs, such appears not to be the case. A recent study conducted in Washington, D.C., by Chaiken (2000) for OJJDP examined the types of delinquent behavior found among boys living in the three most violent neighborhoods in the district, and the role of basic institutions such as families, schools, churches, and youth-serving organizations in the lives of the boys. Chaiken found that, although the Mayor's Youth Initiative maintained a listing of some 618 programs, only 72 were chartered as delinquency prevention and 40 of these provided services to already adjudicated youth or youth who were awaiting trial. Further, not only did Chaiken find that there were comparatively few programs which targeted delinquency prevention, she also discovered barriers to the effective delivery of services, for example lack of coordination and inactive coalitions.

Juvenile Justice Policy

It may be that the disproportionate confinement of minority youth may be less a result of racist or discriminatory practices of juvenile justice authorities and more so a function of get tough juvenile policies that have been implemented across the country these past 20 years. The general public is often frustrated with the perceived volume of crime, and currently, with juvenile crime in particular, regardless of whether crime is actually increasing. Moreover, all too often, the public outcry produces hard-line pronouncements among politicians and lawmakers of "a war on crime." Often, these pronouncements are nothing more than attempts to assuage the fears of the electorate. There has been growing disillusionment with the traditional objectives of juvenile justice and its emphasis on rehabilitation rather than punishment. This disillusionment is stimulated by the image of a "new" type of delinquent. The apparent failure of the traditional "benign hand" of juvenile justice has been challenged by the accumulation of contrary evidence that has prompted many jurisdictions to reevaluate juvenile justice philosophy and procedures. Simply, the disillusionment stems from a recognition that many juvenile offenders no longer fit the prototype of the immature offender who commits only occasional acts of crime, and in fact, many of today's offenders are really indistinguishable from adult criminals except for the fact that they are younger.

For example, Ohlin (1983) noted a distinct shift in juvenile justice policy reflecting a strong conservative reaction to the liberal policies that had been advocated by the President's Commission on Law Enforcement and Administration of Justice (1967). In Ohlin's opinion, the growing fear of crime and increasing demands for repressive action led to more punitive sentencing and to a rapid escalation of incarcerations and the length of sentence to be served (1983: 466). Ohlin further argued that the "just deserts" approach began spreading to the juvenile system as well. He writes:

> In many states we see increasing incarceration even as delinquency rates decline. Juvenile reform legislation now calls for more mandatory sentencing and more determinate sentences for juveniles, lowering of the upper age of juvenile jurisdiction, greater ease in obtaining waivers to adult court for juvenile prosecution, and greater access to juvenile records. (1983: 467)

The shift that Ohlin observed produced more and more "get tough" approaches across the country. At about the same time, Rubin (1985), a noted juvenile law jurist, also discussed a wave of highly punitive-oriented legislation that began sweeping across the country. Naturally, the consequence of transforming juvenile courts into a more punitive venue than has ever been the case, is that more juveniles, perhaps at increasing rates, began receiving more punitive sanctions than would ordinarily be the norm under the traditional philosophy of juvenile justice. In this regard, Krisberg and Austin have contended that: "The increase [in the proportion of young people processed through the juvenile court and juvenile corrections systems between 1980 and 1990] was due to more formal punitive juvenile justice policies that produced more court referrals and expanded use of detention and juvenile incarceration" (1993: 171). In addition to stiffer juvenile proceedings, there appears to be an increasing utilization of transfer or waiver procedures whereby juveniles alleged to be the most "dangerous" are being transferred to adult court. Unfortunately, this "get tough" philosophy is characterized by greater use of detention at the front end of the process, and subsequently incarcerates more youth, both majority and minority, than may be necessary at the final stage. Thus, it would seem to be a prudent time to consider Bernard's (1992) recommendation for a model of juvenile justice in which the objective is to communicate to youth that their actions have consequences by utilizing a multi-stage treatment approach which extends from "counsel and release" at the police encounter stage to criminal court punishment. He has argued that the sanctions should be broadly applied and the vast majority of delinquents should be involved in an extensive network of community-based services. He also sees a need for small, treatment-oriented, secure juvenile facilities as the last resort, but with the potential for better results when used only for the most serious offenders.

My colleague and I (Tracy and Kempf-Leonard, 1996, 1998) have also provided comprehensive discussions of juvenile sanctioning models and we have argued along similar lines to Bernard. We have suggested that juvenile justice must adopt a philosophy of early intervention, but that, if early intervention efforts fail, then subsequent efforts should attempt to deter further delinquency through a set of "progressive sanctions" which gradually intensify the severity of the juvenile court's response. We have further suggested that a system of progressive sanctions should produce noticeable success at each stage. Delinquents can expect to receive a progressively more restrictive disposition each and every time they recidivate, and when such sanctions are not only promised but in fact delivered, some youth may amend their behavior. Moreover, even if there are varying degrees of success achieved through progressive sanctions, a predictable and measured court disposition is far preferable to the unfortunate practice of waiting until it is too late to be effective and the juvenile court response is reduced to mere punitiveness rather than prevention.

It is obvious that, in order for the juvenile justice system to fulfill the goals of accountability and personal responsibility, it is crucial that the responses to juvenile crime reflect a coordinated and comprehensive policy among police, courts, probation, and corrections officials, a system in which information about initial decisions is communicated to those who might subsequently encounter the youth. Juvenile justice interventions must be perceived by offenders as significant and they need to be enacted early in delinquency careers when they can be of the greatest effect, not delayed until after the deviant lifestyle is reinforced. Clearly, a strategic juvenile justice policy, such as progressive sanctions, with its reliance on graduated and gently escalating penalties, would likely reduce unnecessary detentions and incarcerations for all youth. However, of greater significance is the possibility that a strategic juvenile justice policy, like progressive sanctions, would serve even more important goals: (1) the reduction of juvenile recidivism; (2) the disruption of a nascent criminal career; and (3) the prevention of an adult criminal career altogether.

The issue of the differential handling of minorities within the juvenile justice system is extremely important. But it must be determined, not merely speculated, that such differential handling results from discrimination rather than legally permissible variables upon which juvenile justice agents should rely in rendering a disposition. When the disparity is due to racist policies or agents (i.e., "differential selection"), then corrective action must be taken. But, even when the disparity is legitimate and is due to "differential involvement," then corrective action may still be warranted. In this regard, the best possible remedy to disproportionate minority confinement, and more broadly, unnecessarily punitive handling of youth of any race or ethnicity, is a system of juvenile justice that begins the intervention process early and gently, but predictably, and only escalates when absolutely justified. By so doing, dispositions are more predictable and standardized, and the opportunities for differential or arbitrarily punitive handling are thereby reduced concomitantly.

Bibliography

Austin, J. 1995. The overrepresentation of minority youth in the California juvenile justice system: Perceptions and realities. In K. Kempf-Leonard, C.E. Pope, and W.H. Feyerherm (Eds.), *Minorities in juvenile justice* (pp. 153–178). Thousand Oaks, CA: Sage.

Austin, J., Dimas, J., and Steinhart, D. 1991. The overrepresentation of minority youth in California's secure facilities. San Francisco: California State Advisory Group on Juvenile Justice and the California Office of Criminal Justice Planning.

Baily, W., and Peterson, R. 1981. Legal versus extra-legal determinants of juvenile court dispositions. *Juvenile and Family Court Journal,* 32: 41–59.

Bernard, T. 1992. *The cycle of juvenile justice.* New York: Oxford University Press.

Bilchik, S. 1999. Minorities in the juvenile justice system. *Juvenile Justice Bulletin: 1999 National Report Series.* Washington, DC: Office of Juvenile Justice and Delinquency Prevention.

Bishop, D.M., and Frazier, C.E. 1988a. The influence of race in juvenile justice processing. *Journal of Research in Crime and Delinquency,* 25: 242–263.

Bishop, D.M., and Frazier, C.E. 1988b. A study of race and juvenile justice processing in Florida. Unpublished report, University of Florida.

Bishop, D.M., and Frazier, C.E. 1996. Race effects in juvenile justice decision making: Findings of a statewide analysis. *Journal of Criminal Law & Criminology,* 86: 393–414.

Black, T.E., and Smith, C.P. 1981. A preliminary national assessment of the numbers and characteristics of juveniles processed in the juvenile justice system. *Reports of the national juvenile justice assessment centers.* Washington, DC: Office of Juvenile Justice and Delinquency Prevention.

Blumstein, A. 1982. On the racial disproportionality in the United States' prison populations. *Journal of Criminal Law & Criminology*, 73: 1259–1281.

Bodenhausen, G.V., and Lichenstein, M. 1987. Social stereotypes and information processing: The impact of task complexity. *Journal of Personality and Social Psychology*, 52: 871–880.

Bodenhausen, G.V., and Wyer, R.S. 1985. Effects of stereotypes on decision-making and information-processing strategies. *Journal of Personality and Social Psychology*, 48: 267–282.

Bortner, M., and Reed, W. 1985. The preeminence of process: An example of refocused justice research. *Social Science Quarterly*, 66: 413–425.

Bortner, M., Sunderland, M., and Winn, R. 1985. Race and the impact of juvenile deinstitutionalization. *Crime and Delinquency*, 31: 35–46.

Bridges, G.S., Conley, D.J., Beretta, G., and Engen, R.L. 1993. Racial disproportionality in the juvenile justice system: Final report. Olympia, WA: Department of Social and Health Services.

Bridges, G.S., Conley, D.J., Engen, R.L., and Price-Spratlen, T. 1995. Racial disparities in the confinement of juveniles: Effects of crime and community social structure on punishment. In K. Kempf-Leonard, C.E. Pope, and W.H. Feyerherm (Eds.), *Minorities in juvenile justice* (pp. 128–152). Thousand Oaks, CA: Sage.

Bridges, G.S., and Steen, S. 1998. Racial disparities in official assessments of juvenile offenders: Attributional stereotypes as mediating mechanisms. *American Sociological Review*, 63: 554–570.

Center for Substance Abuse Prevention. 1993. Prevention strategies based on individual risk factors for alcohol and other drug abuse (CSAP Technical Report, No. 7). Washington, DC: U.S. Department of Health and Human Services.

Cernkovich, S.A., Giordano, P.C., and Pugh, M.D. 1985. Chronic offenders: The missing cases in self-report delinquency research. *Journal of Criminal Law and Criminology*, 76: 705–732.

Chaiken, M.R. 2000. *Violent neighborhoods, violent kids*. Washington, DC: Office of Juvenile Justice and Delinquency Prevention.

Clegg, R. 2000, July 17. Race and crime. *Legal Times*.

Cohen, L.E., and Kluegel, J.R. 1978. Determinants of juvenile court dispositions: Ascriptive and achieved factors in two metropolitan courts. *American Sociological Review*, 43: 162–176.

Cohen, L.E., and Kluegel, J.R. 1979. Selecting delinquents for adjudication. *Journal of Research in Crime and Delinquency*, 16: 143–163.

Community Research Associates. 1992. Technical assistance materials for the states. Champaign, IL: Author.

Currie, E. 1993. *Reckoning: Drugs, the cities, and the American future*. New York: Hill & Wang.

Curtis, L.A. 1989. Race and violent crime: Toward a new policy. In N.A. Weiner and M.E. Wolfgang (Eds.), *Violent crime, violent criminals* (pp. 139–170). Newbury Park, CA: Sage Publications.

Devine, P., Coolbaugh, K., and Jenkins, S. 1998. Disproportionate minority confinement: Lessons learned from five states. *Juvenile Justice Bulletin*. Washington, DC: Office of Juvenile Justice and Delinquency Prevention.

Duncan, B.L. 1976. Differential social perception and attribution of intergroup violence: Testing the lower limits of stereotyping of Blacks. *Journal of Personality and Social Psychology,* 34: 590–598.

Eaton, A.W., and Kruglanski, A.W. 1991. Person perception by introverts and extraverts under time pressure: Effects of need for closure. *Personality and Social Psychology Bulletin,* 17: 161–165.

Elliott, D.S., 1994. Serious violent offenders: Onset, developmental course, and termination. *Criminology,* 32: 1–21.

Elliott, D.S., and Ageton, S.S. 1980. Reconciling race and class differences in self-reported and official estimates of delinquency. *American Sociological Review,* 45: 95–100.

Fagan, J., Slaughter, E., and Hartstone, E. 1987. Blind justice? The impact of race on the juvenile justice process. *Crime and Delinquency,* 33: 224–258.

Farrington, D.P. 1973. Self-reports of deviant behavior: Predictive and stable? *Journal of Criminal Law and Criminology,* 64: 99–110.

Federal Register, August 8, 1989.

Federal Register, May 31, 1995.

Feld, B.C. 1989. The right to counsel in juvenile court: An empirical study of when lawyers appear and the difference they make. *Journal of Criminal Law & Criminology,* 79: 1185–1346.

Feld, B.C. 1995. The social context of juvenile justice administration: Racial disparities in an urban juvenile court. In K. Kempf-Leonard, C.E. Pope, and W.H. Feyerherm (Eds.), *Minorities in juvenile justice* (pp. 66–97). Thousand Oaks, CA: Sage.

Feyerherm, W. 1981. Juvenile court dispositions of status offenders: An analysis of case dispositions. In R.L. McNeely and C.E. Pope (Eds.), *Race, crime and criminal justice* (pp. 127–144). Thousand Oaks, CA: Sage.

Feyerherm, W. 1993. The status of the states: A review of state materials regarding overrepresentation of minority youth in the juvenile justice system. Unpublished report, Portland State University, Portland, Oregon.

Feyerherm, W. 1995. The DMC initiative: The convergence of policy and research themes. In K. Kempf-Leonard; C.E. Pope; and W.H. Feyerherm (Eds.), *Minorities in juvenile justice* (pp. 1–15). Thousand Oaks, CA: Sage.

Fisk, S., and Taylor, S. 1991. *Social cognition.* New York: McGraw-Hill.

Fleming, R.B., Nardulli, P.F., and Eisenstein, J. 1992. *The craft of justice.* Philadelphia: University of Pennsylvania Press.

Frazier, C.E., and Bishop, D.M. 1995. Reflections on race effects in juvenile justice. In K. Kempf-Leonard, C.E. Pope, and W.H. Feyerherm (Eds.), *Minorities in juvenile justice* (pp. 16–46). Thousand Oaks, CA: Sage.

Frazier, C.E., Bishop, D.M., and Henretta, J.C. 1992. The social context of race differentials in juvenile justice dispositions. *Sociological Quarterly,* 33: 447–458.

Hagan, J., and Peterson, R. 1995. Criminal inequality in America: Patterns and consequences. In J. Hagan and R. Peterson (Eds.), *Crime and Inequality,* (pp. 14–36). Stanford, CA: Stanford University Press.

Hammond, K.R. 1948. Measuring attitudes by error-choice: An indirect method. *Journal of Abnormal and Social Psychology,* 43: 38–48.

Hamparian, D.M., Davis, J.M., Jacobson, J.M., and McGraw, R.T. 1985. The young criminal years of the violent few. Washington, DC: U.S. Government Printing Office.

Hamparian, D.M., and Leiber, M.J. 1997. Disproportionate confinement of minority juveniles in secure facilities: 1996 national report. Champaign, IL: Community Research Associates.

Hamparian, D.M., Schuster, R.S., Dinitz, S., and Conrad, J.P. 1978. *The violent few: A study of dangerous juvenile offenders*. Lexington, MA: D.C. Heath.

Hawkins, D.F., Laub, J.H., and Lauritsen, J.L. 1998. Race, ethnicity and serious juvenile offending. In R. Loeber and D.P. Farrington (Eds.), *Serious and violent juvenile offenders* (pp. 30–46). Thousand Oaks, CA: Sage.

Hawkins, D.F., Laub, J.H., Lauritsen, J.L., and Cothern, L. 2000. Race, ethnicity, and serious violent juvenile offending. *Juvenile Justice Bulletin*. Washington, DC: Office of Juvenile Justice and Delinquency Prevention.

Heckman, J. 1979. Sample selection bias as a specification error. *Econometrica,* 47: 153–161.

Hindelang, M.J. 1978. Race and involvement in crime. *American Sociological Review,* 43: 93–109.

Hindelang, M.J., Hirschi, T., and Weis, J.G. 1979. Correlates of delinquency: The illusion of discrepancy between self-report and official measures. *American Sociological Review,* 44: 995–1014.

Hindelang, M.J., Hirschi, T., and Weis, J.G. 1981. *Measuring delinquency.* Beverly Hills, CA: Sage Publications.

Horwitz, A., and Wasserman, M. 1980. Some misleading conceptions in sentencing research. *Criminology,* 19: 411–424.

Howell, J.C. 1997. *Juvenile justice and youth violence.* Thousand Oaks, CA: Sage.

Hsia, H.M., and Hamparian, D. 1998. Disproportionate minority confinement: 1997 update. *Juvenile Justice Bulletin.* Washington, DC: Office of Juvenile Justice and Delinquency Prevention.

Huizinga, D., and Elliott, D.S. 1987. Juvenile offenders: Prevalence, offender incidence, and arrest rates by race. *Crime and Delinquency,* 33: 206–223.

Jeffords, C., Lindsey, J., and McNitt, S. 1993. Overrepresentation of minorities in the juvenile justice system. Austin, TX: Texas Youth Commission.

Johnson, J., and Secret P. 1992. Race and juvenile court decision making revisited. *Criminal Justice Policy Review,* 4: 124–139.

Kelley, B.T., Huizinga, D., Thornberry, T.P., and Loeber, R. 1997. Epidemiology of serious violence. *Juvenile Justice Bulletin.* Washington, DC: Office of Juvenile Justice and Delinquency Prevention.

Kempf, K.L., 1992. The role of race in juvenile justice in Pennsylvania. Shippensburg, PA: The Center for Juvenile Justice Training and Research.

Kempf, K.L., Decker, S.H., and Bing, R. 1990. An analysis of apparent disparities in the handling of black youth: Technical report. St. Louis: University of Missouri–St. Louis, Department of Administration of Justice, Center for Metropolitan Studies.

Kempf-Leonard, K.L., Pope, C.E., and Feyerherm, W.H. (Eds.). 1995. *Minorities in juvenile justice.* Thousand Oaks, CA: Sage.

Kempf-Leonard, K.L., and Sontheimer, H. 1995. The role of race in juvenile justice in Pennsylvania. In K.L. Kempf-Leonard, C.E. Pope, and W.H. Feyerherm (Eds.), *Minorities in juvenile justice* (pp. 98–127). Thousand Oaks, CA: Sage.

Kennedy, Randall. 1997. *Race, crime, and the law.* New York: Pantheon Books.

Kowalski, G., and Rickicki, J. 1982. Determinants of juvenile post-adjudication dispositions. *Journal of Research in Crime and Delinquency,* 19: 66–83.

Krisberg, B., and Austin, J.F. 1993. *Reinventing juvenile justice.* Newbury Park, CA: Sage.

Kruglanski, A.W., and Freund, T. 1983. The freezing and unfreezing of law inferences: Effects on impressional primacy, ethnic stereotyping, and numerical anchoring. *Journal of Experimental Social Psychology,* 19: 448–468.

LaFree, G. 1995. Race and crime trends in the United States, 1946–1990. In D.F. Hawkins (Ed.), *Ethnicity, race, and crime: Perspectives across time and place* (pp. 169–193). Albany: State University of New York Press.

Leiber, M.J. 1992. *Juvenile justice decision making in Iowa: An analysis of the influences of race on case processing in three counties.* Cedar Falls, IA: University of Northern Iowa.

Lockhart, L., Kurtz, P., Stutphen, R., and Gauger, K. 1991. *Georgia's juvenile justice system: A retrospective investigation of racial disparity.* Athens: University of Georgia Press.

MacKenzie, L.R. 1999. Residential placement of adjudicated youth, 1987–1996. Fact Sheet, #117. Washington, DC: Office of Juvenile Justice and Delinquency Prevention.

Mann, C.R. 1993. *Unequal justice: The question of color.* Bloomington, IN: Indiana University Press.

Massey, D.S., and Denton, N.A. 1988. The dimensions of residential segregation. *Social Forces,* 67(2): 281–315.

Massey, D.S., and Denton, N.A. 1989. Hyper segregation in U.S. metropolitan areas: Black and Hispanic segregation along five dimensions. *Demography,* 26(3): 373–391.

McCarthy, B.R. 1985. An analysis of detention. *Juvenile and Family Court Journal,* 36: 49–50.

McCarthy, B.R., and Smith, B.L. 1986. The conceptualization of discrimination in the juvenile justice process: The impact of administrative factors and screening decisions on juvenile court dispositions. *Criminology,* 24: 41–64.

National Coalition of State Juvenile Justice Advisory Groups. 1987. *An act of empowerment.* Bethesda, MD: Author.

National Coalition of State Juvenile Justice Advisory Groups. 1989. *A report on the delicate balance.* Bethesda, MD: Author.

Ohlin, L.E. 1983. The future of juvenile justice policy. *Crime and Delinquency,* 29: 463–472.

Petersilia, J. 1983. *Racial disparities in the criminal justice system.* Santa Monica, CA: Rand Corporation.

Poe-Yamagata, E., and Jones, M.A. 2000. *And justice for some.* Oakland, CA: National Council on Crime and Delinquency.

Pope, C.E. 1984. Blacks and juvenile crime: A review. In D.E. Georges-Abeyie (Ed.), *The criminal justice system and blacks.* New York: Clark Boardman.

Pope, C.E., and Feyerherm, W.H. 1990a. Minority status and juvenile justice processing: An assessment of the research literature (Part I). *Criminal Justice Abstracts,* 22: 327–335.

Pope, C.E., and Feyerherm, W.H. 1990b. Minority status and juvenile justice processing: An assessment of the research literature (Part II). *Criminal Justice Abstracts,* 22: 527–542.

Pope, C.E., and Feyerherm, W.H. 1992. Minorities and the juvenile justice system. Washington, DC: Office of Juvenile Justice and Delinquency Prevention.

Pope, C.E., and Feyerherm, W.H. 1993. Minorities and the juvenile justice system: Research summary. Washington, DC: Office of Juvenile Justice and Delinquency Prevention.

Pope, C.E., and Feyerherm, W.H. 1995. Minorities and the juvenile justice system. Washington, DC: Office of Juvenile Justice and Delinquency Prevention, Second printing.

President's Commission on Law Enforcement and Administration of Justice. 1967. *The challenge of crime in a free society.* Washington, DC: U.S. Government Printing Office.

Prothrow-Stith, D. (with Weissman, M.). 1991. *Deadly consequences.* New York: Harper Collins Publishers.

Public Policy Research Institute. 1997. *Juvenile justice in Texas: Factors correlated with processing decisions.* College Station, TX: Texas A&M University.

Rubin, H.T. 1985. *Juvenile justice: Policy practice and law.* New York: Random House.

Sager, A.H., and Schofield, J.W. 1980. Racial and behavioral cues in Black and White children's perceptions of ambiguously aggressive acts. *Journal of Personality and Social Psychology,* 39: 590–598.

Sampson, R.J., and Raudenbush, S. 1999. Project on Human Development in Chicago Neighborhoods, 1999 Annual Report. Cambridge, MA: Harvard University.

Sampson, R.J., and Wilson, W.J. 1995. Toward a theory of race, crime, and urban inequality. In J.D. Hagan and R.D. Peterson (Eds.), *Crime and inequality* (pp. 37–54). Stanford, CA: Stanford University Press.

Sampson, R.J., and Wilson, W.J. 2000. Toward a theory of race, crime, and urban inequality. In R.D. Crutchfield, G.S. Bridges, J.G. Weiss, and C. Kubrin (Eds.), *Crime* (pp. 126–137). Stanford, CA: Stanford University Press.

Schwartz, I.M. 1986. *Testimony before the House subcommittee on human resources,* June 19.

Schwartz, I.M. 1987. *(In) Justice for juveniles.* Lexington, MA: Lexington Books.

Schwartz, I.M., Fishman, G., Hatfield, R.R., Krisberg, B.A., and Eisikovits, Z. 1987. Juvenile detention: The hidden closets revisited. *Justice Quarterly,* 4: 219–235.

Shannon, L.W. 1980. Assessing the relationship of adult criminal careers to juvenile careers. Washington, DC: Office of Juvenile Justice and Delinquency Prevention.

Smith, D.A., Visher, C.A., and Davidson, L.A. 1984. Equity and discretionary justice: The influence of race on police arrest decisions. *Journal of Criminal Law and Criminology,* 75: 234–249.

Snyder, H.S. 1990. Growth in minority detentions attributed to drug law violators. *OJJDP Update on Statistics*. Washington, DC: Office of Juvenile Justice and Delinquency Prevention.

Snyder, H.S., and Sickmund, M. 1999. Juvenile offenders and victims: 1999 national report. Pittsburgh, PA: National Center for Juvenile Justice.

State of Texas. 1991. Texas juvenile probation statistical report: Statistical and other data on the juvenile justice system in Texas for calendar year 1990. Austin: Texas Juvenile Probation Commission.

State of Texas. 1992. Texas juvenile probation statistical report: Statistical and other data on the juvenile justice system in Texas for calendar year 1991. Austin: Texas Juvenile Probation Commission.

State of Texas. 1993. Texas juvenile probation statistical report: Statistical and other data on the juvenile justice system in Texas for calendar year 1992. Austin: Texas Juvenile Probation Commission.

State of Texas. 1993. Texas juvenile justice: A system in need of rehabilitation. (SAO Report Number 94-009) Austin, TX: Office of the State Auditor.

State of Texas. 1994. Texas juvenile probation statistical report: Statistical and other data on the juvenile justice system in Texas for calendar year 1993. Austin: Texas Juvenile Probation Commission.

Texas Family Code, Volume 3. 1995. St. Paul, MN: West Publishers.

Tonry, M. 1995. *Malign neglect: Race, crime and punishment in America.* New York: Oxford University Press.

Tracy, P.E. 1978. An Analysis of the Prevalence and Incidence of Self-Reported Delinquency and Crime. Ph.D. Dissertation, Center for Studies in Criminology and Criminal Law, University of Pennsylvania.

Tracy, P.E. 1987. Race and class differences in official and self-reported delinquency. In M.E. Wolfgang, T.P. Thornberry, and R.M. Figlio (Eds.), *From boy to man, from delinquency to crime* (pp. 87–121). Chicago: University of Chicago Press.

Tracy, P.E. 1990. Prevalence, incidence, rates, other descriptive measures. In K.L. Kempf (Ed.), *Measurement issues in criminology* (pp. 51–77). New York: Springer-Verlag.

Tracy, P.E., and Kempf-Leonard, K. 1996. *Continuity and discontinuity in criminal careers: The transition from delinquency to crime.* New York: Plenum Press.

Tracy, P.E., and Kempf-Leonard, K. 1998. Sanctioning serious juvenile offenders: A review of alternative models. In F. Adler and W. Laufer (Eds.), *The criminology of criminal law* (pp. 135–170). New Brunswick, NJ: Transaction Publishers.

Tracy, P.E., Wolfgang, M.E., and Figlio, R.M. 1985. Delinquency in two birth cohorts, executive summary. Washington, DC: Office of Juvenile Justice and Delinquency Prevention.

Tracy, P.E., Wolfgang, M.E., and Figlio, R.M. 1990. *Delinquency careers in two birth cohorts.* New York: Plenum Press.

Vickers, T. 1992. Balancing the scales: A look at the overrepresentation of minority youth in the juvenile justice system. Austin, TX: Criminal Justice Division.

Webb, E.J., Campbell, D.T., Schwartz, R.D., and Sechrest, L. 1966. *Unobtrusive measures: Nonreactive research in the social sciences.* Chicago: Rand McNally and Co.

Wolfgang, M.E., and Cohen, B. 1970. *Crime and race: Conceptions and misconceptions*. New York: Institute of Human Relations Press.

Wolfgang, M.E., and Ferracuti, F. 1969. *The subculture of violence*. London: Tavistock Publications Limited.

Wolfgang, M.E., Figlio, R.M., and Sellin, T. 1972. *Delinquency in a birth cohort*. Chicago: University of Chicago Press.

Index

About the Author

PAUL E. TRACY is Professor of Criminology, Sociology and Political Economy at The University of Texas, Dallas.

www.ingramcontent.com/pod-product-compliance
Ingram Content Group UK Ltd.
Pitfield, Milton Keynes, MK11 3LW, UK
UKHW020817290926
15470UKWH00003B/1206

9 780275 976514